FROM BLUNDER TO BLESSING

JAN D. THOMAS

FROM BLUNDER TO BLESSING

JAN D. THOMAS

ARPress
45 Dan Road Suite 5
Canton MA 02021
Hotline: 1(888) 821-0229
Fax: 1(508) 545-7580

Ordering Information:

Quantity sales. Special discounts are available on quantity purchases by corporations, associations, and others. For details, contact the publisher at the address above.

Printed in the United States of America.

ISBN-13:   Softcover   979-8-89356-304-7

                  eBook   979-8-89356-305-4

Library of Congress Control Number: 2024902951

TABLE OF CONTENTS

PROLOGUE

As I drive through the beautiful fields of the Mesilla Valley in southern New Mexico, I cross a two-lane bridge over the Rio Grande on Shalem Colony Trail. Crops of lettuce, cabbage and melons are checkered between large stands of pecan trees. The corn has already been harvested and most of it chopped up and covered with plastic tarps in silage pits. Onions and chile were harvested during the summer and early fall. Other fields are green with alfalfa that when bailed and taken to area dairies, provides nutritious feed for the cattle that produce milk mainly for a local cheese factory. Many dairies have moved to New Mexico because the environment with generally dry conditions allows irrigation to regulate water, providing a more nourishing feed for the cows. Cotton is being harvested to be taken to the gin to be made into…well, maybe the blue jeans I wear almost exclusively. The Mesilla Valley along the Rio Grande is famous for chile crops, especially to the north around the village of Hatch. Hatch chile has been trademarked for its excellence and New Mexico is very careful to make sure that other states don't tread on its desire to sell only the best chile in the world, and an ingredient in my favorite food. New Mexico ranks in the top three states for pecan production along with Texas and Georgia. Many don't realize the agricultural impact of my home state, but it is substantial. Those who have never been here think of the Land of Enchantment as being only desert. It is that, but much more.

As I approach West Picacho Avenue west from Las Cruces, I am reminded again that the valley is surrounded by the Chihuahuan

Desert. To the east, the Organ Mountains rise majestically to almost 9,000 feet and appear to those with a little imagination to be a pipe organ's ranks of tubes and reeds. A recently dedicated monument, the area has a rich diversity of wild lands and unique history including the Butterfield Stagecoach Trail, Billy the Kid's Outlaw Rock, Geronimo's Cave, World War II aerial targets, and thousands of Native American petroglyphs and pictographs as well as training sites for the Apollo Space Mission in conjunction with White Sands Missile Range to the east. This is home for rocket scientists who have worked at White Sands and developed military weaponry as well as the vehicles that have taken our nation to the moon and beyond.

The Camino Real, the Spanish Royal Road from Santa Fe to Mexico City, courses through the valley and into El Paso, down through the Mexican state of Chihuahua. Ciudad Juárez, one of the largest cities in Mexico, conjoins the West Texas City and between the two populations and Doña Ana County, now called the "Borderplex," there are over two and a half million people who call this home.

To the west, the desert stretches on through Arizona broken by mountain ranges and desert peaks. Cooke's Peak has been a landmark for the Butterfield Trail and can be seen from many angles in the area. The Florida Mountains near Deming are ripe rock hound haunts and many kinds of semi-precious gems have been dug and traded over the years from the Floridas. My father loved the geodes which he found and halved, many of which displayed an array of crystals inside the hollow rocks. At one time, the western boundary of our Doña Ana County extended to the Colorado River bordering the eastern edge of California, encompassing most of what is now southern Arizona before the New Mexico Territory was divided in 1863 and the two became states in 1912.

I am on my way to prison—again! I have been either working at Southern New Mexico Correctional Facility or volunteering my time for nearly twenty-five years. As I drive I reflect on what brought me to this point in my life. Although I am almost eighty, I am not more than a hundred miles from where I was born.

Southern New Mexico Correctional Facility is located off Interstate 10 just southeast of the Southern New Mexico State Fairgrounds. As

I pull into the facility I am greeted by a correctional officer who says, "Hi, Warden Thomas, which side you going to?" I am amazed I'm still called "Warden" by some of the staff. The facility opened in 1984 and I joined its confines as the Deputy Warden in 1993. If I continue straight ahead, I go to the parking lot for the JSU, the unit named for Lt. Joe Silva who was beaten to death by an inmate in 1987. It houses security levels 3 and 4, along with a segregation unit for disciplinary and protective custody inmates. If I turn to the left, I pass the Visitors Hospitality Center initiated and operated by Christian volunteers to help the families of inmates during visits. In a separate part of the facility, the POU, the Paul Oliver Unit, named for an associate warden of programs who died of cancer in 1988, reside inmates in security level 2, who are within 4 years of release. I am headed today for the chapel at the JSU where I will roll my equipment through doors and gates in a wheeled suitcase and walk with the chaplain to a lockdown gang unit to bring hope where there is little. After twenty-five years, I retired from the Corrections Department in 1997 and began a volunteer program that has consumed my time and devotion since. How I got here is the substance of this story.

CHAPTER 1

THE EARLY YEARS

It sounds a little like a soap opera description: "I was born in a small mining town in the west." It turned out to be a hole in the ground from which I sprang. Santa Rita, New Mexico. The town had a history behind it. The Spanish, Mexicans and Americans mined copper from this site for over two hundred years, leaving an open-pit gaping from the bottom and side of a mountain called The Kneeling Nun, a rock formation shaped like a religious figure kneeling before an altar.

Mining began in 1799 by Lt. Coronel José Manuel Carrasco under the laws of Spain, and their mining efforts were fought off by the Apaches. The conflict and the mining operations were inherited by the Mexicans in 1821 who did battle with the Chiricahua Chief, Mangas Coloradas until he was

Santa Rita Chino Mine and Kneeling Nun

murdered by U.S. troops in 1863. The Americans continued with the Apache conflicts and mining until peace settled over the region and the small town of Santa Rita. As a child, Kennecott Copper Corporation dominated the life of my family as well as the rest of the residents. The open-pit copper mine has continued to grow, swallowing up the town which is no longer. All the buildings were moved away or destroyed by the mid-1960's. There are road signs giving directions to "Santa Rita," but no one lives there, it is a working open-pit copper mine.

It was from this beginning I have my earliest memories. My parents met when my mother, who had just migrated from Colorado, saw my father delivering groceries from the Santa Rita Store Company, the only grocery store in town. It also sold almost everything people needed and employees could charge groceries they would pay for at the end of the month. Dad was the delivery guy for the store. The song "I Owe My Soul to the Company Store" has some meaning for those who lived and worked at Chino, the name of the mine.

Clyde Douglas Thomas and Dorothea Frances Peper were married and lived on Booth Hill until after I was born. Booth Hill had a lower standard of housing than the Ball Park, but still higher than Mexican Town, which testified to the segregationist attitude of both the Company and the Anglo community. To my knowledge, there were no black people in Santa Rita or Hurley, but there were a few in other towns in Grant County. Mexicans were looked down upon and seldom selected for promotion to any job other than laborer. That opened the doors for union activity often shutting the mine down on strikes. While the 1954 movie *The Salt of the Earth* describes some of the events in a nearby town, Fierro, concerning another mining company, Empire Zinc, the issues were pretty much the same.

Even though living conditions were disparate and unequal, the schools were integrated as were all schools in New Mexico and many of the Hispanic children excelled in their studies, often becoming much more than their natal environment would have predicted, but not at Kennecott. None of the supervisory or other administrative positions was held by other than Anglo employees. It wasn't an issue, usually, but the thought often underlined the attitude of people living in Santa Rita. Anglo kids didn't step into Mexican Town and vice-versa. Sometimes rock-throwing incidents would occur, or fist-fights would break out at the slightest provocation. Shouts of "dirty Mexican" and "*Gringo salado*," were hurled at each other, but for the most part we got along at school. There was no cross-cultural dating allowed. That was an unspoken rule.

My grandparents and my mother's sister, Theresa (pronounced THREE-sa by the family and those who were told how to say it "right") and her family also lived in Santa Rita. My uncle, Jim Saige, had worked in Mexico for a while and learned of the job opportunities in Southwest New Mexico, obtaining a position with Kennecott as the Carpenter Superintendent. My grandfather, Herman Peper was offered a position as a carpenter foreman and they also migrated to the town from Las Animas, Colorado along with my mother in 1938. That was the year of their marriage and I appeared on the scene in late 1939.

My cousin about two years older, Vance Saige, was ushered into the room where my crib was after I was brought home from the hospital and told in hushed tones, "That's your cousin, Jan." He relates he was less than awestruck at the revelation. Vance had an older brother, Leon, who died in childhood. He was later blessed with another brother, Gerald (who forsook his real name for "Jerry" after adulthood), the object of his older brother's pestering as they grew up.

The family moved to Deming for a few weeks while my father tried selling insurance, an endeavor at which he did not excel, and later to Silver City. Although I don't remember it, I'm told I fell out of the window of the house we lived in while in Deming. I suppose it had no effect on me; however, there are times I wonder if this was the beginning of a strange fear of heights. It wasn't a bad fall, but I have a fear of being in high places. My family grew, my brother Keith was born in 1941, and Dennis in 1943. We called him "Denny" and he was given a hard time by all of us because he was the youngest.

My earliest recollections of living in Silver City, the county seat, were a bit *shocking*. My dad's mother used to gather black walnuts from the local trees which grew wild and removed the nut meat from the hull with a hairpin and ate it. I loved the taste of the nuts and one day, I guess I was about three, I decided the electric plug in the wall looked so much like a black walnut I stuck a hairpin in the holes of the socket and discovered that indeed, it was NOT a nut at all. I appropriated a healthy fear of electricity for the rest of my life.

Dad got a job during World War II at the copper smelter in Hurley, becoming an electrician. I don't believe it had anything to do with my previous experience with the wall socket. We moved there and most of my earliest memories stem from this location. This change in occupations was in lieu of joining the military during the effort to defeat the Axis. My uncle Gene Peper, my mother's brother, joined and became an aviation trainer in the Army Air Corps.

I remember being taught a nightly prayer to say before going to bed:

> *Now I lay me down to sleep,*
> *I pray Thee, Lord, my soul to keep.*
> *If I should die before I wake,*
> *I pray Thee Lord, my soul to take.*

> *Amen*

I didn't quite understand the prayer and I wasn't sure I wanted the Lord or anyone else to take my soul while I slept. But it was a prayer my mother wanted me to pray, so I did.

Dad didn't grow up with any brothers or sisters; he was adopted by my grandparents, Marvin and Minnie Thomas when he was three years old. He was the thirteenth of thirteen children and the story goes that his real father went out for a loaf of bread and didn't come back, leaving the tribe to his wife who couldn't keep up with it all and put him up for adoption since he was the youngest. The family name was Alman, but dad didn't talk about this part of his life. His father returned some years later, but dad wanted little or nothing to do with any of the family. When his biological father died, an inheritance of a few hundred dollars was offered to him, but he returned the money. He had some contact with a sister, but she was Jehovah's Witness and off limits as far as he was concerned. He didn't talk about religious issues and I never heard him mention the Bible or what he believed or didn't believe, although he claimed to be a "Methodist." He would go to church once in a while, mainly to appease Mom, but until later in his life, it wasn't important to him.

My adoptive grandparents followed wherever my dad went. Grandad Thomas had very little education and had to sign documents with an "X" rather than write his name. He could read a newspaper and I used to enjoy seeing his lips move as his eyes skimmed the pages of the paper. He worked for the U. S. Forest Service in the Gila National Forest and was gone fairly often. I never did learn what his job was, but I suspect it was building trails or other tasks assigned to him. He also worked at Ft. Bayard, a former military outpost later used as a tuberculosis sanatorium.

In their home, which was usually a one-room apartment with a sink, stove and a few pieces of furniture, he would sit in a rocking chair, roll his cigarettes using loose tobacco from a Prince Albert can or sometimes a sack of dried tobacco. For him rolling a cigarette was an art. Holding the paper in his left hand, he poured the tobacco—just the right amount—into the dip in the paper formed by his fingers. He put down the tobacco container and, with one motion of both hands, rolled the cigarette and, bringing it up to his mouth; licked the edge of the paper and shaped it into a nearly perfect cylinder. He would then reach for a match and strike it underneath the arm of the rocking chair, firing up the handmade masterpiece, and deeply inhale the smoke it produced. The look of satisfaction always appeared on his face. He had a chiseled face, somewhat dark, black hair and a knot under his left ear that was unexplained, but probably an overgrown nodule left over from a pimple from his youth. His ears were hairy, and he often smiled and laughed when he talked.

Very often he told stories of his past, laughing at some of the events. The stories would be told over and over again with laughs in the same places. He told about a boy who would spell pie, p-s-y-g-k. To him it was hilarious! He was quarter Blackfoot Indian but didn't have papers to prove it. He never drank socially, but at night he would take down a bottle of whisky he kept in the top of his closet, fill a spoon once, twice, and then take a swig—for medicinal purposes. He spoke disparagingly of blacks and other people, most of whom he had little contact with. My dad was also disposed to making racist remarks.

Beside the chair was a coffee can which became simultaneously an ashtray and a place to spit. His lungs filled up with phlegm and he had a deep and raucous cough. It was a ghastly sight to look into the can beside his chair on the floor, but it was a part of him. He would smoke the cigarette down to the smallest butt, his thumb and forefinger always black from the experience. Those who visited usually sat at the table in the kitchen part of the room. If there were more than that would hold, the bed became a couch. Early on they had no refrigerator, opting for a window on the north side of the house to keep anything like milk or butter cool by placing a wet rag around it. The toilet was in the backyard, a wooden shack called a "privy" with a seat built with holes cut in the plank you sat on, hoping the spider lurking underneath would remain tranquil. Toilet paper was a catalogue, usually Sears and Roebuck or J. C. Penney, sometimes Montgomery Ward. Baths were taken inside with water heated on the stove either standing or sitting, depending on your age, in a No. 3 washtub.

Marvin Thomas moved his family from Arkansas to the town of Central (now Santa Clara) in Grant County after being told his tuberculosis was not survivable in a humid climate. Ft. Bayard was a few miles from Central and he was able to get work there. This is where my dad grew up, went to school, and nearly graduated from high school in Silver City. He lacked one credit.

Minnie Thomas washed clothes in the same tub baths were taken, with a rub board and a bar of white soap. A thin woman, she would never tell her age, and while she didn't smoke, she would disappear after meals and return wiping her mouth with a handkerchief she always carried. Sometimes a brownish trickle escaped from her lips, but she would never acknowledge that she dipped snuff—we found out later that she preferred Garrett's Sweet and Mild. She was usually a pleasant woman but could get flustered easily. When things didn't go her way, she would express her frustration by saying, "I'm all blowed up."

Coming from Arkansas they had a number of sayings that flew in the face of the culture they had come into. To close a door, they would say, "pull the door to." You never pushed a button; you "mashed it." If you told them something amazing the response was, "Well, I swan." We never had toys; they were "play pretties." Marvin Thomas had a wonderful way of eating—with a table knife. He ate peas, carrots, whatever, scooping the food up with his knife. My cousin Vance still marvels at his ability to eat this way.

The Peper side of the family had originated in Illinois. My grandfather, Herman, spoke nothing but German until he was about seven years old. A balding, heavy-set man, he was raised in the German community of Ohlman they were always seeking ways to make a living. His parents were born in the United States, but their parents had migrated from the "old country." His father died early leaving him and his siblings to fend for themselves, each working to help support the family. By the time I knew him he had no accent and had forgotten most of the German he had learned as a child. He would, on occasion, sing *Twinkle, Twinkle, Little Star* in that language. Grandad had a job during the early years sorting mail on a railway between Chicago and Buffalo, New York. Lydia, my grandmother was of mixed heritage which included English, Scotch-Irish, and German. Her family with the surname of New came from New York to Illinois, by way of Missouri.

Lydia Peper also had a form of tuberculosis and was advised to "go west." They moved to a homestead near Las Animas, Colorado and farmed a patch of land. Grandad often had to work as a carpenter to supplement the family income, but he was a hard worker and very intelligent. He also smoked cigarettes, but he only smoked the "tailor made" kind, always the Lucky Strike brand. He was heard to say that he did not trust a man who didn't smoke. They lived in a Company-provided home in the Ball Park section of Santa Rita when I was old enough to take notice of where and what we were. Jim and Theresa lived about a block away. The earliest and some of the best memories that have lingered with me come from these towns.

Living in Hurley, another Kennecott provided house, a number of events stuck in my mind. I can remember going to the Chino Club, a recreation center for employees of Kennecott Copper Corporation, Chino Division. The mine is still called Chino mine, named for iron pyrite which in Spanish is called "chino" or Chinese. While some have argued that there was a Chinese person somehow involved in the mine, this has generally been discounted.

My father sent me when I was about five years old to the employee's club, a place where a person could go to play pool, bowl, or have some non-alcoholic refreshment or snack, to buy a pack of cigarettes for him. I set off with ten pennies and as I walked there were puddles of rain water around the bases of trees along the way. I thought it great sport to throw a penny into the water to see the splash. When I got to the club and asked to buy the cigarettes, I didn't have enough money. So, I returned home and announced this to my father who reacted negatively to my attempt to amuse myself with water splashes. I recall returning with the right amount of money and a reprimand on my heart.

Other memories are laced with smells and sounds, some good, some not quite so good. Like the sound of a steam engine pulling cars from the south, up a continuous grade past yucca, cactus and creosote. The terrain is the northern edge of the Chihuahuan desert that slowly rises to a mountain range known as "the Gila" at the edge of the Gila National Forest.

I would stand in my bed, a boy of five winters, and look out my window westward, unable to fall asleep until I got to see and hear the *chuch! chuch! chuch!* of the engine lugging those cars by my house, black fumes belching from its smokestack and steam spurting from the wheel cylinders. I could hear that whistle blow, watching while steam from the boiler was forced through its reed as it signaled the crossing of roads, both to the south and north of town. And as it passed, the smell of coal smoke was left in its wake. I was fascinated by the thunder of it all as it rumbled by. It would signal a short chapter in my life later on.

My Uncle Jim had become a pilot and purchased a military training airplane which he housed in a hangar at the Hurley airport, not far from our house on the west side of town on Romero Street. It has since been moved away from the town, but at that point it was not more than a quarter mile away across the railroad tracks. One day we were in the yard and I was hanging on the fence when we noticed a fire in one of the hangars. A drum of gasoline exploded. The building blew up and a huge ring of fire and smoke went up into the clear blue sky, it seemed like miles to me, but the event was, in my young mind *awesome!* Someone said that my uncle and cousin Vance were at the airport and worry set in. We soon found out that they had escaped without harm and everyone was relieved. I can never hear the Johnny Cash song, *Ring of Fire* without thinking of this event.

My Great-grandmother, Dora Peper, came to visit and stayed with us in Hurley. She was hard of hearing, but with her "hearing horn" she would listen to the news on the radio about the war and when speeches by Adolph Hitler were broadcast, she understood the German and would pound her knee and say things in German that none of the rest of us understood. I don't think they were profane sayings, because no one in either side of the family was prone to that kind of language. They were, however, very demonstrative. She was definitely American, not German in spite of her background.

I have another recollection that ushered in a new age. My brother, Keith, and I were sleeping in the same bed and early one morning, the date was July 16, 1945, we heard a loud booming sound, actually two of them.

"What was that?" my brother Keith asked. I replied that I didn't know. We were dismayed and wondered what it was. Later that day people were discussing the noise and what it could be. A story was released that a dynamite magazine at the mine in Santa Rita had blown up. This was discredited by those who worked at the mine including Grandad Peper and Uncle Jim and knew that nothing of the kind had happened. It was later revealed that this was the test of the first atomic bomb at Trinity Site. Some say the blast was at Alamogordo, which claims the credit, but that is many miles from the point of detonation which was nearer to Socorro and Carrizozo than Alamogordo, but it was about 125 miles from Hurley. Granddad Thomas was working with the Forest Service near Beaverhead in the Gila and actually saw the flash of light in the early morning sky and heard the sound resounding across the hills.

The war ended on August 6 after the bombs were dropped on Hiroshima and Nagasaki, Japan; and Hurley had a celebration! People in cars and trucks were going up and down the streets of the town with American flags waving and horns honking during V-J Day. We all went to the baseball park where a bonfire had been assembled and a post with a straw-stuffed Japanese soldier's uniform had been placed, hung from a noose. The effigy was set afire and everyone cheered. The war had ended. We had endured, and we had won.

During the war many things were rationed: gasoline, tires, sugar, coffee and so on. Families were issued ration stamps and could buy only some of these items in small quantities. Sometimes we couldn't go anywhere in the 1928 Model-A Ford my dad had been able to purchase because we had run out of stamps. No gas, no tires, no go. The end of the war began the change toward a more luxurious time for my family as well as most other Americans.

CHAPTER 2

MOVING NORTH

The end of the war also brought other changes to my family. Dad got a job somewhere out of Santa Fe; he couldn't tell us where and some of the words in the letters he wrote home were blotted out by someone. We found out that he had gone to work at Los Alamos, the birthplace of the atomic bomb. He soon sent for us and we moved to Española, first to a "suburb" called San Pablo on the south end of the town. It was an adobe house with wooden planks for floors. Some of the planks had knot holes in them and there were gaps between the boards. We cooked on a wood stove, had a privy out back and, to make things fun for the kids, my dad hung a rope in a cottonwood tree and tied a tire to it. We had a tree swing! There was no running water in the house and all our drinking and bathing water came from a well not far from the privy. I remember getting sick a lot, earaches, colds, flu, and some things that just made my stomach ache.

Grandparents Thomas followed us and lived a few miles away in Riverside, another "suburb." My dad still drove the Model-A to work at Los Alamos. Soon we moved to another area called Guachupangue (pronounced Watch-a-PANG-gay). We found out what Anglo-Hispanic discrimination felt like in that place! The tables were turned and the folks there didn't like outsiders, especially those who didn't speak Spanish. Keith and I would be playing in our "yard" which really had no distinguishing borders—like a fence. A rock would come out of nowhere and land in our play area. None ever hit us, but we learned to be weary. Marvin Thomas, still disliking anyone who was not like himself, found a friend; a man by the name of "True Hill." He mistook the name Trujillo and called him by the name he had invented. He didn't realize Mr. Trujillo was not Anglo.

At age 6 or 7, my grandparents took me to Arkansas by bus. As we traveled toward the destination, I began to feel sick. We stopped for a short time in Shamrock, Texas. I got off the bus and began puking as I sat on a curb. When we arrived in Quitman, they called a doctor who examined me. He smelled "funny" and they said he was drunk, but he came to the house we were staying at and pronounced to all that I had the chicken pox. I had been at a Methodist church in Española that had a Vacation Bible School and the disease had been transmitted to me during that week just before we left for Arkansas. My feet itched; I itched all over, but after spending about a day or so in bed, I began to come around. I met a girl cousin, several times removed, and she and I began to play together. I don't remember her name, but she was related somehow.

I met my granddad's brother, Frank Thomas, who sat on the porch of the white frame house and chewed tobacco. He would cut a plug of the brown stuff off a cylindrical piece of the foul-looking material, sit back, chew on it a little and spit over the railing of the building. I noticed that the flowers in the bed below the porch weren't doing well, they were mostly wilted and a little brown from the glaze he dropped on them. They laughed and talked all the time, enjoying each other's company. I think it had been a long time since my grandparents had visited with their families. I met the Williams family, my grandmother's clan. I don't remember which family I was spending time with, but one of the families had a milk cow and my grandmother remarked about how good the milk would taste directly from the source. I was looking forward to it. They had also helped me acquire a taste for buttermilk and some had been churned as fresh butter was made. My first taste of the fabled substances was awful! I spit it out and, since I was the first to try this batch, they asked me what was wrong. I told them it tasted terrible. They tried it and their reaction was similar to mine, but there was a proclamation: "the cow had been in the bitter weed again!" So much for home churning… and for cows being the deliverers of delights.

Back home, indoor plumbing continued to be a problem and we had to haul all our water in a little red wagon from a place up the road. Baths were taken in a No. 3 washtub like my Grandma Thomas had and our clothes were washed the way she did it, using a corrugated washboard and a bar of white soap. We were renters and our nearby neighbors lived close by. The streets weren't laid out squarely as they had been in Hurley and were built in helter-skelter fashion, most of them from adobe mud bricks, stuccoed with plaster and either painted or not, mostly not. We dealt with bedbugs in that house, and at one point we put the legs of the beds in cans of kerosene to stop the bug's migration into the bedding and mattresses.

My dad would drive to Los Alamos and, to save gasoline and would stay there in a dormitory which accommodated construction workers and tradesmen. At night in Guachupague an Indian man from the Santa Clara Pueblo, tanked up on red wine which he carried in a gallon glass jug, would knock on the door and announce, "This my house, you move thirty days!" Mom was afraid and kept a hammer close to her pillow at night. I remember one incident where he grabbed me in front of neighbors, held me by my chest and put a pocket knife to my throat. The neighbors laughed to see this little gringo in distress and I wiggled and twisted myself loose and ran home. I told my mother about the event and she didn't believe me. Why, she never told me, but thinking back I could tell some stories that weren't exactly true. Another defect in my character was also developing. The incident, I discovered later, had an impact on me. I began to doubt my value to my family or to those around me. I was an object of ridicule and not even my mother would stand up for me.

One evening the Indian, named Joe Ree-Ree (or that's how it sounded) approached the door, not knowing that dad had taken the Model-A in for repairs, did his knock-knock routine and dad met him at the screen door, picked him up by the collar of his shirt and the waistband of his trousers and deposited him on the other side of the road that ran by the property. I don't recall that he ever came knocking on our door again.

I had been around people who smoked all my life. My grandfathers, uncle, father and most of the men I knew all smoked. When they weren't looking, I would sneak a cigarette butt and go elsewhere and smoke it. I got caught a few times and, when we moved to Española my dad would allow me to smoke one cigarette on my birthday, beginning with my sixth. This would add fuel to a long battle I had with tobacco.

Going to school during the first grade was an ordeal. I had to walk over a mile to Española Elementary School, along with others who hated me and my kind. I would be harassed both going and coming. There was no school bus, no parent to drive me. At school, I didn't encounter many problems, but I do remember a teacher, Ms. Montoya, giving me an outline of an apple to color with a crayon. I colored it in a manner I though was pretty good. She said, "Color it darker." I said, "I don't want to." She got a wooden ruler and hit the back of my hand with it. *I colored it darker!*

I met two girls in first grade; one's name was Elaine, the other Wetherel. Elaine's father owned a grocery store. I don't remember what Wetherel's dad did, but she later moved to Afghanistan where her father established a school and her picture later appeared in a National Geographic Magazine. The point of the story is that, since I didn't have any sisters or first cousins who were of the female variety, I immediately fell in love with both of them. I would kiss one of the girls behind the steps of the school and the other one at a different time. This was fun! …Until I came in late from recess and had to stand in the corner for being truant. Lesson learned, but I still liked them both.

We had a dog for a while, named Shug—which was short for sugar—she had puppies. I loved animals and had moved from Hurley with a cat named Eliza Jane. She was my cat, but after we moved, she ran off and I grieved her loss until we got the dog. My dad was okay with one animal at our home, but more than one was not appreciated. Dad had me do something I *so* didn't want to do. We took the puppies out and killed them with a shovel. I cried, and Dad bawled me out about it. I felt this was wrong, I loved them and now I had to be involved in killing them. Dad never saw the hurt this caused me and glossed over it as if nothing had happened. We buried them just off the roadway going to Los Alamos.

Dad bought a piece of land not far from the school and built a house. Even before it was finished we moved in because nobody liked

Guachupangue. We had no electricity at first at the new home and used gasoline lanterns for light at night. A cousin of my dad, Ira Williams, heard about what was happening and bought a piece of land not far from our house. We also became neighbors to a man named Lujan who had survived the Bataan Death March who was a local butcher.

One day, Keith and I were playing in a nearby arroyo. Digging into the side of the ditch we found some "worms" which we brought back in a jar. When we revealed our find, they were immediately destroyed. They were not worms. They were rattlesnake babies. Another lesson learned. My dad's cousin's wife, Margaret, was going to take us to the store one afternoon with her in my dad's Model A car. The car was running, and Keith and I were left in it while she returned to her house for something she had forgotten. Somehow, we released the emergency brake and the car began rolling backward. She saw our predicament and ran to stop the car before we were injured. And again, another lesson in life. Don't mess with the leavers in cars.

Just as I entered the second grade and turned seven we moved to "The Hill" as Los Alamos was known. I had not been to the place where my dad worked before, since it was a closed city and only those who lived and worked there or were invited by residents could enter. I remember the first time going up the steep, curved road to the Main Gate. My dad had made arrangements for us to be admitted since he had acquired an apartment on Trinity Drive. On the bluffs above the road were anti-aircraft guns pointed eastward. A gun tower stood over the shack housing the soldier who checked each vehicle and the occupants inside. Very impressive to a seven-year-old who had never seen anything like it. After clearing the Main Gate, we proceeded past an airport and into the town.

All of us had to get ID cards with our pictures on them and a thumbprint to prove we were who we said we were. Our apartment was one in a quadraplex with two on the bottom and two on the top. The building was sided with asphalt shingles. Having lived in very sub-standard accommodations for the time in Española, this was like the Taj-Mahal. Central heating, hot running water, a real bathroom with a bathtub and a fireplace! The floors were polished hardwood and there were three bedrooms. Wow, wow, wow! We had made it to the pentacle of life! No more rocks thrown over the roof of the house, no more Joe Ree-Ree telling us to move. No more long walks to school with harassment going and coming.

Behind the building was the gate to Tech Area, where the atomic labs were. I found out years later that about a hundred yards from our apartment building on Trinity Drive the first atomic bomb was assembled and was taken to Trinity Site, as were the bombs that were dropped on Hiroshima and Nagasaki. I had become a witness to parts of our history that, on one hand were a part of the peace the United States has enjoyed, and on the other hand a dangerous, apocalyptic evil that at any moment could be unleashed on the planet. From our bedroom window we had access to a fire escape with a ladder we could play on. We never considered that this had any other use. From time to time we would get balsa wood gliders that we would sail from the back porch, sometimes landing on the other side of the Tech Area fence. It was great fun to beg the security guard to allow us to go on the other side of the fence to retrieve the downed craft.

When we first moved to Los Alamos the Army had jurisdiction over the security of the hidden city. A barracks was located about a quarter mile from our apartment and in the morning, we would hear Reveille bugled on a loudspeaker. At night, it was Taps. I loved Los Alamos, everything about it. We had two movie theaters, a shopping center, a library and school were only a short walk away. I could see the tall water tower with red and white checkers on it warning off any flying objects. We would play in the canyons, rolling the soft volcanic tuft boulders from the side down to the bottom. There were caves to explore, pine trees to be climbed and we had friends we could play with. I immediately made friends with a kid whose family had come from Alabama. His name was Danny Foshee.

Walking to the shopping center we passed by a pond dubbed "Duck Pond," because a group of ducks had adopted it. Once in a while we would discover a duck egg and bring it home to cook. My brother Keith and I found some cattle in a corral that had been in the area of the atomic blast at Trinity Site that were being observed for the effects of radiation they had received. We would climb on the fence to watch them. They were black cattle, probably Angus, but their hair in spots had turned grey.

The radio station, first given the designation of KRS, played music mostly, and the news. Later they added an "N" to make it fit the four-letter designation of most radio stations in the United States. During supper mom would turn on the radio which played classical music. This was "dinner music," and we were now somewhat cultured. At night, the station played network radio dramas or other programming like, *The Shadow.* On Saturday mornings, it was *The Buster Brown Show.* "Featuring Buster Brown and his dog Sparky."

Snow. Ah, the snow. Los Alamos is at an elevation of over 7,000 feet. One time it snowed up to my waist, but we still had to go to school. No "snow days" back then. I remember trudging through the snow, enjoying the novelty of it and relishing the joy of playing in it. When it melted it wasn't so great because things got muddy and the clean snow became brown and black from the substances around it. I know about snow angels, snow balls and, yes, ice balls—once it melts enough to squish together and compact it, just-so it will hurt when it hits. My parents bought us a sled and we would swoop down the icy streets that had little traffic or the slopes of a depression just west of the apartment building. We learned that snow could provide another delicious treat: snow ice cream. Mom would make it from clean, fresh snow using milk, eggs, sugar and a little bit of vanilla.

During the fourth grade, we were offered the opportunity to join the music program at Central School. I always wanted to play trumpet, but when my last name which begins with one of the final letters of the alphabet was reached the only thing left was cello. I had no idea what it was, but I thought I could "blow" one and I raised my hand. Walking home that afternoon I wondered what I had gotten myself into since the cello was almost as big as I was and there was no mouthpiece from which I could blow it. The bow wouldn't fit in my mouth… So, my short music career began. I loved music, but I hated the screeching noises I made.

We made pilgrimages back to Santa Rita. Visits with my cousins were always fun and when it was the Fourth of July we had fireworks to occupy our time. One summer when we were setting off some screamers, a dog decided he would chase them. Until he caught one! It only took one to break him of the habit. Vance and I would crawl under streets that had culverts to prove our manliness and bravery against claustrophobia. We would catch wild burros that had at one time been used to bring ore out of the mine and ride them, using a rope as a halter. Keith and I did this one time when Vance and Jerry were in school. We rode the donkey, Keith siting forward with the rope halter in hand, me on the back facing the burro's south side hitting it on the butt with a length of hose.

The burro was not amused. He inched up under a juniper tree limb and started bucking. I escaped quickly, but Keith was stuck between the bucking burro and the tree limb. I still remember the sound of his hollering. No harm done, though, either to the poor beast or to my poor brother. At one time, Vance owned one of the critters. They were being rounded up for dog food and other purposes to get them under control since they were bad for the gramma grass that grew there. Several times Vance had to bail his donkey out of "jail," but he did it with great pleasure because they were "friends."

We began to go to church, or at least sometimes dad would go along with all of us, sometimes just mom. Usually, though they would send us kids to Sunday school. Los Alamos Community Church was not far away, and "regular" denominations were not found offensive to my mother. Methodist, Presbyterian and the like were all right in her estimation, but Baptists and Pentecostals and Catholics weren't. My friend Danny was Baptist and once in a while I went to church with him, but it was kind of frowned upon in my household.

During the fifth grade my dad lost his position with the Zia Company and we had to move to a construction community, a few miles away named White Rock that had little cracker-box houses. We rented a house of approximately 900 square feet, only two bedrooms, but it did have a bathroom. I went to White Rock School, but I longed for my home in Los Alamos. I tried to continue playing the cello, but the thing sounded so bad, and I hated hauling the big thing around with me, I asked for a violin. Mom got one from the Montgomery Ward catalog. Twenty-five dollars I think it cost, and it sounded even worse than the cello. While I blame the instruments, there was probably a more personal reason why the sound was not so good. I don't think I had a lick of talent in this area, but I did acquire an appreciation for music, especially classical.

My Granddad Peper had a record player with vinyl 78 rpm records, most of them piano concertos and when I was at their house, I loved playing them. I remember listening to *Claire de Lune* and loving this piece of music by Debussy. I would carry this music through my life as my favorite listening music, although I had an appreciation for other kinds of music as well.

Another diversion for us kids came with tobacco cans. Prince Albert and Velvet tobacco were sold in tin cans. My dad would take the can and cut it with tin snips into the shape of a propeller. He then made a device from a spool of thread, without the thread, placed on a stick with a dowel in the middle of one end just the right size to hold the spool. Holes would be made in the middle of the tin propeller and nails had been driven into the wooden spool at just the right place to fit the propeller holes. A string would be wound around the spool, the propeller placed on the spool with the finishing nails to hold it, and if wound in the right direction, the propeller would lift off the spool and fly into the air. Some danger existed, and we were cautioned to be careful, because the propeller could fly in any direction and with a forceable rotation could hit someone and cut them. This never happened, and we enjoyed this inexpensive exercise. Dad also made scooters from 2"X4" boards and fit wheels from roller skates, so we could ride down sidewalks or neighborhood streets. This was an enjoyable time for our family.

CHAPTER 3

THE ALBUQUERQUE YEARS

My dad changed jobs again and we moved to Albuquerque. He learned about a great job opportunity at Yucca Flats, Nevada, so we moved to a rental house on Buena Vista Street, south of the University of New Mexico. It took several weeks for the first paycheck to catch up to our needs. At one point, we had been eating macaroni and cheese, and then cheese and macaroni, then just macaroni. One day I asked my mother why we couldn't have chicken. I wanted chicken. She explained that we didn't have money to buy anything, but payday was coming. I didn't want to wait, so, I made an improvised slingshot out of a piece of leather, a "Y" cut out of a limb of a tree and two strips of rubber innertube to get the stretch I needed. I had some steel ball bearings, fairly large, and I went to Roosevelt Park. I knew there were pigeons in the park and I had heard they could be eaten and tasted somewhat like chicken. I shot two, cleaned and dressed them out and took them home. That evening we had "chicken."

Dad was finally able to send money from Nevada and the cuisine at the Thomas residence rose remarkably. We even had hamburger. My brothers and I attended Buena Vista Elementary School in southeast Albuquerque. The school no longer exists, having been incorporated into the Technical-Vocational Institute, which later became the Central New Mexico Community College.

We bought a house on Euclid Avenue near Broadway and I attended Stronghurst Elementary School becoming one of the Crossing Patrol guards. I had the great privilege of leaving class early, donning a red jacket, white web Sam Browne belt and a yellow cap with red piping. We would march smartly to the street corner where we were to "protect" fellow students and direct traffic to stop or go according to the numbers of those who needed to cross. Our whistles signaled when to put the stop sign out and when to retrieve it in a synchronized manner. The captain of the squad carried the pole which when horizontal stopped pedestrians and when vertical allowed them to pass. The captain also had the whistle and at one point I got to be a captain! I guess after some mishaps elsewhere, not on our watch, they decided to stop the practice in favor of hiring crossings guards who usually are retired people with not much else to do who could use the extra cash. We did our duty without any pay.

Euclid Avenue was a divided street with an irrigation ditch running between the divisions. Most of the time there was water in the ditch channeled from the Rio Grande which ran through the valley. Crayfish inhabited the water under and around the rocks. We called them "crawdads." We never ate them, but they provided many hours of diversion. Did you ever put a crawdad's claw on your skin and see how hard it can squeeze? I never tried a nipple like sometimes is seen on America's Favorite Videos, but I have experienced the pinch.

At one end of Euclid lived a guy named Jimmy. He wasn't very sociable and often hid behind the ditch bank to throw rocks at others in the neighborhood. We would have words and he would throw rocks. A block over on Indian School Road lived a kid nicknamed "Cookie." He had thirteen brothers and sisters. His dad worked for the Santa Fe Railroad and spent much of his off-duty time at a local bar away from the family which was, to say the least, rambunctious. Most of the time Cookie was my friend, but sometimes we would argue, sometimes fight and then make up. He invited me to go to his church once, First Baptist Church downtown at the corner of Central and Broadway. One invitation was to a watermelon feast on the roof of the church. We ate watermelon and threw the rinds over the side down on the sidewalk. We were reprimanded by someone, but it wasn't a harsh rebuke.

I also attended a Billy Graham Crusade at a special building called a "Tabernacle" constructed for the events. This was my first real connection to Evangelical Christianity and I, with whatever understanding I possessed, committed my life to Christ. I knew this was the right thing to do, but my family, while not rejecting the experience, didn't really embrace my newfound faith. We rarely spoke of religious things at home and when we did it was always at the surface level. My mindset was that God wanted me to be good, and I usually justified the things I did as not really being "bad," just maybe a little out of sync with perfection. I could justify most things by reasoning that "everyone did it."

For a while we attended Northminster Presbyterian Church as a family, but attendance drifted off with only me attending events like dances. The church no longer exists yielding to a merger with another church, the building succumbing to urban growth. I really had little grounding of my faith as a youngster, usually following along with whatever my friends did, trying to fit in.

The seventh grade in Albuquerque was at Garfield Junior High School (now Middle School). It was a long walk to school, about two miles. While we weren't poor, we didn't have any money, so to speak. My brothers and I got one pair of shoes a year, at the beginning of school. If that pair of shoes didn't last and a hole wore through in the sole, cardboard was cut in the right shape and put it in the bottom of the shoe, so my foot didn't contact the ground. Sometimes the stitching around the sole came loose and my shoes flapped—embarrassing! I continued to smoke cigarettes, stealing money from my mother's purse to purchase them. Most of the time she didn't notice, and I would lie and cover up when change came back short when I was sent on an errand.

I learned from some of the other students that if you squat down, take a number of deep breaths, stand up and blow on your thumb without letting air out you will pass out. We thought this was hilarious until I did it in shop one day and fell backward, hitting my head on the concrete floor. No concussion that I know of, just a headache that changed my perspective on this activity.

I met several girls that I liked, Becky who lived across the irrigation ditch on Euclid, and Donna who lived next door. I was infatuated with both of them, but really didn't know how to establish a romantic relationship. We were mainly friends, but hormones were kicking in and I had no clue what to do about it. Donna's mother died of cancer and she was raised by her father and two brothers who were seldom home.

My dad continued to work in one place and then another. Paducah, Kentucky; Corpus Christi, Texas; Yucca Flats, Nevada; Farmington and Roswell, New Mexico. He was gone much of the time. He finally got another position in Los Alamos and I was elated to return to the place I loved. I attended the eighth grade at Los Alamos High School. We were called of all things, sub-freshmen. A five-year high school. I did pretty well in school until I got into the math class. They enrolled me in algebra in the eighth grade. I didn't take to it. Other math courses made sense to me, but posing a question like: A train leaves New York City at such and such a time on such and such a date and another train leaves San Francisco at this time and this date, when will they collide? My mind said, "why would you want to ruin two perfectly good trains?"

I continued to find girls enticing. Not since the first grade in Española and Becky and Donna in Albuquerque had I really thought as much about them as I began to discover the surge of hormones. I became friends with Carla who also smoked cigarettes and I contemplated what might become of the relationship, but I was always "chicken," even though she wanted to get more involved. I became adept at hiding cigarettes in various nooks and crannies, like under rocks, in tree holes and under the house.

One evening when I was spending time at the school for a reason I can't remember I walked into the auditorium where the school orchestra was playing. They were practicing Ravel's *Bolero* with lights shining on a screen or curtain behind the orchestra. As the music became louder the lights became brighter and as it became quieter, the lights dimmed. I was mesmerized. I love that piece of music even now. That fueled my affinity for classical music, that and, of course, my Granddad Peper. I would often think of being at their home listening to classical music and piano concertos that Vance and I would play on their record player. I found out that Grandad also liked ballet, although he didn't get to go to any that I know of.

As a boy, it was incumbent upon me to prove myself. A pipeline crossed from one side of a canyon to another carrying either gas or water to another section of the city. It was suspended by cables much like the Golden Gate Bridge, only a lot smaller. But from the pipeline to the bottom of the canyon it was a sheer drop, perhaps a couple hundred feet. We walked that pipeline, holding on to the cables. After crossing, we would hang by our hands on the cable over what was significantly less of a fall, but definitely a fall that could hurt. I managed to do this even though I had serious problems with acrophobia. Scared to death, but more afraid of chickening out, I did what I had to do from that suspended pipeline. None of us was harmed. The last time I checked it had been closed off and gated, as it should have been earlier. Thinking back on the activity sends chills down my spine.

CHAPTER 4

BACK HOME AGAIN—SANTA RITA

Dad lost his job at Los Alamos *again* and we moved for a few weeks to Albuquerque. Valley High School had just opened and for the first two weeks of the school's history, I was a part of it. We chose the school colors, and Vikings became the name of the school's mascot which we voted on. It was a short two weeks and we found out we were again moving, this time back to the Santa Rita area. Dad had a job with Kennecott. The news met with grand approval from all the family which not only included my brothers Denny and now Bruce who was born during our last sojourn at Los Alamos.

He was a surprise. Mother was in her 40's and they received the news that Bruce had a defect. He had Down syndrome. The doctor urged her to place the child in an institution, but she wouldn't hear of it. Had abortions been legal then, I'm sure that would have been an option, but again, this was not a choice for Mom.

We moved to a hilltop in Turnerville, now not even a dot on the map, although Google Maps lists a Turnerville Post Office, under a pile of rocks dug from the Chino mine. It was owned by the Alton Turner family. We had our own well and a pump put water in our water tank. We bought our first television while living in Albuquerque. It didn't work very well in Los Alamos, and the picture was almost non-existent in Turnerville. That is until we began to move the antenna around. Finally, after trying to get decent reception I put the mast down on the cyclone fence. "That's it!" my mother shouted from the house. The antenna was pointed downward into a canyon where we tied it down and it stayed. Sometimes we would get a "skip" program from distant places like Mexico City and Miami. Most of the time we watched television stations from El Paso, a little over a hundred miles away.

Our house was only a short walk from Santa Rita; down our road into the canyon, cross a road and then walk a trail up the other side to the Chino Club on a hillside just west of Santa Rita. Most of the time I chose to walk the trail to join my friends at the club where we could shoot pool, set pins for spending money or bowl ourselves. We could get a milkshake or a coke and watch TV. Sometimes there were bingo games or dances, but most of the time we had the run of the place as long as the person in charge had no objection. We were usually respectful, knowing that misbehavior would warrant a call to our parents. The club had the right to ban anyone it deemed a nuisance. Sometimes the walk in the dark was without incident, but I was always aware that "something" was out there in the blackness. Once in a while a bird would fly off or a cow would moo. I knew it wasn't anything harmful, but still my heart would race, and my breathing get short when I was startled.

It was while we lived at Turnerville that I learned to drive. We had a 1952 Dodge station wagon with standard shift drive. My dad drove the car to a clearing near the house, showed me the gear sequence, got out of the car and told me to practice until I had it down. I was to drive back home when I thought I had it mastered. The first time he rode with me while I was driving I was 22 years old. I taught myself to drive on winding curving mountainous roads, the best thing I could have done. I learned well enough to get my driver's license at age fifteen and a half. I was on my way to becoming a "real person." My mother rode with me a few times and had to stifle the desire to "help" me see the curves ahead or to watch out for this or that object she was afraid I would hit. I was a good teacher to myself in the skill of driving. I never hit anything of any importance…

When the mine was on strike, we all suffered the loss of income. On one occasion my dad had made friends with a neighbor who owned leaching rights in an arroyo through which water mixed with sulphuric acid that had been filtered through copper ore flowed. Most of the time the water was channeled into concrete vats filled with iron shards including tin cans with the tin burned off. Through a process called *precipitation*, the iron changed to copper as the mixture came together. If properly done, the copper precipitate was nearly pure.

We boys were recruited to gather tin cans and other iron shards wherever we could and put them in a dammed up area along the arroyo and then let the water run over them. We had to be careful when summer storm clouds gathered. If a sudden rainstorm hit the area and washed out the precipitation dam, all our efforts would be lost, so often we slept in the car I drove to the site. We blocked the rainwater and protected the copper.

At the end of the summer we loaded the copper, about a ton, into a truck and hauled it to El Paso to the ASARCO smelter where we sold it. We received enough money from the endeavor that we were able to pay the food bill at the Company Store. Keith, Denny and I rode in the back of the truck with the precipitate as Dad and the neighbor, Mr. Oliver drove.

My brother, Denny, was the youngest of the family and we all picked on him. I'm not sure why, but that was common. After we returned from delivering the copper to El Paso Denny became ill and he was taken to a doctor. We weren't sure what it was, but mom and dad stayed with him in the hospital in Silver City. On the second day of his hospitalization my parents returned in the evening without him. Dad broke down in tears, the first time I had ever seen him do this. Denny died at twelve years old. He had bulbar polio and it had taken his brain. The rest of the family was called and Reverend Harold Johnson also came to the house for prayer and consolation. We were devastated. I felt guilty for my actions toward my brother and now there was nothing I could do to change what I had done.

We were members of the Santa Rita Community Church and I attended most Sundays, joining the youth group, called Pilgrim Fellowship that met on Sunday evening. The church was affiliated with the Congregationalist denomination which descended from the Puritans who came to America to settle this land. It was liberal in theology and teaching, but the pastor, Reverend Harold E. Johnson was a revered member of the community everyone looked up to and respected. Drinking was *verboten.* During the War, he volunteered and served in the Red Cross. He was the leader of the Boy Scouts, Pilgrim Fellowship, led services at the Ft. Bayard hospital, and had founded a youth camp named Camp Thunderbird, about 22 miles up a mountain road through the small town of Mimbres.

Left to right: Granddad Peper Jan Thomas, cousin Gerald Saige, Keith Thomas, Rev. Harold E. Johnson

Rev. Johnson enlisted all of the people he could to build the camp, and those who helped most were the youth group from the church. We would spend weekends and many days during the summer to help with all of the tasks that needed to be done. All the kids and most of the adults called him simply, "Rev."

Grandad Peper had been recruited as the caretaker of the camp and we helped mold two buildings that had been moved from the mine into a cottage for my grandparents to live in. Camp Thunderbird had two pre-World War II Dodge Power Wagons which had been acquired from Army Surplus. I felt like a "somebody" driving those old trucks. They dated from about 1938, as I recall. The camp became a launching pad for us when we hunted deer, wanted to hike through the forest, or just enjoy a skinny-dip in a near-by cattle watering tank.

We found a friend living in a shack not too far from the camp, an old Mexican man who invited us to share coffee and beans with him. We were never sure what he did out there, but he was friendly and accepted us gringo kids. The coffee and beans were welcomed, and he always seemed to enjoy our company.

Not far from there was a shack where we found a cache of dynamite. I have no idea why it was there or to whom it belonged. We took a stick of the explosive and tried to figure out ways to set it off. We were afraid to do it, but to chicken out wouldn't have been "cool." We threw it, but nothing happened. We knew a blasting cap had to be inserted, but none were available. I don't remember what happened to the stick, but it didn't blow up and we were not harmed in the process of trying to understand how to get it to do what it was designed for. I'm sure I wouldn't be telling you this if we had completed our experiment with it successfully.

For a week in the summer we had camp, all of the Congregationalist churches in New Mexico and El Paso, Texas, joined together. I loved the camp experience and once, by the material presented, considered again my commitment to Christ. But it only lasted momentarily. I had too many other things on my mind; like having fun with my friends who included my cousin Vance and his brother Jerry. And there were girls; I was always interested but feared rejection, so most of them became fantasies in my mind. There were strict rules about boys staying in boy areas and girls vice-versa, but we always managed to try to find ways around that.

Vespers were always inspirational, especially when we would hike up the road to the top of a hill where we could look down on the Sapillo valley below. Sunset, with the spectacular colors in the sky were a beautiful setting to sing hymns, say prayers and think about the world God had made. I was aware of the Creator, but I still didn't know much about Him and I was too busy growing up to learn. Besides, there wasn't a lot of teaching going on apart from Sunday school and, of course, camp. Rev. Johnson taught the youth Sunday school, and it was about as boring as his sermons that were always read. I can't remember a single sermon. Once I was asked to be the youth preacher and I used the 23rd Psalm as my text. I had memorized it in class at school. You could do that back then.

My freshman year of high school was the last year of the old Hurley High, 1954-55. The two-story building was old and shook during class change. It was phased out and a new school building was constructed in Bayard, a few miles to the north which opened in the fall of 1955. Hurley as a typical smelter town, had acrid smoke pouring out of the smokestack when copper was in the process of being refined. During temperature inversion weather conditions, the smoke came down on the town and breathing became an issue. It smelled like sulfur and had a high content of the element. I hated these days and my lungs felt raw.

If I would have thought about it, or if some of the anti-smoking advertisements would have been made then, I might have stopped smoking, maybe not. I kept getting caught by my parents until one day, when Dad had a cigarette rolling machine, he asked me to roll some cigarettes for him; and by the way, I could roll some for myself. From then on, it wasn't a forbidden vice, just an unhealthy one. Most of my friends smoked, there was even an approved area for us to smoke outside the high school building, which we frequented often.

High school was a mixture of a lot of things that didn't necessarily include learning. I mentioned earlier that algebra was not something I understood, nor did I want to know more. I flunked the algebra class in the eighth grade. I had to take it again my freshman year. Mr. Hendrix was the teacher and he was deathly afraid of the students. This made for great sport.

His appearance reminded us of Porky Pig in the cartoons, and he stuttered, especially when he became nervous. We could *easily* make him nervous. Vance found another use for the copper wire they used in the physics lab. You could fashion it into a spiral, make a loop at one end with a note tied to the other end. One or another of the students would see him in the restroom hovering over one of the waist to floor urinals, doing what guys normally do standing in front of the receptacle. As he bent over, he never looked around him and it was easy to slip the loop of the copper spiral through his belt loop. When he returned to the classroom, the copper "pig tail" dangled with the note at the end. Hendrix would turn around and stutter, "I-I-I-I ddddon't kknnow what yer lllaphin' at. Iff yyyou dddon't stop, I'mm gggonna tttake yyyou ttto thhe ppprincipal." Nobody ever got taken. The note at the end of the wire had a simple message: "oink oink."

Sometimes we would stand up in our desks and move them out into the hall as we changed classes. There were magazines, even back then, with centerfolds that would somehow get taped to the rear wall of his classroom. Hendrix would never say anything but, with his book held at eye-level so he wouldn't have to look at anyone, he would walk to the back of the room… a tearing sound was heard… and the centerfold crumpled, taken to the trash can and disposed of. Although I wasn't involved, his car was jacked up by some of the other boys and put on blocks; or watermelon rinds would be put under the rear tires. As he tried to drive off, the car would just spin tires and wouldn't move. I have repented of this kind of behavior but think fondly of the man who tried to teach us math, although I never really got it because of my wayward character. I opted for general math to meet my requirement for graduation.

My grades were abysmal and my attitude toward academia was even worse. I had no appreciation for the process and I was headed for a life of pick and shovel, little more. I wasn't afraid of work; I just didn't appreciate the learning process. My parents were concerned about my lack of enthusiasm about making good grades, but they didn't know what to do about it. It seemed that blue collar work was all the family had known and we were always encouraged to get a job. While some of the jobs were not what would be allowed presently under our child labor laws, back then it was not really a problem. We did things that kids today would never be allowed to do.

When I was fourteen some of us boys got a "real" job during the summer as painter helpers at the mine's locomotive shop. A painting contractor wanted help and he wasn't picky about who he hired. We were to clean the motor housing on an overhead crane in the electric locomotive shop at the mine. This required climbing up iron girders, about 40 feet up, walking on railings to the carriage area and scraping grease off the crane that picked up the heavy locomotives that moved the ore from the mine up miles of tracks. It was dirty work, required a solvent to help remove the yucky stuff and our shoes became slick with the sludge we were removing. But hey, we made a paycheck! My payments into Social Security began at that point. I'm glad it did, retirement isn't bad!

At sixteen a friend of ours, Bob Mallard, told my brother, who was fifteen, and me about an opportunity to work at a sawmill near Beaverhead in the Gila Forest. It paid a dollar an hour. We jumped at it. By that time, I had a car of my own, a 1948 Dodge sedan with Fluid Drive. But there were problems: the clutch slipped, the tires were worn and there were a few other things that showed up the more it was driven. The car was only eight years old, but right after the War the quality of craftsmanship in the United States was less than impressive.

Planned obsolescence it was called. This vehicle was a disaster, but hey! It was mine. I paid $500 for it.

Keith and I started out to the sawmill site after being told we were hired and, not far from Camp Thunderbird, we had a flat tire. No spare. We walked back to our grandparents' cottage at the camp, repaired the tire, and borrowed the spare for their car a 1946 DeSoto, that had the same wheel configuration as our Dodge since it was also a Chrysler product. We set out again, but the slipping clutch made it difficult to go up the mountainous road. But we made it.

At the sawmill we were given the job of pulling lumber off the assembly line and stacking them in 2X4, 4X4 or 2X6 stacks, according to the cut made by a skilled worker. It was called the "green chain." We placed logs which had been loaded on a skid onto the saw carrier to be cut into slabs by the giant circular saw. We used a tool I had never heard of, a *cant hook* to grip the log and get it moving onto the carrier. I worked up to the job of "off bearer" which required pulling the slab from the saw as it was cut, turning it on a side and sending it down the rollers to be cut into widths. Sometimes a log would be full of little black ants that would spray all over everyone and smell like urine. They had a name with a more common term that reflected the smell.

On the days we worked we came back to our one-room slab shack exhausted. We had to catch a nap before we could make supper, which mainly was soup out of a can cooked on a wood stove. There was no electricity and, hence, no refrigeration. Our food items that needed cooling were placed in a clean garbage can, set in a square enclosure that was about three feet high and filled with sawdust which was kept wet with water to help with cooling. Occasionally we would get fresh venison from a worker who had poached an animal for food. I don't know if it was legal or illegal, probably illegal, but it was food and game wardens didn't check anyone.

Most days we worked, but if a saw was broken or the sawyer had been jailed for being drunk, we didn't. No work, no pay. Rather than to drive back home on weekends, if we had a chance, we would ride with some of the other sawmill workers who usually drank as they drove into town. We never had an accident, which was a good thing.

After having a lot of days without work, Keith and I decided we would quit. The superintendent wasn't happy but wrote us a $40 check for the hours we had accumulated. We needed gasoline, but he said we were on our own, he would neither give nor sell any gas to us, so we started back knowing that a less mountainous route existed, but it was by going north, not south, catching a paved road, NM-12, which would take us to Horse Springs, into Reserve, Glenwood, Silver City and home. The Dodge wouldn't make many more mountainous roads.

The car continued to have a hard time going along dirt roads, up small hills—and we were running on gas fumes. I wasn't sure we were going to make it, and after going down into an arroyo, one of the tires gave out. I looked out on the rocks outside the car and discovered we had entered a Gila monster lizard hangout. Gila monsters are not numerous, but here they were. The black and pink mottled skin was a dead giveaway. No way was I going to change a tire in this dry gulch! We drove on until we saw no more lizards, got out and were in the process of changing the tire when a gasoline truck, headed south, stopped and asked us if we were having trouble. I told him about my concern about running out of gas and he got out and filled a five-gallon can and put it in our tank. We only had the check for $40, and he wouldn't cash it, giving us his address for us to send money after we got back. We agreed to do so, and we followed up that promise, probably surprising him. It wasn't much at about a quarter a gallon, but we honored our promise.

After changing the tire, we tried to start the car and the starter began slipping. We looked at it and it was hanging on by one bolt which was loose. We had no tools, even if we would have had a wrench, the threads were stripped. My brother held the starter in place while I cranked the engine and we got it going. I felt that things were looking up until I put it in gear and the gear shift didn't catch. Keith looked under the hood and the shift leavers had become uncoupled. He managed to get them back together and we actually got going. I felt better when we reached the paved road and began driving toward home. As we crossed the San Francisco River I heard a bang and smoke came from under the hood. We stopped and tried to figure out what had happened. Keith explained that he saw the oil cap off to the side of the engine. Puzzlement! He put it back on, held the starter, made sure the shift linkage was connected and I started the car. We went a little further, and again the bang, the cap was off, and I began to notice the oil pressure gauge was showing low pressure. We got it into Reserve, pulled into a service station where there was a hydraulic lift and had the mechanic take a look at it. He shook his head and said there was nothing he could do. It was an internal problem in the engine.

We were using oil like crazy. Just outside Glenwood I decided that it was really going to be impossible to go up any more hills without help. We parked the car alongside the road and decided to get back home by hitching a ride. We got into Glenwood and called home. Dad had gone to work at the mine and would be working all night. We tried to cash the check, and no one would do it for us. We both looked like bums, dressed in khaki's.

Well, could we get a ride home? We tried and walked about 10 miles out of Glenwood toward Silver City. There was very little traffic and those who did pass, had no intention of picking up anyone who looked like we did. It was well after dark when we decided to start catching a ride back into the town we had had no luck in getting even a bite to eat. After a few cars passed us, one did stop and took us into town. We tried getting a room at several hotels that would not touch the check that we had.

Finally, a motel owner, having pity on us at that late hour, decided to look at the check and recognized that it was probably good. We slept. We called home the next morning and Mom told us Dad was on the way. After breakfast he appeared to our relief and we discussed our situation with him. We drove out to where we had left the clunker, got a case of oil, put some oil in it, Keith held the starter and we got it going. As we drove along, the jalopy slowed down going uphill, and dad would move in behind us and give us a gentle push to get over it. Bumpers back then had a real purpose. Every once in a while, the oil cap would blow off, smoke would emerge from under the hood; we would stop, put it back on and head off again.

We got to Silver City—familiar territory—and, guess what? The oil cap blew off again; smoke signal… and I prayed silently that nobody I knew was watching. We were in the middle of town at the intersection of West College and North Pope Street. If they saw us, they never said anything. This was not a "cool" thing and we always wanted that element to be an expression of who we were. We got it home and us boys who had taken auto shop and knew almost nothing other than how to put oil in a car and drive it, removed the engine head and discovered a hole on the top of one of the pistons, so big you could put four fingers through it up to the first knuckle. The cause of the engine explosion was that the gasoline fumes from the carburetor went into the oil pan and the sparkplug set the mixture off, blowing the oil cap off and creating smoke from the burnt oil. We were home, safe and with a tale to tell. It took some time to gather money to get the car fixed. We did what our limited expertise could accomplish, but transmissions, especially Fluid Drive eluded us.

Drinking, beer was definitely cool and whenever we could scrape up enough to get a six-pack we would find a bar that would sell it to us. One bar down below Mimbres, at a settlement known as San Juan had no problems as long as we had the money. We termed the place "Uncle Johnny's" and we bought many six-packs there. My cousin Vance, a few other boys and myself skipped school one day and drove to Palomas, Mexico, south of Deming and Columbus where we bought several bottles of a rotgut rum and brought them back. I don't remember how we were able to get them back into the US through the Immigration officers, but we did. We drank all the way back to Bayard. I think Vance looked old enough to bring it back and since we didn't have to show any identification it worked.

Vance and I had one of the bottles, actually a jug, hidden in the rocks of a hill not far from where we lived. We had seen a movie of two old cowpokes that had a jug and one of them pointed a gun at the other one and said, "Take a drink." Under protest the other fellow drank a swig of the foul liquid. Then the one with the gun gave the sidearm to the other guy, took the jug and said, "Now you make me take a drink." We played that scene out several times as we made ourselves sick. We stayed at Vance's house that night since his parents were out of town. I threw up and made a mess, but I was scheduled to work as a sacker at the Company Store the next morning and I dutifully did. Everything smelled like that awful rum. I made it through the day, but I made a resolution that I would never drink that stuff again. Beer was another thing.

Skipping school, while not a regular event, did happen occasionally. I had learned to forge my mother's signature on an excuse note and was able to get by with this behavior. One time, we decided just after lunch to skip a class and sit in Jim Billings' car and smoke. We had been out the previous night to Camp Thunderbird to help thaw out pipes at the camp. Water was not getting to my grandparent's' cottage, so we took an arc welder out there and hooked the ends to frozen steel pipes and finally got the water going. The temperature was below zero and it was cold. We did get some sleep that night before going to school, but while sitting in the car somebody yelled, "There's Haggerson." Nelson L. Haggerson, Jr. was the principal of Cobre Consolidated High School in Bayard, New Mexico. He was younger than we thought he was, but at younger than thirty, he was the epitome of a "no nonsense" school administrator. He had red hair and a ruddy complexion. When he got "steamed" he became redder.

I was sitting in the passenger seat, Jim in the driver's seat of his Ford sedan. We all slumped to the floor of the car, hoping he wouldn't see us, but my hopes were lost when I saw Jim's eyes focus on Haggerson just as he opened the door on my side of the car. We were caught! Soundly commanding us to go to his office we meekly complied, no longer recalcitrant in our demeanor. Oh, the horror!

He asked us why we were missing class and we instantly cited our wonderful behavior of thawing out my grandparent's water lines. It worked! We were warned never to do it again, and we were not expelled, but our parents were told. Nelson Haggerson went on to get his Ph.D and taught at Arizona State University in Tempe, Arizona. He would come back for class reunions, the first time in full "hippie" regalia with long hair, beads and all. We enjoyed getting to know him as the person he was. He wrote several books on education issues and became distinguished far beyond his tenure at Cobre High School. He died in 2009, at 82 years old and had been at a reunion with us in Silver City a year or two before his death, dancing with his former students. I will remember him fondly.

Another teacher, Lola Knight, who was a member of the Santa Rita Community Church had an effect on me that planted the seeds to rethink my attitude toward renouncing academic pursuits. She asked me to stay after class one afternoon, sat down at a desk near me and told me my grades so far in the class were a low "D." I was pretty sure it was close to that, but I didn't think I needed anyone to tell me. I had just entered my junior year. My GPA was abysmal. I was sure that the teachers in the teacher's lounge were taking bets as to whether I would graduate or not. At that point I didn't care one way or the other. She told me something no one else had ever mentioned. She said, "I know you are a smart kid. I know you can do better. Promise me you will begin to do your homework and let's see if we can get this grade up." I promised her I would. And I did. I went on to get on the Honor Roll the last two years of high school in spite of getting another job. Lola Knight was named New Mexico Teacher of the year, and she saved me from self-inflicted mental wounds that almost kept me from being more than a blue-collar worker for the rest of my life, not that that was necessarily a wrong career choice since all of my ancestors had gone this route, but it was not who I was able to become. Thank you, Lola for your encouragement to me. I'm sure you are in heaven. She was a member of our church and a great friend of Rev. Johnson.

I had other teachers who were competent in their teaching skills, but occasionally there would be miscalculations in lab experiments. I enjoyed chemistry and did pretty well in the class. We did have some events that in retrospect were humorous. Mr. Hornbaker was demonstrating the properties of solid sodium. He took a piece of the volatile metal from a container which surrounded it with kerosene. I never understood how kerosene kept the sodium in check, but it does. Placing the sodium in a beaker filled with water, he captured it with a glass tube and, as he lighted the end with hydrogen being released from the water by a reaction of the sodium with the water, the kerosene ignited around the dancing sodium and the piece of sodium shot through the glass tube and up—into the ceiling panel! It continued to burn into the acoustical tile and a janitor had to be called in to cut the piece of sodium out of the ceiling. The look on the teacher's face was priceless.

On another occasion Hornbaker was demonstrating how cupric oxide would react to something—we never got to the "something"—when he took an upright rod used to hold Bunsen burners and began to crush the substance into water in a thistle tube. Shortly after the demonstration began, the teacher got a strange look on his face, pulled the upright out of the thistle tube and we saw it foaming as he laid it on the table. It had a reaction with the aluminum in the upright, which became hot in the glass container and began burning his hands. He was not injured, nor was anyone else, but we enjoyed the demonstration.

I almost got knocked out with the smell of burning sulfur someone placed below my nose, and I burned my arm with a piece of something we were told not to get on our skin, because it was highly caustic. I, being the skeptic, placed a piece on my arm. I still bear the scar from its eating out my flesh in that spot. I also have a mark in my left palm where someone was challenging me with a pencil and I slapped it out of his hand, the end of the pencil penetrating my hand and bringing blood. The graphite from the pencil became the only "tattoo" I have placed on my body, either on purpose or accident. I had previously thought of getting the Marlboro man's tattoo on one of the back of my hands, but I grew out of that desire before I had the opportunity to be engraved forever with this foolishness.

During my junior year I learned of an opening at the Atchison, Topeka and Santa Fe Railroad that needed workers to move the ore from the mine in Santa Rita to the smelter in Hurley. My early fascination with trains became a reality when I filled out an application, took tests in El Paso and was given my battery-powered railroad lantern to begin work as an assistant switchman. I was in! I had a job making $96 a week and I worked the "extra board" which usually meant I worked the graveyard shift. My assignment was to hook gondola cars up after the ore had been dumped into a bin to be pulverized by the ball crusher on its way to being turned into copper ingots.

The car dumper was designed to receive a car, clamp the bottom of the wheels, turn it over and empty the contents into the abyss below. As soon as the car was empty, the engine at the head of the spur track would push it out of the way, placing the next car on the dumper clamps. My job was to hook up the empty cars after they had been pushed out of the dumper. Sometimes that was a real thrill… especially when the brakes wouldn't work right. A wheel on the end of the car was turned until it stopped… or was supposed to stop. The first car was ridden down the track, braked to a stop, an iron tie spike was placed under the wheel, the brake was released, and it rested there until the next car was pushed out. I had to run to catch the next car, brake it down, gently bring it into a clamp with the knuckle of the first car, connect the air hoses, and then catch the next car and so on, hooking up 50-car trains to be taken back to the mine at Santa Rita to be again filled with ore.

Depending on how far away the first car stopped, it could be a hard run to catch the next one. We were taught how to get on and off the car. Sometimes the car would be going faster than it was safe to get off, and a reprimand from the supervisor was required. My limbs could have been severed by a miscalculation by being run over by a car's wheel or my fingers caught by the knuckle as the cars were hooked together.

Getting from work to school was usually a quick change of clothing while driving from Hurley to Bayard after getting off at 8:00 a.m. Class started at 8:35 and it took me a little time to get from the parking lot to class in my now repaired Dodge. I was never late to class and, while my hands might be dirty from work because I didn't have time to wash up, I was ready to learn. Homework was done after school, a nap was taken before I had to go to work again, and I managed to work a month and a half before I got *the call*.

The assistant trainmaster called me one evening and asked me what my date of birth was, I told him what I had entered on the application. He responded that they had checked with the school and I was off by a year in my calculations. I was born in 1939, not 1938. I owned up to it and he told me I had been doing a great job, but the insurance company for the railroad wouldn't allow a 17-year-old to work. I had to be 18. He said he wanted me to apply again when I was old enough, but by that time the railroad was laying people off and my railroad career was forever finished. I needed to concentrate on getting through high school and I did.

I had to take an additional correspondence course taught by the Assistant Principal, Mr. Phillips, in order to graduate. Even though I was on the honor roll the last two years of high school, my first two years seriously affected the first two. We met after classes were over and Mr. Phillips tutored me through the course. I don't remember the class content, but it was enough to get me over the hump and to receive my diploma. The night of graduation, I made a statement that was completely overturned by events which followed. I said: "If I never get into another classroom, it will be too soon!"

Graduation was a hoot! We went to Cherry Creek and had a picnic; all the administration and teachers who taught senior subject were there. We climbed rock bluffs, waded into the creek and managed to dunk several of the adults, including Mr. Haggerson. I proudly walked across the stage on graduation night and received my diploma.

The family moved immediately after my graduation to Albuquerque. Dad was tired of working for Kennecott and had other union opportunities there. The year was 1958. Vance and I tried to find work in the area, but had difficulty; there was a recession on and jobs were scarce. We worked for a few days in Grants, insulating houses that were being built. I hated working with the glass wool that we had to install because the glass beads went through clothing and irritated anything that had a nerve. It was a booming uranium mining town about 80 miles west of Albuquerque. Vance was not doing well at New Mexico State University (at that time called New Mexico College of Agriculture and Mining, in Las Cruces). He was pursuing a career in agriculture since he was involved in the Future Farmers of America while at Cobre, raising sheep and pigs in his back yard, or just outside his back yard, in Santa Rita during high school. He rethought the career choice and had lost interest. Pigs just weren't his style.

CHAPTER 5

THE MILITARY YEARS

We began exploring the military since we were draft eligible and the possibility that we could be called up, could surface in the future in the middle of something else. We decided to get it out of the way and were headed to the Navy when Jim Billings came up from Santa Rita. He and Vance began to talk about going into the Marine Corps. I had seen movies: Marines hitting the beach at Iwo Jima, getting shot at; slogging through the jungles, getting shot at... I told them to go ahead into the Marines; I wanted to check out other options.

I talked to the Army recruiter who tried to get me to sign the application, telling me I would be sent to basic training the next day. I held off. I talked to the Air Force recruiter who told me that if I signed with them there would be a six-week wait, since there were many who wanted to select this branch of the military. Thinking about getting shot at in the Navy, Army and Marines, I decided that since there were so many more who wanted to go into the Air Force, that was the outfit I wanted to enlist in. I didn't relish being shot. I signed my name. At the time I was working for a combination drive-in restaurant and gas station near the University of New Mexico, earning seventy-five cents an hour for the privilege. When I mentioned joining the Air Force to the owner of the establishment, he questioned my reasoning. I told him that driving to work daily was eating up my earnings, since I was paid such low wages. He didn't offer to up my salary, and my decision to join the Air Force was reinforced.

The time came to go to basic training and I got my first ever airplane ride from Albuquerque to San Antonio. There were no airline jets in 1958, only 4 engine propeller aircraft. Landing in San Antonio, I along with others who had enlisted from New Mexico, was met by a bus from Lackland Air Force Base. One of them was from Albuquerque, his last name was LaCour, and he and I became part of the same training group. We were in for a rude awakening after being driven to a mess hall about midnight to have "breakfast."

After eating, I leaned back and fired up a cigarette. A uniformed guy across the room jumped up from his table and shouted: "PUT THAT CIGARETTE OUT! You will smoke only when you are told you can smoke." I gulped and quickly put the lighted instrument out. We were herded to a building and given an olive drab flight jacket and a cap. We were then lined up and told we were a bunch of nothings that had wandered into the best outfit in the world: THE United States Air Force. If we were to make anything of ourselves, we had better jump when told and keep our mouths shut unless asked something. It was about two in the morning and we were marched to a barracks and allowed to lay down—but not for long. At 0500 we were blasted with revile and told to stand in formation outside the barracks.

Again, we were told how pitiful we were, not even human beings, less than the lowest animal on earth. Maybe not even an amoeba. I learned to say, "YES, SIR," and mean it. The Training Sergeants led us through learning how to march, break down M-1 rifles, and shoot them. After six weeks, I was placed aboard a bus and transported from San Antonio to Biloxi, Mississippi, Keesler Air Force Base. I was headed to tech school to become a radar operator! I was now a *somebody*. I learned how to read a radar scope, write backwards on a clear plastic board with range, azimuth and grid lines which correctly placed the location of flying aircraft. I learned weather, and again how to shoot a weapon.

After graduation, I was told my first assignment would be—drum roll—not anywhere but smack dab back in New Mexico, a little over a hundred miles from where my parents had bought their home on 57th Street NW in Albuquerque. Join the Air Force and see... *New Mexico*? I had lived here all my life! But Continental Divide Air Force Station would be my first assignment, almost halfway between the cities of Grants and Gallup. Less than a couple hundred personnel manned the site which was located off the highway, south of what used to be Route 66, now Interstate 40 at Top of the World. Not much around to do.

Radio during the afternoon consisted of Navajo music from a radio station in Gallup. Once in a while you could hear an advertisement from nearby car dealers and other establishments, but for the most part it was unintelligible to the English-speaking ear. At night radio stations that covered the American West, the "big boomers," came in loud and clear. KOMA, Oklahoma City; KOA, Denver; KOB, Albuquerque; and one I liked a lot, XERF, Del Rio, Texas. Sometimes we could get a station from Shreveport, Louisiana; KWKH-AM and FM that played *The Louisiana Hayride* followed by *No Name Jive*. Since I liked Country and Western as well as Rhythm and Blues and the Rock and Roll that started in the '50's, I was okay with that. Vance and I had discovered a young singer on the *Hayride*, named Elvis. At one point he came to Silver City and was the opening act for Hank Snow while we were in high school. My only time seeing him in person.

Being a radar operator, I worked shifts, three days, followed by three swing shifts, and then three days off. The next cycle would have three days, followed by three graveyards with three off days. I didn't like the midnight to eight shifts, but they would be with me for all of the rest of my time in the Air Force, with the exception of when I became a bus driver, and we'll get into that later. It was a bleak place to live and work. On my days off, I would often hitch-hike into Albuquerque in uniform, which usually got me a ride without waiting too long, not like the time in Glenwood.

I finally saved up enough money to buy a car, a 1957 Mercury that looked much like a car my Uncle Jim and Aunt Theresa had. It was the same color, but only a two-door. And the transmission worked! I got the privilege of being one of the few in the unit to own a car, so I was compelled to drive people into town, and they paid for the gas I put in it. I got along with most of those stationed with me except for one Puerto Rican guy who didn't get along with anyone. He and I went out behind the barracks one day to settle an argument, but it only resulted in shouts at each other because an NCO broke up the conflict before blows could be struck.

I was disciplined once for my use of language as my mouth had gotten pretty foul over the years. One day, sitting at my position in the Operations Building, I heard over my earphones, "Thomas, report to me after you are relieved from your position." I recognized the voice of a captain who was our shift supervisor. "You know you're not to use profanity over the land-lines and during work, don't you?" he said. I acknowledged that somewhere back in my memory of how we were trained I had heard that.

"I'm writing you up for cussing on the lines," he announced. I replied with a very military, "Yes, Sir!" The result was that I was restricted to the site for several weeks and my days off to go to Albuquerque would not be available. Nor could I go anywhere, and in addition, I had other duties assigned to me during my time off, like KP (Kitchen Police, for those who never had the experience) and cutting weeds. I was duly chastised, and my language was cleaned up—at least while I had the headset on. Lesson learned.

Once, in October of 1959, we were assembled in formation, an event very rare for the Air Force, at least at radar sites, for a visiting Colonel. As we stood outside in formation, in our summer uniforms with short sleeves, it got colder and colder. At an elevation of over 8,000 feet, this time of year it could get cold. The snow started, and we waited for the bigshot to show up. Minutes passed into hours and still we stood, shivering in the cold, snow falling all around us. He had not yet entered the facility. Finally, a vehicle drove into the site and the occupants went into the BOQ (base officers' quarters for the uninitiated). After what seemed like weeks, we were dismissed and never reviewed by the brass. That's the military way of making sure humility is a part of the enlisted experience.

Gallup had and still has a terrible problem with alcoholism within the Native American people. Going into that city was an adventure. At night a panel wagon driven by the police Department would pick up drunks who had passed out on the street and haul them to jail. It was kinder than leaving them there in the winter to freeze to death, which claimed the lives of some. Occasionally a fight would break out which added to the amusement of a group of airmen who would go into town, most of the time I would be with them.

In one incident, a man and a woman were arguing in Navajo on a street corner. The man shoved the woman into the street (fortunately there was no traffic). He turned and headed down the sidewalk and when she got up; she chased him down and kicked him squarely in his hindquarters. She turned and ran the other direction with him following. They turned a corner and---we never saw the end of the conflict.

My roommate, whose name I can't recall, decided that these people were fair game and talked about "rolling" them for their money. Even back then, I knew this was a stupid thing to do and I don't know if he ever did it or not, but one day the Gallup police came onto the radar site and arrested him for stealing money from an employee of the only drive-in restaurant in that fair city, the Curb-n-Go. He followed the person around after the money bag had been removed from the café and, when he stopped before going to the bank, my roommate reached into the car and took the money. He then raced back to the radar site with the police in pursuit.

Coming into our room, out of breath, he told me what had happened and asked me to get his horse from a ranch about 10 miles from our base and put it in a corral which was a part of Continental Divide Air Force Station. He was taken off in handcuffs and the next day I had another airman drive me to the place where the horse was kept, knowing he didn't have a saddle, only a bridle, and I rode that horse the ten miles or so to the corral. I am thankful that the horse was gentle and that I had had some practice riding burros back in Santa Rita, but for the next two weeks my legs reminded me that it had been a long time since I had ridden an animal and that it would be a long time before I would do it again.

In December of that year a buddy told me there was a TWX (military talk for a teletype message) giving me orders to go to Spain. At that point in my education, I knew it was a country that had populated my part of the United States, but I really didn't know where it was. My name had been placed on a list of those wanting transfers after I had put in for a transfer to Labrador (why I put my name in for this part of the world, I can't imagine, but I wanted to see some place other than New Mexico while I had a chance).

Later that month it snowed hard and deep. The temperature was minus 8 degrees and I was assigned guard duty. Now military, at least the Air Force, had guard duty but the guards were never armed. It was an exercise in discipline, I suspect, but here I was outdoors in below zero weather "guarding" something that at that time I was sure nobody wanted. I was issued a parka which had fox fur around the face and it kept me relatively warm, but my feet nearly froze off. The .45 caliber side arm I was issued never came out of the holster.

I checked out where Spain was and found it to be in southern Europe, which sounded warm to me. I was given two weeks leave around Christmas that year and orders to report to McGuire Air Force Base near Trenton, New Jersey early in January. I traveled to New York City, hoping to meet a fellow airman who had been stationed with me at Continental Divide who borrowed twenty dollars from me and promised to pay it back. We were to meet at Grand Central Station.

In my high school year book under my senior picture it stated that I wanted to go to the Empire State Building in New York, and on that trip to Spain, I was able to do that, even having only twenty dollars to my name when I arrived there with four days to spend. It was 1960, cheaper times, and I found a flop-house on Times Square for three dollars a night, purchased my bus ticket to McGuire AFB, which cost less than four dollars, leaving me about four dollars for the fine cuisine that could be found in the largest city in America at that time. I walked a lot, went to the Empire State Building and took in all the sights that had a military discount or allowed military in for free. I remember ordering at the lunch counter in Walgreens Drug Store just off Central Park.

I was looking for the cheapest meal I could find that would help the hunger slowly overtaking my body on the second day there. Noting the offerings on the menu list above the counter, I selected grilled cheese and French fries. The guy behind the counter said, "Whadda ya wanna drink?" I looked for the selections and said, "Uhhh…" "UH," he quickly retorted, "we don't got no *uh*, here!"

"Well, just give me a Coke," I said, shocked by the rudeness of the man. Coming from the southwest, while we may not have had all the cultural skills we should have had, we at least were not rude to customers or strangers who meant us no harm. New York seemed huge, impersonal and I felt lonely in the midst of the millions of souls wandering around Manhattan. I went to a Congregational church I had looked up in the phone book. Maybe I could find someone to relate to there. No luck. They were just as impersonal as the others I had encountered.

I rode the subway, saw a flea circus and gained entrance into Ripley's *Believe It or Not,* museum—and went to Grand Central Station looking for the guy who owed me the twenty bucks. Every day. I searched the faces of everyone, but he was not among them. My last day I ate one candy bar, it cost a nickel back in those days. I didn't starve, but when I rode the bus from Port Authority Bus Station to McGuire I was thinking *boy, could I go for even the worst meal they serve!* I checked in and was able to get a meal before I expired.

The flight from McGuire was on a C-54 aircraft with seats facing aft. I'm told the reason for the reverse seating is in case of crash, it's safer. Fortunately, we didn't need to test the theory. We were given parachutes in case we had trouble and had to bail out. I didn't quite understand the logic, since we were over the Atlantic Ocean the whole time. We boarded the plane and settled in for a 16-hour flight to the Azores, then on to Torrejon Air Base at Madrid, Spain. While not sleeping, we played cards and talked about whatever came to mind. We landed during the night at the airfield in the Azores, got off the aircraft for a little while and, after boarding during the daytime, we looked out of the window at water below while still on the runway during takeoff. It appeared to me that we would crash into the Atlantic! *That's why the seats were facing the rear of the aircraft,* I thought. The runway was built out into the ocean and we lifted off without incident.

Landing at Torrejon Air Base in Madrid, we were taken to the mess hall and given a meal, and afterward we were put on a bus which took us into the city to spend the night in a hotel set up for American military personnel. Along the roadways I was astonished to see workers with picks and shovels working, but they were in coats and ties. A little shabby, some of them, but overly dressed, in my estimation. I was definitely in a different country. It wasn't the first time I had been out of the United States, since I had been to the Mexican border towns of Ciudad Juárez and Palomas, but Spain wasn't anything like Mexico.

We traveled overnight by train from Madrid to Sevilla and were met by a bus from the Constantina Air Force Station, the 872nd Aircraft Control and Warning Squadron. The traffic in the city was horrendous and it was different than anything I had ever experienced. We were transported northward about 65 miles through hilly country; small towns and villages along roads surrounded by cork and olive trees, with occasional vineyards along the way. I would have to get used to the metric system somewhat, but I still thought in terms of feet, yards, miles and pounds. Women were often in black dresses, signifying they were either widows or mourning a loved one in their family. Men almost always had coat and tie on. No woman was ever in pants, always dresses or skirts. *Very formal people*, I thought to myself.

Entering the gate at the radar site, we were deposited in the middle of a quadrangle and taken to our quarters. This would be my home

Constantina Air Force Station, Spain

for over two and a half years. Thinking back on it, I loved the place, it was far from home, but apart from that I quickly took to the challenge of getting acclimatized to the culture, the language and the people. I found very few of them unfriendly, most wanted to get to know us, and we them. Apart from a short orientation, we were told we would be given lessons in Spanish, we were not to talk politics or religion with the locals and we were to be in coat and tie in the evenings when off-duty and off base.

Our duties were shared by members of the Spanish Air Force who were expected to have learned some English, at least enough to function in the world of military aircraft. Their dormitories were on the same grounds, but separate, as was their mess hall. We didn't like the food they ate, and they weren't fond of ours either. When we had corn on the cob, the workers in the kitchen would peek out of the doors and make comments about us eating food they only fed animals. I guess it would be similar to someone watching other people eat dog food.

Our work area called the Operations Building was located on top of a hill about a quarter mile from the living quarters and mess halls. We boarded a 29-passenger school bus for the trip up the hill for every eight-hour shift, with an American airman assigned as driver. At the bottom of the road leading up the hill was a guard station manned by a Spanish airman with a *loaded* rifle. This military didn't kid around like the U.S.

Spanish lessons were taught by an instructor who lived with us from the province of Castilla. His pronunciation was with the Castilian accent; his name was Antonio Griñán. The sounds of Castilian Spanish sound a little "sissy" at least in my mind. The word for the number five, cinco, is pronounced *thinko*. Plaza is *platha*. We were, however in Andalucia and the pronunciation was more like Mexican, with the exception of chopping off the "s" sounds at the end of words. Cinco would be *sinko,* and plaza would be as understood elsewhere, but the speech would be rapid and cut; the ll, which usually has a "y" sound was pronounced like a "j" in English. I decided I would learn Spanish with more of a Mexican accent, and that is what I practiced. Turns out I have more like a Mexican-gringo accent. I never figured out who "Joe Quiero" was. *Yo quiero* means I want in English.

During times of low numbers of aircraft in the Spanish skies, we would teach each other our languages, sometimes drawing a picture of a dog or some other animal and the Spaniard would say *perro* and we would say "dog." We went through a lot of napkins, grease pencils and other writing materials learning the languages. Antonio would give us grammar lessons and we would get more vocabulary from our counterparts.

We also learned Spanish when we went into town. We had a favorite hangout named *"Venta Pepe Gordo"* or Pepe Gordo's Bar. I quickly learned to order *vino tinto,* or *vino blanco,* depending on whether I wanted red or white wine. Hard liquor was not available, but they had cognac, anise, and other liquors, including brandy. Their beer tasted less than good, somewhat like kerosene to me, so vino is what I mostly drank. Local wine, made there. We could get the hard stuff at our Airman's club on site and the cost was reasonable. When I ordered food, it was usually boiled shrimp *"gambas"* or *un bocadillo de jamón y queso* (ham and cheese sandwich). Often the ham slices were cut from a hanging ham with flies on the outside; we got used to it.

Water off-base was not recommended for drinking. I forgot a few times and got a case of "turista" which lasted in the bowels for about 24 hours. After a couple of these episodes, I think I got some immunity.

My first excursion alone into Sevilla was an adventure. I got a *pensión* for the night for a dollar which included breakfast and the evening meal. I ate what they served, trying not to question the ingredients. It was during the *Feria de Abril,* the April Fair, which is a big blowout for the local people.

Sevilla, Spain. The smell of jasmine and orange blossoms wafted through the April night overwhelming me as I walked along *Avenida Flota de Indias.* Tall apartment buildings on the left, the fairgrounds on the right, the sun was setting behind me as I walked toward the *Rio Guadalquivir.* The sounds of flamenco guitars and high-pitched Andalusian singing rang from the loudspeakers as I meandered through the crowds of people standing along the sidewalk or sitting on benches. Women and girls in beautiful traditional dresses, were escorted by men in coats and ties. Perfect night, exotic in its effect on this young American.

I had been in Spain only a short time, but I had come to love its people and especially the joy they seemed to have by just coming together at this *Feria,* held a couple of weeks after Easter. It was a time to show off their native ambiance; their beautiful dresses and horsemanship, the carriages and *casetas*—the quickly constructed tents they would inhabit during the festivities.

As I walked along a couple of young men drove up in a motor scooter and in broken English asked me if I was enjoying the event. I replied in the affirmative and we went into a *caseta* they invited me to. We drank a little and talked. They found out I was American and in the Air Force and asked if I would go with them to the *Exportadora* where the U.S. military exchange store was and existed for American military in that area. I agreed, and we bought several bottles of whisky, a substance they could not get on the local market and brought them back to the *Feria.* Although I saw no evidence, they told me they were members of the *Guardia Civil, the* elite police force which Generalissimo Francisco Franco used to keep order in this amalgamation of provinces, each with its own ethnic history and culture.

Francisco Paulino Hermenegildo Teódulo Franco Bahamonde, was his full name and as a monarchist, he wanted to preserve the nation which had factions that even presently could tear the country into various parts. The Basques in the north, mainly in the Pyrenes Mountains, have always wanted their independence and prefer their own language to Spanish. The northeastern part of Spain, Catalonia, also has its language which is similar to Valenciano in the southeast and they have repeatedly asked for independence. Andalusia considers itself the "heart" of Spanish culture and is the seat of flamenco music and dancing. Other areas such as Extremadura, the poorest part of Spain, and Galicia in the northwest surround the provinces of Castillo and Leon, which believe they hold the culture of the nation. They also have the Castilian accent. The native language in Galicia is more akin to Portuguese spoken in Portugal just to its south.

The policemen left, and I went into another *caseta* and was approached by a young Spaniard speaking English who asked me where I was from. Feeling a bit inebriated, I told him I was British and began to try to use a British accent. I don't think he caught on to my inconsistencies in speech and a little later came back and in an excited voice told me there were some other Brits there and would I like to meet them. My brain said, "NO!" but my mouth went the other direction and I was introduced to a very tall Englishman who asked me where I was from. I uttered, "Birmingham" with absolutely the wrong accent, more like the Alabama pronunciation. The Brit looked at me with distain and said, "What part of Cedar Rapids are you from?" I immediately looked for a large crack in the floor to fall through but found none. I was busted! Even though the alcohol had dimmed my inhibitions, I was still embarrassed to be caught in such a stupid lie. The man didn't know me, and I don't know him, but I'm sure he will remember the stupid American in Sevilla.

Back at Constantina, I continued my drinking. Several of us drove the bus to another small village which had a *feria*, Alanis, not too far from our site. A sergeant who had a keen eye, and I went to a shooting gallery that used air rifles to shoot objects. Winning resulted in a shot glass of anís, a licorice flavored liquor. He won a whole shelf of the drinks and he and I began to put them away. I remember getting back to my room, rolling over on the floor and puking my guts out. I think I swore off that beverage forever at that point. I don't even like the candy now, although the spice is put in the local Christmas cookies here in New Mexico, called *biscochos* or *biscochitos,* depending on which part of the state you are from are still on my menu.

One evening a couple of the Spanish airmen and I decided to go into town for the evening. We had a pretty good time and we walked the four miles from the radar site to the town and back. Returning as it was getting dark, we had thought about stopping at a *venta* for another few drinks, but the place was closed. We stood outside talking

Guardia Civil with tricorno hats

and we saw a person with a flashlight walking down a hill telling us to stop. It was a *Guardia Civil,* with his *tricorno* hat. Their hats were a distinctive shape and highly polished. He had a machine gun slung over his shoulder and a pistol on his hip. When they tell you to stop, you stop!

He asked us who we were and what we were doing, and we explained, or the Spaniards did the explaining, I listened. The *guardia* knocked on the door, getting the owner up out of bed, telling him it was time to drink some wine. We went in, talked and laughed a bit and I put the *guardia's* hat on, I'm sure not looking as menacing or as official as the officer, but it was a pretty good fit. After a while, the *guardia* said it was time to go and we paid the tab and left. We had been told that whatever a police officer told you to do, to do it. They had the right to shoot and ask questions later. I never questioned the wisdom of this direction from the military.

Another encounter with the *Guardia Civil* came as several of us were on our way to San Pablo Air Base near Sevilla to pick up supplies. I was driving the crew cab pickup and a *guardia* flagged us down, asking for a lift into the next town. He entered the pickup and we headed off toward Sevilla. Now, you have to understand that the traffic laws and customs in Spain are different than in the U.S. Usually roads were narrow, were not often marked with lines, and trucks had a tendency to want to take everyone's space, not letting vehicles behind them pass. I honked for the truck ahead of us to move over, so we could pass since he was traveling at a pace not much faster than a tortoise. No response. Again, a honk—again no response. The *guardia* in the back seat said to pass him on the left shoulder of the road, and I did. After getting in front of him, I was told to slow down and stop. I did as I was told. He got out, went back to the truck driver and had some words with him. I have no idea if a ticket was given or just a bad cussing was meted out instead, but he got back in the pickup with a grin on his face. I kinda liked these guys!

The drinking on base began to get out of hand and in one incident a fellow airman was challenged to drink 10 shots of Lemon Hart rum 151 proof—one after the other. He won the bet but lost his life. He went up to his room in the barracks and choked to death on his own vomit. This slowed us down for a few weeks, but after while we were back at it again. We had warnings from the brass that this would not be acceptable, but while I didn't get drunk again after that, I continued to hang out in the club.

CHAPTER 6

A LIFE CHANGER

It was in 1961 that I met a man who changed my life. He was from North Carolina, his name was Billy Hill, at that time an airman first class (now sergeant). He said if you switched his name around it was hillbilly and that was what he was. He always had a smile on his face and a kind word for everyone. Once in a while a Bible verse would come out, not in a negative way, but always in a helpful manner. He was a technician on the radar equipment. Billy invited me to join him and several other airmen in a Bible study. It just happened (I think not) that they were on the Gospel of John. I had read John 3:16 before, but I had never put my name in the "whosoever" place. One night in 1961, laying in my bunk I prayed something like, "Okay, God. If you are really there, I want you in my life. I give myself to you." It felt like Jesus was sitting right on the end of my bed.

The next morning, I got up and didn't feel any different. I wondered if my prayer had really begun changes in my life. Walking down the corridor of the barracks I saw a piece of paper on the floor. This was unusual. In a military barracks paper on the floor was never found. If it was, it was immediately disposed of. I reached down and picked it up. It had writing on it and I read it—a Bible verse! I can't tell you what it was, but it confirmed to me that God had been listening and that began my walk with Jesus Christ. I told Billy what had happened, and he was pleased with my experience. He invited me to chapel services and, while we didn't have a chaplain, the chaplain from Moron Air Base near Sevilla brought up materials, including 16mm films of "The

Chapel of the Air," a series of sermons helpful for those on remote outposts. We took turns leading Sunday School and I found out that there were others in my squadron who were also Christians. Some were NCO's and some were officers, as well as airmen like myself. I wasn't lonely any more. I had family.

I was invited to Thanksgiving and Christmas dinners at the homes of those who had families and were able to have housing at Constantina Air Force Station. Billy and I grew to be close friends. We took courses offered by the University of Maryland in additional Spanish courses, Spanish History and Culture and speech classes. Antonio Griñán taught all of the language and culture classes. While he was a bit "sissified," I learned to respect and learn from him. I was definitely not on the road I had earlier chosen on graduation night. I was in classrooms again— and enjoying the experience. My new relationship to Jesus Christ had now begun to direct my paths and Proverbs 3:5-6 became my life verse: *Trust in the Lord with all your heart, and lean not on your own understanding; in all your ways acknowledge Him, and He shall direct your paths.* Back then I was reading only the King James Version. That was all I had. I wrote this verse in the flyleaf.

We took field trips. When we studied the Roman influence in Spain, we drove to the ruins of Italica not too far from Sevilla. The Roman General Publius Cornelius Scipio Africanus, after wars with the Carthaginians and Hannibal, constructed a retirement community for his soldiers which at the time was quite ornate. Floors in homes and other buildings were mosaics laid with colored stones; a coliseum was built with concrete and marble veneer; streets were lined out and delineated. During the Moorish invasion of Spain anything of value was taken or destroyed by the Islamic forces. The floors of many of the homes remained, however and the basic structure of the coliseum was intact, complete with moat for "sea battles" and other spectacles, but the marble was gone. We walked through the tunnels underneath the stadium. Nearby were niches where stone boxes kept the ashen remains of long-dead Romans.

On another excursion we went to Córdoba where the city had also undergone an invasion and settlement by Islamic Moors in 711 AD. They had torn down the Christian cathedral, replacing it with an ornate mosque with many arches and pillars. Conquering Spain, they set up a Caliphate that lasted for 525 years. At the base of one of the pillars the guide made special note of a cross scratched, according to legend, by a Christian who had been chained to the pillar and used his fingernail to trace the emblem of his faith, taking much time to complete. The mosque was reclaimed, however during the *Reconquista* of Spain by the Christians in 1236 and only a portion of the mosque was torn down to build the cathedral called *La Mezquita* (The Mosque) that now stands in the middle of the arches and pillars of this beautiful building. The last of the Moors left in "*El Gran Año*" the same year Columbus sailed for America, 1492. Their presence on the Iberian Peninsula lasted 781 years.

Billy and I often went to Sevilla and stayed in a pensión near the Catedral de Sevilla. It is the largest Gothic cathedral and the third-largest church in the world. It is also the largest cathedral in the world. La Giralda is the bell tower of the cathedral that is 343 feet high with a square base of 44 feet long per side. It was the former minaret of the mosque that stood on the site under Muslim rule, and was built to resemble the minaret of the Koutoubia Mosque in Marrakech, Morocco. After the Reconquista it was converted into a bell tower for the cathedral, although the topmost section dates from the Renaissance; it was completed 1198, with the placement of four gilt bronze balls in the top section of the tower. After a strong earthquake in 1365, the spheres were missing. In the 16th century the belfry was added and the statue on its top, called "El Giraldillo, " was installed in 1568 to represent the triumph of the Christian faith. We remarked that with all the gold, silver and precious stone treasures on display in the cathedral, the church could take better care of the poor we saw all over the country.

Another day trip took us to Almodóvar del Rio castle built from the ruins of a Roman fort in the 1200's on the top of a hill not far from Córdoba overlooking the town of Almodóvar below. We were told that the castle had been occupied until the Spanish revolution in 1936, and even had electricity installed to light the building. One could see slots in the rock walls that allowed arrows to be shot through, protecting the archers inside. During the revolution, the furniture and other possessions of the occupants were thrown down and destroyed on the rocks below.

Antonio was very knowledgeable in the history and culture of his country and was always a gentleman and a great teacher. I think I grew to love this country more through him than anyone else I met there. I would like to again experience this time in my past, but with a more mature attitude and understanding, but the past is gone, only memories last. What was can never be revisited, only recalled.

I was given an assignment during the last year of my presence in Spain. I was technically a radar operator, but now I was now a bus driver! A 29-passenger school bus designed for military use, but still a school bus. I learned to drive this "baby" through streets full of hazards. Our first practice was in a field not far from the radar site, close to a small stream that ran through the hilly country covered with cork and oak trees along with stands of chestnut trees scattered about. In the stream we discovered a lot of frogs and retrieved some, removed their legs and had them cooked and served to us by the NCO club. That was the first frog legs I ever ate and, yes, *they taste a lot like chicken.*

The biggest issue in driving a vehicle this large was to maneuver through the streets of towns and not hit balconies or pedestrians. Burros were used by many of the people for transportation and moving goods from one place to another. Often an individual would be riding a donkey or walking along the highway or streets and it was the driver's responsibility not to hit the person or the animal. Highways were paved by using burros to haul material to be used in the construction of the pavement and the animals would know how to go to where the rocks were dumped and return for another trip which would continue throughout the day. Very seldom was heavy equipment seen and it was only for specialty work.

Constantina had one main street that narrowed to one lane in the middle of town. Whoever got to the middle first had the right-of-way and the other person had to back up and let the earlier person pass before he or she could go forward. I can remember a couple of times I brushed a burro, moving it slightly as I drove the bus through town. One owner raised a fist at me, but that was the extent of the problem. There was a penalty for clipping a balcony along the street, however. The person who did it, including the American driving the military bus, had to pay for the repair. We were warned that it would come out of our pay which at that time was $120 a month including overseas pay. I was always very careful and did not hit any structure. The burros survived and were not injured.

Coming from New Mexico I missed the Mexican food I had grown up on. The closest to anything with a bite to it was *gambas al ajillo*. Snacks in Spanish are called *tapas* and this *tapa* was shrimp cooked in olive oil, garlic and cayenne pepper. There were many *tapas* available and I sampled a lot of them. Sometimes we would sit in an open-air *venta* along the streets and eat *gambas* boiled in salt water and served in a pile that cost roughly a dime in American money. We spent *pesetas* on the economy which we would exchange at our site at the market rate.

Paseo de la Alameda

Along the walkway in the middle of Constantina, called *Paseo de la Alameda,* on Sunday afternoons, we would *dar el paseo* (walk back and forth) along with others in the town. The young single women would look at the young single men (of which I was a representative) and *dar piropos* (give flirtatious complements) which usually were stated in opposite terms. For instance, if you thought a young lady was pretty, you called her ugly. In turn they would return the "complement." I got a few *que feos* as I walked along and gave a few *que feas* back. The gals would look embarrassed and would keep looking back if they liked you. We would stop for *gambas* and wine and watch the girls, most of whom were very pretty. After my commitment to Christ, I stopped drinking any alcoholic beverage, but I still liked the shrimp. At that point it wasn't hard to stop the drinking. Christ in me had given me complete victory over it all at once. I don't think at that time I was an alcoholic, I just wanted to fit in.

With just a taste of spicy food, I was elated one day to be invited to the NCO Club for enchiladas. Tortillas made of corn had been sent from the States in tin cans and I looked forward to the meal. My first taste, however, was extremely disappointing. They had used spaghetti sauce on the corn tortillas. While it was edible, it wasn't what my mind had been wanting, so I had to wait until I got back to New Mexico to have my favorite food. I did see "tortilla" once on a menu in a restaurant. I ordered it and discovered that it was an omelet with potatoes in it. Again, a disappointment.

My favorite food off base was a *bocadillo de jamón y queso.* Otherwise known as a ham and cheese sandwich. It was hard to mess this up. Bread generally was pretty much what we would call *bolillos,* buns that are available throughout the United States.

The biggest problem we had was that respectable ladies never "dated" in the sense that Americans are used to. You would have to get to know the family and have someone in the family chaperone the two wherever they went.

There were houses of prostitution, but the chance of catching a social disease was very real. One of my buddies came down with syphilis and after treatment he was warned severely about his activity, given an Article 15, and was told that if a second occurrence would happen he would be disciplined even further and could be discharged from the Air Force for bad conduct. I shied away from this activity and didn't have problems like this.

I did "date" María, one of the workers on the base who worked in the snack shop fixing hamburgers and other sandwiches along with cokes and other goodies. It seemed to me that the name, Maria, was given to at least half of the girls in Spain. Her sister went with us. We saw the movie *Terror of the Tongs* in Constantina at the movie theater there. It was dubbed in Spanish and I was at least able to understand most of it. I thought about what it would be like to marry María and bring her back to the States, but she had a hard time learning English and I don't think it would have worked well, especially since I have been married to a woman I met much later for over fifty years who spoke English very well.

During my tour in Spain the distance from home seemed greater during times when there was illness and death. Both Grandads, Peper and Thomas died, not too many months apart. I was not able to attend their funerals and my loss seemed greater. These men were so much a part of my life and I missed them. Grandad Peper had bladder cancer and within a short while after the diagnosis he died in the hospital. Grandad Thomas had a heart attack and died suddenly.

My cousin, Jerry, who did not go into the military because he had eye problems, bought a Triumph sports car after he graduated from high school. He ran off the road, hitting a post which catapulted him into the trunk of a tree and was in a coma for several weeks. I tried to get a telephone call back to the states to find out how he was, but this was not granted, and I didn't have the monetary wherewithal to pay for it. So, I waited for letters to come from home. Two weeks between sending and receiving; to get an answer required at a minimum a month. It was agonizing in my experience away from home. I finally got word that he had come out of the coma and he was learning to speak again with the help of a dog that kept him company during his recovery. His speech is still slower than it was before that happened. He's now in his mid-seventies and still ticking after taking that licking.

Getting back to the bus driving, I worked two 18-hour shifts a week, most of which was waiting to drive the next shift to work and the Spaniards who worked on site to and from town. There was a lot of time off during the day and working two days in a row, I got the next two off. I was able to take my University of Maryland classes without interruption. I also got away from the less than exciting job of watching "blips" on a radar scope, plotting their trajectory by writing backward on a clear plastic board with maps, range and azimuth markings on it and recording these moves for posterity on logs that were kept somewhere and may still exist in some long-forgotten warehouse or not. Who knows? They may be located near the "Ark of the Covenant" portrayed in the Indiana Jones movie, *Raiders of the Lost Ark*.

Upon graduating from a speech class, we had dinner at a local hotel and restaurant owned by a Belgian couple who had sided with the Nazi's during World War II and had to exile themselves to Spain to escape the repercussions of their former alliance. The place was pretty nice for where and when it was. There was a swimming pool and rooms that could be rented for the night, but we never needed to do this. We did use the pool and ate at the restaurant occasionally.

The meal was very nice and each of us were to give an extemporaneous speech during the banquet. The speech class was a good one for me, since the instructor absolutely would not tolerate the speaker to say "uhhh" between phrases while thinking of the next thing to say. He instructed the class to tap their pencils on the desks at the least hint of an "uh" being uttered. I have all but stopped this habit as I speak now, well, maybe not completely…

Billy and I had leave coming and, after the dinner was over we drove to the Naval Air Station at Rota to catch a hop from Spain to England and later to Italy. Before being able to board the airplane, I began to feel sick and remembered eating potato salad at the banquet that had been sitting for a while. I was in the throes of a major stomach poisoning episode and, refusing to back out of the trip we had planned, I boarded the C-47 which took us to London. During the flight I mentioned the stomach problem I was experiencing and the sailor who was the attendant thought I had drunk too much and had an oxygen mask placed on my face. It didn't help.

Arriving at the Naval Air Station outside London, we boarded a bus to an American military hotel in the city. I needed something to help my stomach, so I began looking for a drug store, walking along the streets of London. I was generally aware that the Brits called these by another name, so I looked for pharmacies or other places that might have Kaopectate or Pepto Bismal, or some other help for my discomfort.

I walked around the city for what seemed like a long time and it finally dawned on me that all of the "chemist shops" I had passed were actually drug stores. I entered one of the shops and pled my plight to a pharmacist who mixed up a concoction which I paid for in British currency and left the store. Now I had to find my way back to the hotel. I had no idea where it was from my location. I just knew it was the Barkley Hotel, so I approached a cab and told the driver where I wanted to go. He drove a short distance, let me out in front of the hotel. Putting out his hand he said, "Two bob!" I suspected it was like" two bits," but more than that in US money, and held out a handful of money and let him take what he needed from it. I have no clue if he cheated me or not, but at that point, I didn't care. Going to my room where Billy was, I took some of the mixed concoction and it tasted much like Kaopectate. I felt a little better, but not much. I don't remember wanting to eat anything that evening. I stayed in bed.

The next morning, we got up, I felt a little better, but my stomach was still rebelling against the Spanish potato salad. We booked a tour of London and set off seeing the sites of Mother England. I tried fish and chips, and while it looked good and I ate some of it, I couldn't eat the whole meal. My stomach was still not cooperating with the rest of my body.

The downtown London tour included Westminster Abbey, Buckingham Palace and a number of other places, including Parliament. At one time, while in Westminster Abby, we got so interested in looking at the historical landmarks the tour bus went off and left us. We continued to look anyway, managed to get to Buckingham Palace in time for the changing of the guard, and took a cab back to the hotel.

On Sunday morning, we went to church at Bloomsbury Central Baptist Church. This was the first church service I had attended outside of our chapel services since my commitment to Christ. The pews were curved, and the pulpit was on a raised platform. As I looked down the pew we were sitting on, I noticed the ugliest pair of bare knees I had ever seen, but then realized it was a Scotsman in a kilt, dressed for Sunday worship. That was something I had never experienced, and it was a novelty to me, but probably not to the others in the church service.

After the service was over we went to the basement for coffee and tea and for a talk about how we in America could help the church financially, since it was "an historic monument" in the city. They were not concerned about their witness to London, just the historicity of the place. It was my impression that they were more interested in promoting their building which went back to 1848 than in sharing the Good News of salvation through Jesus Christ. It may have been me, or just the Sunday, but that's my memory.

We flew back to Spain and caught another Navy hop from Rota to Barcelona, then to Niece, and on to Naples. My stomach was still bothering me, but I managed to enjoy as much of the trip as I could. My first encounter with Italians were the kids who "wanted to take my luggage." We had been warned of people wanting to "help" and then running off with the belongings of those who they helped themselves to, and pickpockets who also wanted to help themselves to other's belongings. We went to a hotel and then began to explore this new country.

Ah, Italy! Home of some of the greatest food in the world. I wanted a *real* Italian pizza, so one was ordered. I was not amused. It had dead minnows on it instead of pepperoni. I was told these were anchovies and they were traditional on pizza in Naples. With stomach problems, this was definitely NOT going to be what I ate. I flicked the "dead minnows" off my delicacy and ate only a little of the rest. I really did NOT like their version of pizza. I liked American pizza much better. This, however, did not ruin my culinary pursuits. Naples has the best ice cream in the world. I have never tasted better.

We went to the Blue Grotto in a small boat. Beautiful! The sea water was clear and blue and the cave with the blue reflection coming through the Mediterranean was magnificent. Then on to the "Isle of Capri." CAP-ree, it is pronounced. We left from Naples in a small power boat and landed on the island which is a protrusion of rock sticking up out of the sea. While there we met an American girl, who wanted Billy to put suntan lotion on her back. He complied, but it was her intention to go a litter farther. Billy, being a Christian gentleman, politely declined the offer and we went about our sightseeing.

Returning to Naples, we got a tour of Pompeii. The devastation left from Mt. Vesuvius in 70 A.D. was almost unimaginable. Petrified bodies in fetal positions were visible as we walked down the ancient streets. At one point the women were told to remain in one area while the men went down a side street. We were shown the pornography of the ancients with phallic symbols and drawings on walls. It was obvious that the city buried under the ash of the volcano had its social problems, not dissimilar to those we experience in the 21st Century. The tour guide, however, was more interested in getting us to vendors rather than in us being able to observe and absorb the archeological and historic site. At one point, we spent nearly an hour in a cameo shop listening to why the wares in this shop were far superior to those anywhere else. I did buy a cameo which I sent to my mother.

We decided to go by train to Rome and traveled in a car with some American naval officers talking about where we were going and where we had come from. One of the officers asked us if we had hotel reservations in Rome and we assured them we did not. This, in their experience, was a problem. We had never had trouble getting rooms elsewhere, but Rome was another matter. Everyone wanted to go to Rome and not to have reservations meant you would likely have no place to stay. Sleeping on the street was not an option.

They offered to help get us housed in the YMCA where they were staying, and we readily agreed that was a great offer. We followed them carrying our luggage from the train station to the YMCA. These guys must have been Seabees or Navy Seals. They went at a breakneck speed we struggled to keep up with, but we made it huffing and puffing carrying our bags. Air Force, or the kind of airmen we were, weren't used to the physical part of military life. Sitting and watching blips on a radar scope or driving a bus didn't require much exertion.

The first night Billy and I were split up and given cots in rooms shared by these Navy guys. The second night we were in a room together. We set out to see Rome and again took a tour. Our itinerary took us to the Coliseum and the Tivoli Fountain as well as other sights in the Eternal City. Sunday afternoon we were at the Vatican in St. Peter's Square when Pope John XXIII came out on his balcony and blessed the crowd below. It would have been a much more spiritual moment had not the vendors been there trying to get the tourists to buy their religious trinkets which were sold to have the Pope "bless" them. I doubt if a special prayer was said for the medallions, but some of the tourists bought them with that in mind.

We toured the Basilica in the Vatican seeing the great statues of Michelangelo's David, Moses and the Pietà. They were not guarded as they are presently with barriers protecting them from vandals. We could walk right up to them. The painting on the ceiling of the Sistine Chapel was etched into my mind and the sense of a long-gone era when there was a devotion to spiritual verities, even though some of them were misdirected, was very present as I contemplated the beauty of the seat of Roman Catholicism. I will always cherish this time in Rome.

We returned to Spain by way of Navy hops from Naples to Sicily and through the Strait of Gibraltar to Rota. I can't remember when Billy and I toured Gibraltar, but I suspect it was when we traveled to Chipiona on the southwest coast of Spain, near Cádiz. We spent a couple of days on the beach of this town, not too far from Rota. Billy had purchased a car that we took when we did the traveling in Spain. As we drove into the seaport town, the Atlantic sparkled in the sunshine. Billy and I met two girls who claimed to be Christians, not of the Roman Catholic variety.

We took them out to dinner and then to the beach at night. I, being a newly formed creation in Christ, wanted to be true to my commitment to my Lord and I just sat there. I still wasn't sure how to deal with the feminine side of humanity. We talked a little, looked at the lights on the ocean and…, well, I didn't know what to do. Walking back to town the girl I was with said she was cold and I gave her my sports jacket. A Navy Shore Patrol officer stopped us and gave me a chewing out for not having a coat on. I thought I was in compliance with a tie around my collar, but that was not enough. I took my jacket off the girl and we parted ways. I never saw her again. I don't even remember how we met these gals, but I do remember that it was an awkward time for me.

Not far from Rota was the city of Huelva and across the river, Palos de la Frontera, from which Christopher Columbus is said to have set sail on his historic voyage, discovering the island of Hispaniola; leading to the further finding of new continents called America, North and South. Billy and I supposedly stood on the very spot from which the *Niña, Pinta* and *Santa Maria* left on the epic voyage. Nobody is absolutely sure of the location, but at least we were close. Nearby were the cities of Jeréz and Cádiz, all not far from Gibraltar.

Gibraltar was a great place to renew my use of English on the economy. It was a relief to be able to buy things and order at restaurants in my native language, even when they spoke with a heavy British accent. We went up on "the Rock" and saw the Barbary macaques, the famous apes of Gibraltar. We crossed from Spain to Gibraltar through La Línea, the Spanish town, from which the story goes, the Spaniards heard the British soldiers sing as they marched, *"Green grow the rushes, ho, I'll sing you one ho..."* It is said in that part of Spain that that is where the term "gringo" came from. Well, "gringo" and "green grow" are similar in sound... There are other accounts for the derivation of the word that I won't go into. The Brits took "the Rock" from Spain in the early 1700's which sparked a dispute between Spain and Great Britain that continues since then. Great Britain still flies the Union Jack on the southern tip of the Iberian Peninsula while Spain stops at La Línea.

I bought a couple of tapestries I sent home to Mom. One of them of a Russian in a sleigh fending off wolves which I still have, and my mother hung on the living room wall in her Albuquerque home for over forty years.

I hated to leave Spain, but I was still homesick. I hadn't had a *real* enchilada in two and a half years. (That's 10,000 years in a New Mexican's life!) I had lived in a different culture, enjoyed it, but I wanted to go home to..., well, I didn't know what. I had taken a number of college courses and I knew I wanted to continue at the University of New Mexico. But beyond that, I didn't have a clue.

Returning was much easier than my trip to Spain. I was flown on a C-47 from Morón Air Base near Sevilla, to Torrejon Air Base in Madrid, and not seated on a train with square wheels overnight. There were a couple of days of waiting during which I spent time in Madrid, taking in the Lights and Sounds program at the *Palacio Real* and other sites around the city. But then I got aboard a *jet* airliner—a Boeing 707, the first of my experiences in these aircraft. In around four hours I was at McGuire Air Force Base in New Jersey. It took about eighteen hours to fly to Spain going, and a fraction of that time returning.

While waiting to receive my discharge papers, they reminded me that I was still attached to Uncle Sam and so I cleaned toilets and floors... wherever they told me to. I didn't want to do anything that would cause a delay. Finally, I left McGuire in a Greyhound bus, headed toward home, but other destinations were in mind along the way.

First was Washington, DC. I had always wanted to visit the U. S. Capitol and I was able to go to the White House, Capitol Building and the monuments on the Mall. John F. Kennedy was president and I remarked with tongue in cheek that while I went to his house, he wasn't there to greet me. I saw parts of the Smithsonian Institute and, during a time when things were relatively calm in America, I didn't see any protesters or agitators.

I wanted to visit my Uncle Gene and Aunt Merrie in Danville, Illinois. The closest the bus would get me was Terre Haute, Indiana. Gene and Merrie drove over to pick me up and I spent a couple of days with them in their beautiful house with a "woodsy" back yard. Through a bank of windows, I could see squirrels scurrying through the trees. I could see why they loved Illinois so much. Gene showed me some of the roads he had helped to engineer. Many of them were in the Interstate system. I was proud of my Uncle Gene Peper and what he had become.

I remember my mother talking about how much their home had cost them in the 1950's. Thirty-two thousand dollars. That was a lot of money back then. Gene had served in the Army Air Corps during World War II, got the GI Bill and went to the University of Illinois to get a civil engineering degree. Merrie worked in an office and, having no children, they lived very comfortably and compatibly. They were a couple of my favorite people and I had a great time with them. They took me back to Terre Haute, to again travel on the bus toward home.

My next stop was to see my second cousin, Connie (Peper) Stevens in Boulder, Colorado. She had gotten married to John Stevens and they were building a home in the mountains west of the city. She was very happy to show me some of the fine shopping establishments that had been built recently in her town. She was especially ecstatic in showing me a grocery store that was huge compared to the Santa Rita Company Store I had grown up with. She was my only "girl" cousin and we had gotten to know each other as kids. I didn't have a sister and she became the closest I ever had to one. She had written me while I was in Spain and I had appreciated her letters to me.

Catching another bus, I traveled from Boulder down to New Mexico. I knew I was in familiar territory when we stopped for food at Ratón. In the café a juke box played Mariachi and Rancheros music. I hadn't heard this music in a long time and it signified that I was home. A few more hours and I was in Albuquerque, back with Mom, Dad and Bruce. It felt good. Albuquerque had grown significantly while I was gone. As a twelve-year-old, I remembered the city at a population about 45,000. Now it was over 200,000. Several tall buildings like the First National Bank Building on East Central and San Mateo caught my attention. We were no longer in a small city, it was expanding all over the place!

CHAPTER 7

LEARNING TO LEARN

It was September 1962. I enrolled at the University of New Mexico, not sure what I would focus my academic interests toward. My time in the Air Force had earned me sophomore status. The courses I took in Spain and my military experience was sufficient to eliminate my freshman year. The Spanish I had already learned qualified me to pursue a degree in Latin American Affairs, also requiring me to study Portuguese. Well, that was a start. So, I started. My student advisor was Dr. Sabine Ulibarrí, a student of everything Hispanic. I walked into his office for my first counseling session and called him Dr. YOU-la-berry. He quickly set me straight on the pronunciation of his name: OO-lee-va-REE. It was a Basque name and he was quite proud of it. He had a passion for his cultural background and the sayings of the people in northern New Mexico, *Cuentos de Nuevo México* became published and well known in the Latin American academic community.

The Baptist Student Union at the University became my social and spiritual connection and I joined Trinity Baptist Church not too far from where I lived with my parents. I had sent home enough money to take me through one year of studies. Not having much to spend on other endeavors, I often took the bus to school and borrowed my parent's 1958 Packard for anything else. Hey, it was transportation and I didn't have a macho image to protect, so no big deal. I was interested in the girls, but serious about getting through school without entanglements. I dated one girl who suggested we get some beer and

I suggested otherwise. We met at the BSU, but this wasn't the kind of girl I wanted to continue to date, so one time did it.

One day I had some business in the First National Bank building and who did I meet? My squadron commander from Spain who had given me a citation for my work for the good of the squadron with the chapel while I was there! He and his wife had returned and came to New Mexico when the Department of Defense decided to close the radar site and automated the radar work we had done manually. I was surprised to see them and had no idea they were retiring to Albuquerque.

University life was hectic, and I spent a lot of time in Zimmerman Library studying. One afternoon in November 1962 I left the library to go back to the BSU and I noticed clumps of people standing around transistor radios listening to something. I didn't think much about it and walked into the BSU where a black and white television set was carrying a newscast of something all of the students were watching intensely: President John F. Kennedy had been shot in Dallas! We watched in horror as the events unfolded before us. Police were searching for an assassin in that city and we followed news clips throughout the evening and next several days. I had never considered such an event occurring, especially to a president that most people liked. Sure, he and his brother, Robert, were rooting out Mafia operatives and were involved in the racial struggles going on in the Southern states, but this kind of event shook me, and I remember listening to the accounts through my tears of the parade, the shots fired and Jackie Kennedy holding her husband in her arms as they rushed to Parkland Hospital where he was pronounced dead.

The sentiment at the BSU and generally on campus was one of shock. This was not the America I had defended with my life if necessary. Lee Harvey Oswald was soon arrested and talk about this man who had spent time in the Soviet Union dominated the airwaves. When he was killed by Jack Ruby, some conspiracy theories were suggested, along with Lyndon Johnson and J. Edgar Hoover being involved in the assassination. None of this was ever proved, but this issue occupied a lot of time of students, I among them.

In high school I had done well in an art class and my teacher, Joe Goforth, had encouraged me to pursue a career in fine arts. He was a survivor of the Japanese war camps during the War and had been able to help other buddies to get food and other things they needed by being able to draw pictures for the Japanese soldiers who guarded them. He often complimented me on my work and suggested better ways to present my ability. I considered this career choice, but decided there were too many starving artists already and I didn't need to become a casualty.

At the University I had the opportunity to take drawing classes, which I did. I was shocked to find out that we would be drawing nude human figures. The first time one showed up and took off her robe I dropped my charcoal stick that I was drawing with and nearly turned over my pad of newsprint on my easel seat. This was something I had not expected, and I reacted with not only extreme surprise, but my fantasy life took on a new dimension. We were encouraged to draw all kinds of things, but I found out I liked figure drawing the most.

There were times I would take my drawing pad and pencils and walk down to the edge of the Rio Grande where massive cottonwood trees grew wild. I drew for hours and walked back home. This gave me exercise as well as fueled my desire for drawing. Looking back over this time in my life, I am somewhat dismayed that I didn't take more art classes, but that would have changed my life's direction and I wouldn't be who I am. I still like art, looking at it and drawing or painting sporadically.

Portuguese language and culture classes were taught by a man from Brazil, whose name I have forgotten. At one point I considered going to Brazil to live, but for some reason my mind said I didn't want to take a job away from someone in Brazil who may have needed one. I had some difficulty in Portuguese because Spanish and Portuguese share common words or words that look similar but are pronounced differently. Often, I would get the two confused and blunder out Spanish when the Portuguese word was quite different.

In December I was asked to participate in my brother, Keith's wedding. He had met a girl while going to New Mexico Western University in Silver City and I was asked to be his best man. Vance was already married and Keith was next. I agreed and Keith and Margaret (Meg) were married on New Year's Eve in 1962-63. It was a formal wedding and for the first time I rented a tuxedo and wore it. Grandma Peper was staying with us in Albuquerque and she was doing what she could to manage the event. The pre-wedding dinner was at our house in a former garage-turned-dining room. Meg's parents, brothers, sisters, and my family gathered around the table, the room was very crowded, but a lot of fun. Meg's parents, the Tillotson's, felt a little awkward around our gregarious family but made the most of it. Meg's dad said, "aren't we going to toast the bride and groom?" Grandma Peper, without hesitating said firmly, "No, this is the way WE toast people, as she drank her iced tea." She was a tee-totaler and expected everyone else to be as well.

The wedding was held in All Saints Episcopal Church, the Tillotson's home place of worship. It was very formal, communion included, and lasted longer than I would have liked for it to. Patti, Vance's new wife sang for their wedding.

While pictures were being taken, myself, Vance and Jerry picked up and turned Keith's small car sideways between two other cars, making it hard to get out to start the honeymoon. We all had a great laugh at his plight and when the car was finally untangled, they drove off down the street with tin cans dangling from strings. There would be payback for my actions, I was sure.

I met a fellow student at the BSU, Ron Brown, who had been in the Army in Italy and had returned to the States about the same time I had come back from Spain. Ron was working at a parking garage in downtown Albuquerque and suggested that I could get a job there as well. I applied and started off cleaning the lobby and restroom area and driving the sweeper up the 4 stories of the building. We worked together for a while as cashiers in the booth that allowed cars in and out. The manager, Jack Darling, was a pleasant guy to work for, although a little worldlier than Ron or I. Ron had also become a follower of Christ while in the military and we became good friends, at one point sharing a basement apartment with pipes as part of the ceiling. Mrs. Hoy, the owner of the house, had converted the basement into a living area and she also had other sections of her house that she rented out.

She wasn't crazy about having two men living there, but we assured her that we would exhibit Christian values and she gave us the keys. Women students also lived in the large house, but we didn't see them often. The rent was affordable and the location wasn't far from the UNM campus. Ron and I shared duties, he did most of the cleaning and I cooked. It worked well because I wasn't much of a "clean freak" and his culinary skills left something to be desired. We nicknamed the apartment "Pipesville."

Things began to change for us. Ron got another position leaving the parking garage and I took over his duties as well as my own, working 13 hours a day, as *the* cashier, six days a week. Jack bought a lot in the downtown area, starting his own parking operation. Airport Parking Company was looking for someone else to manage the operation and, guess what? I had worked every position in the facility and knew the business, from cleaning toilets to getting the receipts ready for banking. The general manager flew in from Houston and began talking to me. I told him I wanted the manager's position and, since he didn't have anyone else to consider, I got it.

This worked well. I could go to classes as scheduled, come back and check on the operation, get the receipts ready to go to the bank and do the paperwork all within the day. I hired others to be cashiers, some of whom didn't have the work ethic I had and needed from them. I hated it when I had to go down and run the operation because someone didn't wake up who was supposed to be there or was sick. I was paid about a hundred dollars a week and that was sufficient to buy a car, my first new one. It was a shiny red Volkswagen bug. I paid $1200 for it and it became my only means of transportation. It was not expensive to run. Gasoline in that era was about 24 cents a gallon and sometimes there would be "gas wars" where the price would dip to 15 cents. I even drove to Santa Fe once to get this cheaper gas price.

I joined Trinity Baptist Church as soon as I returned from Spain and that became my church home. Tom Sumrall was pastor and he and his wife, Jane, became good friends. They had been raised in Mississippi and he graduated from New Orleans Baptist Theological Seminary. Tom was a decent preacher, but he had a high pitch to his voice that sometimes irritated my ear drums. This mattered little to me, because

I loved the Word of God. The doctrine was sound, and I soon found myself teaching Sunday School, the high school group. I was baptized in this church and loved the people who attended.

Between the BSU and Trinity, I learned much about the Bible and doctrine of the church. At the BSU, Dr. Richard Cunningham taught Bible classes. He was a graduate of Southwest Baptist Theological Seminary in Ft. Worth, Texas, the largest seminary of any denomination in the United States. Once in a while an announcement was made that a church in the area needed someone to fill in for an absent preacher. Ron and I often got called on to go and preach, even though I wasn't sure I was to be a preacher. Ron told me, yes, he believed I had been called and that began my change to switch majors from Latin American Affairs to whatever got me out the quickest so I could go to seminary. Since I had studied Spanish and Portuguese, this became my major and minor as I completed requirements for a B.A. in languages.

One of the churches I was sent to asked me to be the interim pastor until they could find someone else. I agreed, and in December, 1964, I began a six-month trek to Corona, about a hundred miles southeast of Albuquerque twice weekly to serve the Corona Baptist Church. Corona was a ranching center and had been a pinto bean farming area until drought took the beans out. It had a school, K-12 in one building, one grocery store, a pharmacy, a couple of gas stations and a few other sundry businesses. Three churches, Baptist, Presbyterian and Catholic, took care of the spiritual needs of the community, at least for those who were spiritual.

There were some characters and there were saints who lived there, and the two groups got along well... pretty well. The first family I met at Corona Baptist was the Lackey family. There were two families of Lackeys, Paul Lackey's group and his brother Fred Lackey's family. Some of Paul Lackey's boys were fellow students at UNM. Both families were ranchers, Fred was a fire spotter in the Gallinas Mountains west of the village. Paul had 6 sons, each of them solid in the Faith, as was Paul and his wife, Grace. All the boys grew up to be either a teacher or a preacher or both. One of them is almost related to me since he married my wife's first cousin.

My first Sunday preaching was of some note. I didn't pass out from fright, neither was any object thrown at me for breach of doctrine. I did notice what I thought to be a family sitting in a pew together on the third row back. The young man had a prominent nose and was seated with a very pretty woman and two children. I thought very little of it, learning that the man was one of the Fred Lackey clan. Two sermons were preached and during the afternoon between them I visited with a family who fed me dinner. They were teachers, the main vocation the village had to offer other than ranching and their last name was Slaughter. The salary was low, but housing was provided in homes owned by the school. I very much enjoyed the day and looked forward to being with the church the following Sunday.

Sunday came and I made the two-hour trip to be with them. I got up to preach and I saw the lady with two children and a different man. This guy was much larger than the one I had seen her with the previous week. I thought about asking the burning question in my mind, but thought I should wait to find out in a more natural way, without upsetting anyone. This went on for several weeks, most of which she sat with the two children alone or with another woman I learned was her mother.

One afternoon in January, I was in the back yard of the teacher couple who had invited me to dinner with them, helping clean out a horse stall when that young lady came to ask me a question: Would I accompany her to the Valentine's Day Sweetheart banquet at the church? She was very pretty, dark hair, a smile on her face… and before I really thought it through, I said, "Yes, that would be nice." She didn't stay long and after she was out of sight, I asked the question I had thought about earlier. "What was the deal with her, two kids and two guys?" Mr. Slaughter explained to me that her name was Fern Stees and her husband, Jim Stees, had died of cancer almost a year earlier leaving her with two young children to raise. She was living with her parents, David and Clodell McCloud. Clodell was in the services I had preached. I felt much better knowing I had not agreed to a date with a married woman. She was a widow… other problems, but not that! I had managed to reach the age of 25 without entanglements, one reason was I hated being rejected by girls, and the other wanting to complete school, fearing burdens I couldn't handle. We attended the banquet, which that year was on Sunday. I then invited her to go to a movie with me in Albuquerque, I would come and get her. She said she was going to Albuquerque the next week with her dad and he would drop her off.

We met at the parking garage and she walked with me to put the daily deposit in the bank. The day was cold… really cold! I took her hand and put it in mine and then both of ours in a pocket of my jacket. We talked about all sorts of things and I found it easy to talk to her. Very natural. We went to my parent's house for supper and then to a movie, and dutifully I drove her back to Corona in my VW Bug, returning early in the morning.

I could hardly wait to go back the next weekend for services. There she was, daughter Penny and son, Jimmy in tow. I went to her parents' house for dinner and we drove around that afternoon just experiencing being with each other. Now, at this point the conversation is somewhat muddled… I think I asked her if she wanted to go get a Coke, and she thought I asked her to marry me… Well, since I thought what she understood was better than what my mind remembered, I let it continue. She explained that after her husband died she wanted to wait several years before getting remarried. I began to rethink my stand on entanglements. I really liked this girl! But I had to take on a whole family. I thought and prayed about this and the more I considered it, the more it seemed right. Was this God's answer to my prayer that I marry the one He wanted me to have? I brought the subject up to my parents subtly and, no objection was made, even though they had met her only once. The way I put it sort of startled me *and* them: "I could make you grandparents in one swoop!"

Now Grandma Peper was another story. I had a phone conversation with her and she told me this was a bad idea. She told me I had a mandate to finish my studies at the university. And seminary as well. Marriage and kids would end that. She said in no uncertain terms that I should scrap the idea and not pursue it. Nobody in the family had *ever* hung up on Grandma. I did… And I meant to. I was angry! I loved my Grandma, but this was over the top! She could pour my uncle Jim's booze down the drain. She could give me a spanking for something I didn't do, but not this. I wasn't thinking good thoughts about this lady.

I proposed to Fern and we bought a ring together. It wasn't one of those "romantic" proposals down on my knees. We just agreed that this was what we both wanted. We went to a jewelry store in downtown Albuquerque. The sales person showed us a selection of rings and explained the quality of each and how to tell the cheap from the well-made. He did one other thing. He said, "Now I don't want you to buy this ring right now. I want you to go to other jewelry stores and look at their rings. If you find a ring that suits you better, buy it. If not, come back."

We went to Zales and a couple other jewelry stores asking to see wedding ring sets. After looking at the quality as it was explained by the other jewelry salesman, we went back and I spent all my savings, all $350 of it on this ring! Turns out it was a great purchase. The quarter carat diamond set in platinum has continued to increase in value and was recently evaluated at over $2,000. She lost the ring once having it slip off her finger, but found it on the floor a few months later which brought joy back to her life.

We showed it to her mother, Clodell McCloud, also called "Granny" and her comment was, "Where did you get that, out of a Cracker Jack box?" It kind of took the wind out of my sails, but she seemed to be pleased that we were going to get married. Fern's dad, David McCloud, kind of smiled and grunted an assent, but "Papa" wasn't one to use a lot of words at a moment like this. He was a "jack of all trades," and had a lot of irons in the fire to make a living. He painted the homes owned by the school district, worked a small ranch, cut firewood and most anything else to put food on the table. Papa was anything but lazy.

Their house was a small wood structure with propane gas heating… using open flame heaters. I was always afraid something would catch on fire and burn the house down, but it didn't happen. They had a freezer in a shed out in the back filled with fish he had caught on numerous fishing trips, an activity he loved. There was also beef from cows that had been slaughtered after being raised on the small ranch owned by another family member north of Corona. I stayed at their house many times, sleeping in a bed shared by her brother, Kenneth. Fern and her two children, Jimmy and Penny were housed in a separate structure to the northwest of the house. Jeanette, Fern's sister lived in another bedroom. "Papa" and "Granny" had an upstairs bedroom. I was the interim pastor of Corona Baptist Church and our romance stirred several elderly members to discuss that we were not keeping ourselves pure until marriage, but we were.

I was ordained at Trinity Church in Albuquerque with a presbytery of deacons and pastors asking me doctrinal and personal questions as I sat in a lone chair by the pulpit with others looking on in support. I have never felt so naked and frightened since then. I was only a few years into the faith and I sure hadn't gone to seminary, and I certainly hadn't memorized the Bible, nor had I studied the great Christian scholars who had thought through the issues of theology. But, even though I felt inadequate and unprepared, I was ordained and a charge was given me by some of those I had grown to respect in the Central Baptist Association in Albuquerque. My future bride was there to witness my formal entrance to ministry.

My cousin, Jerry, was married in Silver City a few days after we announced our engagement, to Ellen McFarland and we drove down to be a part of the wedding. We were a little reluctant to announce our engagement because we didn't want to take away from the celebration of their nuptials. But we *did* announce it. On the trip to Silver City we went over the Black Range in the Gila National Forest at night in late winter. I remember seeing the sky without a moon at the top of Emory Pass. The stars were spectacular. I was in love and my bride to be was with me as we stopped and kissed on this beautiful nightscape on the mountain.

The wedding was a beautiful one. Jerry married the daughter of the owner of a telephone company and a man who established the first radio station in Grant County worth listening to—at least in our minds. The only station in Silver City, KSIL, back in out teen-age days, was mainly news and boring music that only broadcast during the daytime. It was silent at night. KNFT, McFarland's station was not boring, but it didn't exist until after we had become adults and Ellen's dad built it. He didn't like the music it played, but it made a pretty good living. Jerry married well. Mr. and Mrs. McFarland were very pleasant people and Ellen was always smiling and had an easy laugh.

She still does. Our announcement was not a douse of water on their wedding, but instead it became what I felt was the icing on the cake.

Our wedding was originally planned for June after the university ended the spring semester in 1965. I was 25 and she was 21. But the date got moved up. We wanted to start the marriage as soon as possible. So after meeting the previous December, beginning to date and becoming engaged in February, we were married on April 17, 1965. Not a long time of courting, but it has become a long time marriage. The wedding itself was memorable because of the lack of elegance. We paid for our wedding, nobody pitched in, which made it all the better.

I was a member of Trinity Baptist Church in Albuquerque and Tom Sumrall was my pastor. He did the honors shared by my good friend Ron Brown with whom I had shared the "Pipesville" apartment. Ron was also a Baptist student preacher and was ordained at about the same time I was and we have remained friends for over fifty years. I could not have had a better wedding.

I needed a suit to preach in so I bought one for less than a hundred dollars and we found a gown for Fern that cost around twenty-five. We made the wedding cake ourselves, baking it in the oven at my parent's house. Now you have to understand that neither of us had any training in baking or the other finer arts of life, so when it came to putting the layers of the chocolate cake on each other we had no idea that cardboard was inserted between the layers. We just put chocolate frosting on top of a layer, placed the next smaller layer on, then frosted it and so on. Four layers, as I recall. But there was a problem. The top layers kept slipping off. We would straighten them, and again they would slide. Finally, I took a tinker toy stick that belonged to my brother, Bruce, and stabbed it through the middle after we got it straight again. It did slide a little, but we put the little bride and groom plastic figurine on top of that and called it good. At the church we found a thin song book that we put under the lower side to make it look straight. The rest of the reception was 7Up punch, nuts and hard candy. No food. Everybody was on their own.

Fern had a hairdresser appointment the morning of the wedding and I had something I had to do, so I dropped her off at the salon. When I went back to get her, she was still in the chair with someone working on her hair. The time for the wedding was getting close and we were still not dressed. So, I waited. And waited. Finally, she was done. She looked gorgeous, but we were late already and had to go to my parents' house to get dressed. There were no cell phones, so we couldn't let anyone know what the problem was, and we showed up a half hour late. Everyone seemed relieved and we explained what caused the delay and the wedding was on! The right words were said, she did and I did and that settled it.

Pictures were taken by my brother, Keith, and after everyone gorged on nuts, candies and punch, we were showered with rice, probably killing some of the local birds in the process, and headed for the red Volkswagen. It had been painted with white lettering with "just married" and the other happy sayings, but was parked horizontal to the sidewalk—on the sidewalk. As we drove off, rubber gloves had been attached to the tailpipes of the red Volkswagen and we left on our honeymoon; big hands waving, then popping, tin cans rattling on the pavement. We got as far as Belen, about 40 miles south of Albuquerque, and decided to put the car in a carwash. We discovered that the brushes used to paint the congratulations on the car had been used previously in regular enamel paint and had balls of sticky stuff that had to be scraped off with our fingernails. It took over three hours to clean that little car before we could head off after grabbing a Lotta Burger from the drive-in next door.

Arriving in El Paso after dark, we went to a motel on Dyer Street that has since been demolished to make way for other changes in this city. We were finally married and this was our time! The car was clean, Penny and James had been left with Fern's sister, Jeanette and we were happy.

The next morning was on Sunday and, in 1965, Texas was under the "blue laws" that closed stores on the Lord's Day for everything that was not "essential." Fern had not packed her hairbrush and we went looking for a place to buy one. The only open store was a Rexall drugstore and we had to sign a document stating that buying the hairbrush was necessary— Did you ever meet a woman that did not find it *essential* to brush her hair? Not my Fern!

Our objective was to drive to Chihuahua City where we would spend our honeymoon. Driving south from El Paso was not difficult and the roadway was adequate, just not quite the quality of U. S. Interstate highways. I wanted to be able to use my Spanish skills, or at least hone them somewhat and I could do this quite well South of the Border.

We arrived in Chihuahua before the sun set and found a motel with the right name: Santa Rita. The name of my birthplace. We had a few disturbances during the evening. A knock on the door was met by a request to buy goods, *¿Usted quiere un sarape, señor?* The man asked holding up the small multi colored blanket for inspection. *No quiero*, I responded. Didn't this guy know I was on my honeymoon and had no use for the piece of cloth? After several more interruptions, I bought one of them just to send him away. Probably not a great way to satisfy my need not to buy it, but it worked!

We went out the next day and drove around the beautiful city. I nearly got in trouble which would have made the trip less pleasurable. I made a left turn on a green light and a police officer blew his whistle at me and motioned for me to stop. I did. He tried to explain to me that I could not make a left-hand turn at that intersection unless there was a green arrow directing me to do so. I gave him a blank "gringo" stare as if I understood nothing. It worked, and after chewing me out, he finally told me to go on. I did. No disobedience from this guy. Just looking stupid did the trick and that didn't require much more than my normal appearance.

Returning to the United States by way of the Bridge of the Americas into El Paso, we were told to wait after learning that we had been beyond the 15-mile zone into Mexico. We needed proof of vaccinations which we did not have, so we were given shots for whatever we could have picked up in Chihuahua. We didn't even pick up the well-known *turista* that so many gringos fall prey to. I had enough experience from Spain to know not to drink the local water, or brush my teeth in it. And we didn't.

Our next objective was to drive to Carlsbad Caverns. While Fern had been there on a senior trip her graduating year, I had not. This was a great time to see what I had not yet experienced. I had been to

Europe and to the Blue Grotto near Naples, I had been on the Rock of Gibraltar and in the ruins of Pompeii beneath the Vesuvius volcano, but I had not been to Carlsbad. I stand in amazement every time I descend into this magnificent abyss. I had seen pictures, even those in 3-D through viewers, but up close and personal is a wonderful way to experience this work of God's magnificent natural beauty. We returned home through Corona, visiting with Fern's parents and picking up the kids from Jeanette. Not long after we were married, Ron Brown married a beautiful and bright lady who had grown up in Grants, New Mexico. Her name was Myrna. I participated in his wedding as well.

Married life was not as much of a struggle as I thought it would be. I did have to drop out of school a semester to work. Fern received a small military pension from her first husband's death since he was on active duty when he became ill with cancer, but it wasn't enough to live on. We moved into a house on High Street in Albuquerque, just behind the Baptist Convention of New Mexico building on Central Avenue. It was an old house, but adequate and just across the street from a drive-in restaurant. I found a job with a convenience store next to a liquor establishment. One evening before I went home for the night, I saw a red light flashing outside. I looked out the door and saw a person lying on the sidewalk. He had been shot by the manager of the liquor store who caught two men trying to shoplift booze. One escaped, the other did not. The manager was harassed by those friends and family of the person who was killed and finally had to find some other place to live and work.

Then I got a job with a finance company, Southwestern Investment Company. They advertised a lot on television and radio with the catch phrase: SOS for SIC if you needed money. The finance company wanted me to repossess vehicles and furniture that had been purchased and not paid for. I was given a company car and set out to do good for the company, but I struggled to meet the demands and had a very difficult time emotionally taking a person's furniture or their vehicle.

On one occasion, they sent me out to the Navajo Reservation to find a truck belonging to a person named Ben Yazzie. No address, no phone number, nothing but a license plate and a locality where he received mail. I started with the post office. Yes, they had many "Ben

Yazzie's" but which one was I looking for? It was a common name on the "Res." I didn't know. It was winter time and I staked out several places this fellow may have resided in, but I saw no truck with that license plate number.

I drove into places that I thought might be where Yazzie lived and went down a dirt road through piñon and juniper trees. It had snowed several days before and most of the road was clear, but I could see that if I continued down this one dirt road it only turned around and there was still snowy ice on it. The roadway I had taken to this point was frozen, but I decided it would be better for me to back down the hill and turn around. As I backed down, the right rear tire slid off the road and began to take the car over an embankment. I opened the door and got out quickly as the car went backward, hitting a piñon tree at the bottom. My heart sank. I could see no one and I had not seen any traffic in quite a while.

I stood and looked down an arroyo and saw smoke. Walking a little further I became aware that the smoke was coming out of the chimney of a house not too far away. I walked to the door and knocked. A pleasant looking Anglo man greeted me and I explained my plight. "Well," he exclaimed, "We can't do anything on an empty stomach, can we? Come on in we were just about ready to eat. Would you like trout?" I assured him that his invitation was gracious and appreciated and as we sat down at the table with his family, he thanked the Lord for the food and for my visit.

I learned that the family was Quaker and they were missionaries to the Navajos. We talked, got acquainted and after dinner, he said, "Let me get my truck and chainsaw and let's get you pulled out." We drove to where my company car was pinned by the tree. The bumper and trunk lid were bent. He cut the tree off at the ground, the car was pulled backward by his pickup with a chain hooked around the bumper bracket. I thanked him and offered payment for his efforts which he refused, saying that it was a blessing for him just to help me. I thanked God for his blessing to me and expressed my gratitude to him. It was afternoon and I again set off in search of Ben Yazzie.

I was getting very discouraged and was about to give up when a truck passed me with mud on the back of it. I could see some of the numbers on the plate, but not all of them, and the description and some of the numbers and letters I had seemed to match. I followed the pickup to a trading post across the Arizona state line and a Navajo man got out. "Are you Ben Yazzie," I asked?

"No, he replied." "He's back in Window Rock."

"I need to see him, where is he?" He looked at me and said he would take me to Ben. He did and I told Ben I needed some payments on the truck or I would have to confiscate it. He came up with enough to satisfy my superiors in Albuquerque, so I had accomplished that mission.

When I tried to explain the damage to the car and how that had happened, I was not met with concern for my wellbeing, but with a certain disdain for causing damage to the vehicle. A couple of days later I was told that my employment was terminated. This was the only time in my life I was fired, with the small exception of my railroad career that ended because of the slight deviation in my date of birth when I was 17.

I worked at several other jobs, including a company that specialized in checking insurance references, which required me during one of my checks to travel to the town of Chama in the northern part of the state and then to another village north of Taos, Questa, to interview the persons wanting to be insured. Trying to minimize my time getting from one place to another, I knew of a road that went from Chama to Taos through the Rio Grande River Gorge. It was unpaved and I had driven it before, but not in winter. It started snowing, but the snow wasn't sticking so I decided to keep on going.

Traveling a little way, I discovered that the dirt road was no longer dirt, but a muddy bog and if I turned around, I would get stuck. So, I kept going, sliding into and out of the ruts that were already there from previous travelers. As I began to descend into the gorge which had no guardrails; the fear factor began to creep up on me, but on I went. *This could kill me,* I thought. I regretted the decision I had made to take the shortcut. The mud was slick and I slid several times, but not so far that I was in danger of going off the cliff. Arriving at the bottom, I crossed the narrow bridge that, like the road, had only one lane. The driving lane across the bridge was made of planks placed across iron girders. It was sturdy, but less than adequate. I crossed the Rio Grande and began up the other side, again steep drop offs on the left side. The farther I went the better I felt. I was exhilarated to top out on the other side, just a little southwest of the village of Ranchos de Taos. It was dark by this time and I went on to Questa, accomplished the task there and headed back for Albuquerque through the snow that kept falling but didn't stick on the highway. A very long and tiring day. I didn't get home until after midnight. This job didn't last long because I didn't like it. I quit.

I got a job working for Valley Gold Dairy servicing a delivery route. I liked this job! I got up early in the morning and drove to where the truck had been parked overnight in a secure area. I had loaded it the night before and was ready to go by 4:00 a.m. My route was the southeast part of Albuquerque, from University Boulevard to Kirtland Air Force Base. I had keys to some of the houses I serviced since the customer wanted the delivery person to go into the kitchen and check the refrigerator for a standing order which I filled; the company sending them a bill at the end of the month. One home had rabbits that left their droppings all over the floor making the house smell like a rabbit hutch. Another home had a little black dog that, when I would approach the house, stayed silent—but when I left the milk on the door step and turned my back—would bark ferociously, hitting the screen door. I knew what to expect but each time the dog startled me sending my heart pounding back to the truck. The company did the billing and most of the payments were mailed in. Those that got behind, I had to try to collect from. There was only one setback for me. I could drink any product on the truck I wanted. I only had to leave the empty carton. I gained weight. I really like chocolate milk…

Fern and the kids did well. I loved my new family and proudly took them to Trinity Baptist on Sundays and usually for the Wednesday night prayer meeting that was more of a Bible study than actual prayer. My new son, James, we called him "Jimmy," sometimes was a handful. He had a strong will of his own and I tried to break him of the habit of trying to open the car door by gently slapping is hand. He would pull back, look at me and reach for it again, and again. Slap, slap, slap!

Penny was well-behaved and required little maintenance. Somewhere we got a dog. The landlady lived next door to us and if I didn't keep the poop cleaned up immediately, she complained and I tried to comply as best I could. Our house, as I previously mentioned, was just across the street from a drive-in restaurant that was frequented by teenagers who got noisy. One night a group of them were on our lawn making a lot of racket while I was trying to sleep. My usually quiet nature was provoked and I, in no uncertain terms, told them to get off my lawn. They replied with a rock through the plate glass window on the enclosed porch. My bluster was called and I huddled with the rest of the family on the floor and called the police. It took them some time to respond and when they did, no one was outside to confront. I made my report and immediately bundled the kids up and we headed to my parent's house. We moved the next day to the west side of the city. I had no idea what the future here might bring and I didn't want the family to be subjected to it. Besides, the landlady didn't like dog poop.

The G.I. Bill was reinstituted and I could go back to school with the two incomes from the government. I changed my major to Spanish with a minor in Portuguese to get my bachelor's degree sooner and go to seminary. Dr. Richard Cunningham, BSU Director, said he was headed to California to teach at Golden Gate Theological Seminary. He convinced me that should be where I worked on my Master of Divinity degree and that became my objective. I became interim pastor of a couple more churches, one in Quemado, New Mexico for six months and another in Cuba. The stipend covered little more than my transportation, but I enjoyed getting to know the people and honing my preaching skills, such as they were. In Quemado we had a mobile home we could stay in after driving down on Saturday. The trip took about 3 hours one-way. Cuba was about half that distance. Winter provided opportunity to practice other skills, such as driving in snow and ice. Ron Brown was also one of the "preacher boys" that was sent out from the BSU to preach at pastorless churches. He was interim pastor at a small church in Pie Town, not too far from Quemado. Pie Town achieved its name from a bakery established by Clyde Norman in the early 1920s for making dried-apple pies. Pie Town still holds a "Pie Festival" on the second Saturday of each September. Located north of the Gila National Forest, you pass the Plains of San Augustin, the location of the Very Large Array radio telescope located along U.S. 60 as you travel from Socorro westward.

We also were asked to preach at the Albuquerque Rescue Mission on South Second Street. Rescue missions receive their "congregations" from off the streets—in all kinds of conditions. One night a couple of drunks got in a fight over a hymn book. On another occasion a man passed out and fell into the isle between the rows of chairs. This was a little disconcerting, but I grew to like working with those who struggled.

Since Fern's dad loved to go fishing, we would join him occasionally, and sometimes went on our own. I took the family camping at Fenton Lake in the Jémez Mountains and little Jimmy kept going off into the water. We worried about him and I found a dog harness that I put around him and tied a rope to it which I attached to a tree. He could go so far, but not to the water and that made him angry. He soon got used to it, but still wasn't happy.

One day I talked to Fern about going camping and she opened up and told me how she felt about it. While I thought it an enjoyable experience, she explained that her living conditions while growing up resembled camping. They lived in a slab shack that in the winter was so cold she and Jeanette would heat rocks on the wood stove to put in the end of their bed. There were cracks in the ceiling that let snowflakes fall through into the room. No running water, only a cistern to catch rainwater and hold it for their use. Their bathroom was what I had known also as a child, the" privy" in the backyard. For years they had no electricity and relied on either kerosene lamps or gasoline lanterns. She had to chop wood to put in the stove and to heat the water they used for washing clothes, like my grandmother and my mother had done. She has a scar on her ankle from the ax slipping off the chunk of wood and slicing her. Her duties were to milk two cows every day. This became one of the sources of protein the family enjoyed. Her dad had ulcers and the food had to be bland so he could eat. Pinto beans, mashed potatoes, biscuits and gravy with chicken occasionally was the family fare. Once I understood her problem, we learned to camp in places like Motel 6 or Holliday Inn. We couldn't afford Hilton at this point.

It was during this time that conflict erupted in northern New Mexico. A Texan by the name of Reyes Lopez Tijerina, who was an itinerate preacher from a cult-like church commune began to launch an attack on the United States government for taking land grants from Spanish colonists and their descendants. He went to Spain in 1966, learned much about the Spanish laws governing land grants. He returned to New Mexico and formed a movement called the *Alianza* which became his base of operation. It had grown to as many as 20,000 members and with this group he planned a March on July 4 from Albuquerque to Santa Fe. During the march, some white New Mexicans shouted epithets at them. Some even shot at them. Arriving in the capital, they met with the governor and delivered a written demand for an investigation into the theft of the communal land holdings.

Failing in this attempt, the *Alianza* decided to take direct action. In October 1966, they occupied some of the "Echo Amphitheater Park," in the Carson National Forest that had been part of the San Joaquín del Río de Chama grant. They proclaimed this region the "Republic of San Joaquín del Río de Chama." Many of their members were descendants of the original settlers. They elected officials, and, according to some accounts, issued visas to passing tourists. When two forest rangers attempted to remove the occupiers, they were arrested by marshals who had been newly elected by the *Alianza*. The rangers were tried, convicted of trespassing, given suspended sentences, and released along with their trucks. Tijerina, his brother Cristóbal and three other *Alianza* members—were subsequently arrested and charged with assault on the Rangers and converting government property to personal use. They were released, but by no means were they through.

CHAPTER 8

CALIFORNIA, HERE WE COME

The year was 1967. On June 5, Tijerina led an armed raid on the Rio Arriba County courthouse in Tierra Amarilla. When we heard the news, Fern was pregnant and we were on our way to California in our 1965 Datsun station wagon. The National Guard had been called out and tanks and other equipment was deployed to subdue the rebellious group. I would have more dealings with these folks and others in the future. But for now we were on another adventure.

I had two classes I could not complete during the fall semester, but Golden Gate accepted me with the stipulation that I would complete these courses either in California or back at the University of New Mexico. It was June and hot. Little 4-cylendar cars had no air conditioners, but we were happy to be going to a place we had only heard about. San Francisco.

We had water and cloths to wipe ourselves with as we drove through Arizona and California. The temperature was somewhere between "hot oven" and "scorching grill." We were pulling a 4'X 8' U-Haul trailer with everything we owned in in. Some things we sold, other things we had given away. We had no health insurance, no promise of a job, only an agreement that the seminary would help with job leads.

The Datsun with the trailer load managed to get up to 45 miles per hour—going downhill. Uphill was a much slower proposition and about 25 miles an hour was a good chug. It took us three days to get to the Bay Area and we had only maps to get us around once we got there. The clutch began slipping on the car, but it wasn't a terrible problem, only a problem. Penny and Jimmy had bouts with "when are we going to get there" anxiety and were restless and argued with each other about—almost everything.

Once we arrived on the East Bay freeway I had no idea how to get to Mill Valley. Fern had the maps, so I asked her, "Which route do we take?" I was met with silence. I repeated my request. Silence. I did so again with a little irritation in my voice. I was tired and confused. Silence. I looked over at my dear wife and she had tears streaming down her face. "What's the matter?" I asked.

"I don't know how to read a map," she said through her tears. I immediately felt guilty for my irritated assumption. I didn't know. I pulled off the freeway to look at the map she had been holding in her lap. I apologized and guiltily tried to find which way I was to go. I had to go from the 580 freeway, cross the Richmond San Rafael bridge and past San Quentin Prison to the 101 and Seminary Drive in Mill Valley. I managed it. Arriving in late afternoon at the Golden Gate Seminary campus. Our apartment was not ready, but we were here and they had a temporary housing assignment for us until the following week when all would be ready.

On Saturday, we ventured into San Francisco for the first time. The seminary was less than 5 miles away from the Golden Gate Bridge and we were anxious to see this famed city and the bridge that the name was taken from to designate our new school. Magnificent! Seeing the bridge as we drove over it was an amazing experience. It was a toll bridge and we paid our quarter as we entered the city. June was summer to us and we didn't take jackets. This was a mistake. Someone once said that the coldest winter he ever experienced was a summer in San Francisco. Whoever said that hit the target! The wind was chilly, so we spent most of the time in the car driving around. Cable cars were operating and we learned that the system ran on cables under the street that the car would hook up to and be carried to the next place and the next, uphill and down. Tall buildings loomed as we went downtown. The clutch had been damaged in bringing the U-Haul out with us, making it difficult to negotiate stop signs placed on uphill intersections. I had a few learning curves to add to what I considered good driving skills.

Lombard Street, the "crookedest street in America" was exactly that, switchbacks down a long hill. Going back to our seminary apartment we crossed the Golden Gate without paying; you only pay going into the city, not out of it. The Bay was beautiful, sailboats out enjoying the windy power they used to maneuver. Occasionally a cargo or Navy ship would be seen churning through the waters into or out of the Bay. Alcatraz island with the abandoned prison was easily seen, along with the larger Angel Island, not far from Strawberry Point where the seminary was. We immediately fell in love with this, our new home.

Seminary proved to be challenging. Moving into our small apartment required the purchase of some used furniture with what little money we had. I went to the office of student affairs and received job possibilities on the following Monday morning and went in search of work to support the family. I found a job the first day and began the next day which was Tuesday. I was now working in a candle holder making factory. The job I had was to fill in around colored pieces of glass that had been glued on to fancy glassware; like brandy snifters, wine glasses and so on. The patterns often had a theme: golfing, fish, random or whatever. The fill that was used was grout mixed with iron oxide, which made it look like lead around the edges of the glass. When a candle was placed in the glassware, the light shined through the colored glass chips, making a great ambiance for, well, whatever the owner wanted. Now, for those who don't know about iron oxide, it is black. Very black. I looked like I had been working in a coal mine after making the glassware look pretty. I didn't look at all pretty and I had to put newspaper on the car seat as I drove home.

I was paid so much for each piece I completed to the owner's satisfaction; fifteen cents for smaller pieces, a quarter for larger ones and thirty-five cents for the largest ones. I got good at it and had enough to feed the family AND pay the hospital for Paul's upcoming birth. Remember that we had no insurance—and the hospital required we have the cost covered before Fern went into labor! I thanked God for the job and the ability to make what I needed at the time I needed it.

I took a summer class in beginning Greek. I needed that class to get started with the studies that were to follow. It was an 8-week course and, guess what? Fern went into labor as I was studying for the final.

Greek, unlike Spanish or Portuguese, uses a different alphabet which had to be learned. I passed the Greek and she passed Paul, almost at the same time. Granny and Papa came out to visit with the new grandchild along with Fern's brother, Ken.

The birth, while long, was not complicated and she was in the hospital for the then required three days. The day she and Paul were discharged everyone wanted to go to Stinson Beach, except Fern, as I later learned. She was game and we all went to watch the waves come and go, but she was tired when we got home. Fern never wanted to let her situation deter others from doing what they wanted to do and as I learned, she would put her feelings or needs aside quite easily to accommodate others. For those who have never been to Northern California, the water and the beaches are usually cold. Even in the Summer.

We had decided to call Paul by his middle name, Scott. He was named for the biblical apostle, and a neighbor living in the next apartment who was a great guy and his name was Paul, so that was our way of coming up with a name. Our address was 3-C Judson Lane, named for Adoniram Judson, the first significant missionary to Burma in the early 1800's.

Seminary was even more difficult than the University of New Mexico had been. Not only did I have to learn Greek, but Hebrew as well. If I thought Greek was difficult, Hebrew was worse! My friend, Dr. Richard Cunningham, the BSU Director at UNM, was my professor of Systematic Theology, he kept me encouraged as I continued to work and go to school, both taking almost all of my time and energy.

In December at the end of the semester, we had to return to New Mexico to finish the two courses I needed for my bachelor's degree. I had checked into the possibility of doing the classes at a California university, but the cost was too high, I couldn't qualify as a California resident. We stored some of the furniture under the apartment with the approval of the seminary and headed back to Albuquerque. I heard on the news that I-40 through Flagstaff, Arizona, was closed because something like 102 inches of snow had fallen. I am pragmatic, can drive in snow, but not that much and certainly not when the highway is closed. We headed for a southerly route, through Needles and Parker,

Arizona. I still had a half tank of gasoline and I decided to press on. Bad move! There were no other places to get gas until I was almost in Phoenix.

The gas gauge was pegging empty. No gas stations in sight. I began praying, "Lord, I need your help." Still nothing in sight. The car went up a hill and began lunging, using up the last fumes in the gas tank. I crested the hill and began the downward descent and the engine died as I coasted. I prayed and as I neared the bottom I saw what looked like a gas station. It was! I drove in and pulled up to a pump with the engine not running. "Thank you, my heavenly Father," I mouthed as I got out of the car and grabbed the fuel hose. In that instant I learned that the God of the universe was also the God of the foolish and unwise who commit themselves to serve Him.

Phoenix also experienced some snow, but it didn't stick. Tucson also had snow and some of it was on the ground. We went through Silver City to visit Jim and Theresa and Jerry and Ellen. Snow was piled up fifteen to twenty feet high in the center of the town after being scooped from the streets.

We went on to Albuquerque and stayed with my parents until we could rent a furnished apartment on the east side of the city while I finished my bachelor's degree. The nearest church was Hoffmantown Baptist Church, named for a sub division in that area of the city. We joined the church the next Sunday after our return. The church was not as stodgy as some Baptist churches tended to be. They had lively music and an orchestra. Most churches in that era were traditional and, if you had not experienced anything different, it would not have been any problem to worship. The church in years to follow would move from this location, keep its name, and become innovative in worship experiences and ministries, one of the largest churches in New Mexico.

We rented an apartment that was already furnished, since much of our furniture and belongings had been left in Mill Valley ready for our return. The University was as I had left it and the two classes I needed were completed.

At the end of the semester I, along with what seemed like half the population of Albuquerque, assembled in "The Pit" which is the name of the famous arena built to house the winning teams of Coach Bob

King which opened in December 1966. It was a dug-out design which cost only a fraction of what similar arenas of different designs would have cost, but without pillars it afforded basketball fans an unobstructed view of the games while providing a noise level that terrified opposing teams and their supporters. We graduated and I received my Bachelor of Arts degree with a lot of personal satisfaction. My family and Fern's family were there to share in my accomplishment. So much for the admonition I gave myself the night I graduated from high school. I DID step into many classrooms and I DID have the ability to earn a degree in higher education. Now, I had to finish seminary and earn the Master of Divinity degree at Golden Gate.

Returning to California, we retrieved the furniture we had stored under the apartment building and moved back into the same apartment we had moved out of. We had different neighbors this time. A visiting professor, Dr. Donald Bell, was our neighbor for one semester, as were other students and their families. Now I needed another job. The candle holder making company wasn't hiring and I got names of other possibilities. The junior high school in San Rafael was needing a janitor. I needed a job. We came together and I became a custodian along with several others, my head custodian was a big fellow from Sebastapol, California, named Roy Berry. Roy was a little bit rough around the edges, but a good boss. We got along well. He had a hard time with certain words, like "condensation." He pronounced it con-sen-da-tion, mixing up the letters of the word. So, I got used to hearing about "consendation" pipes that returned cooled steam to the boilers during winter which heated the building.

I had a certain number of classrooms to clean and restrooms following that. At the end of my shift, if everything was completed, I could use some time to study. My shift was from 3:30 to 11:30 p.m. A full day. After a full day of classes! I would use the time between classes to study and usually my first class was at 7:30 in the mornings. By the weekend I was exhausted, but often I would have to spend the weekends studying. I was given some interim pastorates in the area to preach on Sundays. Two of the longest assignments were at First Baptist Church, Livermore and at Halcyon Baptist Church in San Leandro. Halcyon church was down the street from a coffee roasting plant and, just about 11:30 on Sunday morning we got a whiff of Maxwell House coffee being roasted, which reminded everyone in attendance that Sunday dinner would almost immediately follow the sermon.

One night, as we went into the apartment after arriving home from being at the church all day, I noticed some dishes that were stacked on a table that started to rattle. It seemed like a puff of wind came through the window and to me it was something odd. We got the kids ready for bed and we went to bed as well, watching the 11:00 news. Just after the newscast started the picture on the TV made a movement and the newscasters commented that they believed an earthquake had struck and said, "We are going to a commercial break… we'll be back after that—we hope!" Almost immediately our bed gave a heave as the earthquake went through our part of the area.

Each time we drove through San Francisco on our way to and from San Leandro, crossing the Golden Gate Bridge and later the double-decker San Francisco-Oakland Bay Bridge and under the Nimitz Freeway, also on our route, I thought about the possibility of an earthquake. This was the bridge and freeway that collapsed during the earthquake of 1989. If that happened, what would I do to save my family and others? The only thing I could think of was about saving water in the hot water heater under the apartment for drinking purposes. Beyond that there wasn't much to do but trust God, the same One who had "placed a gas station in the desert" when I needed it in Arizona. So, I learned to trust since there wasn't anything I could do to prevent such an event. And it didn't happen for another 20 years! I now think of the *Prayer for Serenity* by Reinhold Niebuhr: *God grant me the serenity to accept the things I cannot change; the courage to change the things I can; and the wisdom to know the difference.* Sometimes I'm a slow spiritual learner, but my God is always faithful, even when calamity strikes.

Occasionally I took some alone time to think—and fish—off the seawall at Sausalito. Just the need to rest became something I had to do. Sometimes I caught fish, sometimes I didn't recognize what I had caught. I was used to fishing in New Mexico. Trout, bass, bluegills and such. In the Bay I was catching what I thought was the ugliest fish known to man. They had ugly knobby heads which were big and then they became slenderer after the gills. I would throw them back.

One day a guy who was fishing near me said, "Don't you like those fish?" I asked him what they were and he replied: "Rock cod. Good eating." Cod I had heard of, but I didn't associate it with "rock." I took some home, cleaned them and we ate well. I used prawns as bait. Once in a while I would hook a small shark that would cut my line with its sharp teeth. As I fished, I watched people walking on the sidewalk above me. There were restaurants on piers jutting into the Bay, one was named the "Trident." I understand it is still there after a couple of closings, a name change, and a reopening with its original name. The point of my fishing was not so much for the fish, but to rest my body and my mind after full-time school and full-time work.

God can do many things with those who rest and listen. I tried to listen and sometimes I heard, sometimes I didn't, sometimes I just ignored what He said. I did hear the cries of those who were trying to find themselves in the crucible of the "Age of Aquarius" in and around the city of San Francisco. I took in the sights and sounds of those striving to find meaning in the life they had been given, and looking in all the wrong places. It was a time of "free love," psychedelic substances and putting flowers in your hair as you drove your VW bus full of other countercultural seekers… wherever. The Haight-Ashbury district in San Francisco was ground zero. *The New York Times* dubbed it "Hashbury." Jefferson Airplane, Janis Joplin and The Grateful Dead all lived a short distance from the district. Strippers danced in belfry windows along the neon lined Broadway that ran through North Beach. Glide Memorial United Methodist Church seemed to celebrate the cultural revolution and received attention from the media for its efforts. Most Methodists were chagrined that this church was a part of the denomination. All of this was no more than eight and a half miles as the crow flies from the seminary where we lived.

Hippies died from overdoses and brutality not only from those outside the culture but also from within. Freedom was not so free and they tried to make the lifestyle appear as something it wasn't. The movement spread to communes across the country. I would later encounter these folks again, just under different names and circumstances.

When not preaching at churches I had a chance to serve, we attended Tiburon Baptist Church, not far from the campus. Many of the professors and students were members there as well and we got to know many of them informally. Penny went to the elementary school almost walking distance from the seminary to attend Kindergarten. The other two were in the preschool at Golden Gate. Things were good.

I was offered the pastorate of a church in the East Bay, Balboa Park Baptist Church in Richmond, and began to try to become the leader of the flock there. The family moved from Mill Valley to an apartment complex near the church to be closer. This made our drive to the seminary more of an effort as we had to travel across the Richmond-San Rafael Bridge on school days, passing by San Quentin Prison as we entered Marin County. Alcatraz had long been abandoned, but it could be seen from almost anywhere close to the Bay. I often thought these were ominous places, places I would not want to enter for any reason. Several of the seminary students had found employment there and this got them through school, but I didn't think this was for me. The toll for bridges then was a quarter, not much in today's economy, but probably about the same if you reckoned the effects of inflation on the pocketbook. We loved looking at the sea lions below us as we crossed the water and wound our way back on Highway 101, getting off at Seminary Drive.

Balboa Park Baptists were good people who loved God and others. We tried to reach out into the community and on one attempt distributed the newly retranslated gospel of John in modern English to nearby neighborhoods. At one home, we handed a gentleman a copy, he looked at it, saw what it was and threw it into his yard. He then went to where it was and kicked it all the way into the street. So much for the love of Christ in that home.

Fern's uncle Bill and aunt Ruby McCloud lived in El Cerrito, not too far from where we were. We saw them often. Ruby's younger sister, Betty, lived with them and had for many years and considered her older sister like the mother she never had. She had a boyfriend, Billy, who ate with them and traveled with them, but Betty was reluctant to get married. Except for living and sleeping together, they were for all intents and purposes a couple, but she didn't want to commit. She was in her late 30's and Billy in his 40's. Bill and Ruby had a spider monkey that ran roughshod through the house most of the time. Sometimes he was in his cage, but often either escaped or was let loose to scamper up the curtains or hang from a chandelier. The kids loved to see Bill and Ruby—and the monkey.

Bill worked at a shopping mall at a key shop. Ruby weighed well over 400 pounds and had difficulty walking. She filled an arm chair and ate most of her meals there which were brought to her. The family bank was in Ruby's ample endowment just below the top of her dress. Whenever anyone wanted money for any reason, Aunt Ruby would place her hand in the "bank" and retrieve whatever was needed. She was the matriarch and pretty much ran everything in that household in a pleasant manner.

The church was a joy and we grew to love the people there. One of the children of the Giese family had kidney disease and had to be taken several times a week into San Francisco for dialysis treatments. We learned that if we got enough Betty Crocker coupons, a machine would be donated and placed in the East Bay. Well, coupons back in that day were important, so we advertised as best we could through Baptist Press and other means and the coupons started rolling in. From everywhere! We received mail bag after mail bag of them and they had to be placed in bundles of 50 or 100, I can't remember which, so we got busy. We were so busy the Boy and Girl Scouts helped us. Then other churches. It was amazing! Finally, the magic number of coupons had been received and Betty Crocker came through. The award was made by one of the most famous baseball players in history: San Francisco's own Willie Mays. A real honor and a fitting finish for this effort.

Moving away from the seminary we lived in an apartment house that would accept pets and we had missed having a dog in the family. We looked in the newspaper classified section and found someone wanting to sell a dog. It wasn't very expensive, something like fifteen dollars, so we went to see the advertised puppy. What a mess! She was cowering in a backyard pen that was dirty and covered with fleas. She was said to be a beagle, but that was doubtful. Probably a beagle mixed with something—terrier? We didn't know, but looking at her she seemed to say, "Please take me out of this awful place." And we did.

We named her "Lucy" after the Peanuts cartoon character. We couldn't call her "Snoopy" because she was a female and that wouldn't be right.

I bought a bar of flea soap and we went to work or her. Even after the bath we still had to pick fleas off her. In a day or two she was a different puppy. Smart. Loving. We immediately discovered we had made a good choice for sure and she is a dog we will always remember. I still think of her and miss her although it has been many years ago that she departed this world. Although Scripture doesn't say anything about pets being in heaven, we have a hope that God, in his mercy and grace will allow us to enjoy her when we arrive.

The music minister Paul Mauldin, a second cousin to World War II cartoonist famous for his "Willie and Joe" soldier editorial cartoons, Bill Mauldin. Paul was a student at U.C. Berkeley majoring in electrical engineering. His wife, Cindy, was a delight who worked during the day to support herself and her husband. Paul had taught himself music by playing classical guitar and was very bright. At one point, he was about to work toward a Ph.D. in bioelectrical engineering, but discarded that idea when he discovered there was only one place of employment for this career: Blood Services of the Red Cross. He went to work for Pacific Gas and Electric trying to learn how to send massive volts of electricity through underground cables. Last I heard they had blown up a lot of transformers in this attempt.

We were invited as a church on February 13, 1971, to participate in a march on Sacramento's Capitol Building showing solidarity of the Christian community. Proclaimed "Spiritual Revolution Day" by the state senate, many churches showed up and the number of people were estimated at about 7,000. California, not even a hole in the Bible belt, made this a large undertaking we showed up and sang, *They Will Know We are Christians By Our Love, Amazing Grace*, and other songs as we held a rally on the capitol steps. Several of the police officers who were helping to control the crowd sent us "thumbs up" signs and other ways of expressing that they were with us. One police lieutenant was quoted in the Baptist Press as saying, "How can you oppose something like this, it would be like saying you hate your mother." One of the youth, Vicki Allman, from our church who was 13 at the time was quoted in the same article saying that the reason she was marching was, "I love Jesus—I came."

On an outing to get away from our studies and church events, Paul and Cindy along with Fern and I drove to Reno, Nevada, just because we had never been there. We didn't intend to gamble, but when we heard that they were giving away free nickels we collected as many rolls as we could and had enough money to eat on while we were there. Hotels were inexpensive and this was a cheap way to have a time away from our responsibilities. We were not particularly impressed with the gambling resort and never returned. But hey! Free money is free money…

Paul had purchased a used sports car that ran well, but didn't have a pleasant exterior. The paint was faded and there were a few dings in the fenders and doors. Paul smoothed out the bumps and with cans of automobile spray paint, made the little car very red. Not a bad job for spray paint cans. What few bloopers there weren't noticeable by the untrained eye.

A Japanese family moved into our neighborhood and wanted to attend church. They were mainly interested in learning English better, but we exposed them to the gospel of Jesus Christ as best we could. Dr. Fujiwara, a professor at Osaka University, was taking additional classes at Berkeley and his daughters seemed to love being in our Sunday school and just hanging out at the church. We enjoyed getting to know them. The church was multicultural, reflecting the demographics of the East Bay. We had a Philippine family, the father was a chef in an Oakland restaurant; blacks, a Mexican couple, and a few scattered gringos. A Chinese woman played the piano for our worship. Pot luck dinners were wonderful! One deacon in the church had donated the carpeting that went between the pews and an organ. One Sunday as I stepped up to the pulpit to bring the message, I realized I had left my notes in my study. I prayed, asking the Lord to bring to my mind what I had prepared… and He came through. I felt relieved when the service was over and one of the congregation told me it was my best sermon yet. Back then, my preparation was done on a legal pad. I didn't type well, but I could read my writing—just barely. If my scribbling had been any worse, I could have been a medical doctor.

The deacon who had given the carpet and organ to the church died leaving his accumulations to his second wife and children. While getting ready for the funeral someone told me that his son from the first marriage had threatened to shoot both his step-mother and me because his dad had cut him out of the will. This made me a little uneasy, so I prayed for protection. During the eulogy, the son stood up in the family section of the funeral home off to my left while everyone else remained seated. I looked him in the eye and kept on talking. He sat down looking sullen and angry, but he did nothing. We still had the graveside service and that was completed with no actions on his part. I tried to talk to him after the service was over, but he was having none of it. As far as I know, he never made good on his threat to anyone. God was good!

The culture began to change along with the Viet Nam war. Campuses were hotbeds of hatred and conflict. Tear gas was used to disperse crowds. Those who had served the country in time of war were looked down upon, sometimes spat upon or assaulted. Drugs often became the way of escape and the world I had grown up in was beginning to fade. I didn't realize how much until some years later, but "the times they were a-changing," wrote Bob Dylan about that era. We were in the cradle of the change in the Bay Area. I didn't really appreciate how much the change would explode world-wide and how all I had accepted as truth as a child would be considered another time, another culture away.

Ron and Myrna Brown came to California to see us and to check out Golden Gate Seminary. He had been attending the seminary at Denver University, a Methodist institution, since he had decided to become a Methodist. Baptists had become very traditionalized and sometimes hardened to reaching out to others. Not so much as a denomination, but as individual churches. He had had enough. He was impressed and moved to the Seminary to complete his Master of Divinity Degree. Upon completion, they moved back to Albuquerque and he was pastor of Paradise Hills United Methodist Church.

It was in 1971 that Billy Graham had a crusade in Oakland and our church participated in the preparation and the campaign itself. I had had my life influenced by this evangelist when I was twelve years old and loved his ministry and I would have loved to have been there. We left the Bay area before the crusade in July and August, but I would see a campaign later in Albuquerque.

Graduation came in May of 1971. My parents came out in their 1957 Packard Clipper. This was a real celebration for me. My graduation from the University of New Mexico was a bit of an anticlimax, buried in the Pan Am arena with thousands of others. Not very personal and certainly not an event I would want to repeat. I would have been just as happy had they mailed my diploma to me. But Golden Gate was different. It was personal and it was a celebration. I was honored with the Master of Divinity hood along with the diploma. This was so much more meaningful than UNM.

Following graduation, we decided to go to Yosemite to see the Falls. The kids wanted to ride with Grandma and Grandad and they climbed into the Clipper. We were headed toward the famed National Park with Dad following me. At one point on the 205 Freeway I looked into the rear-view mirror and I didn't see them. I pulled over onto the shoulder and waited. Still they weren't coming, so I backed up on the shoulder until I saw them coming. Dad flashed his lights and we got out to meet them. Mom was holding Paul who was about two and a half years old at that time, shouting: "He fell out of the car." The Packard Clipper had a "suicide door" that opened from the center post backward. He had managed to get the door open and fell out, the wind plastering him against the door at 70 miles per hour. As Dad slowed down, he came off the door and rolled onto the shoulder of the highway.

Getting him into our car, Fern wrapped him in one of my old jackets and kept talking to him to keep him awake. I had to find a hospital and I had no idea where one was. I was driving 90 miles an hour and finally saw a police car parked at a phone booth. I slowed down, pulled up to the phone booth and said my boy had fallen out of the car and I needed to find a hospital. He leaned out of the phone booth, took the phone out of his ear and said, "Keep going. It's in Stockton. I didn't tell him what I thought of his nonchalant attitude, but I headed at the same speed in the direction of Stockton following the road signs pointing the direction. In Stockton, additional signs pointed us to the hospital and we got Paul into the emergency room.

They looked at him and saw the road burns on his little body along with gravel that had been ground into his flesh. They shook their heads and began working on him. We heard his painful cries as they scraped the rocks and dirt out. The x-rays showed only 3 small cracks in the bones of one of his feet. He was kept in the hospital overnight for observation and the medical staff remarked that this was a real miracle that he fell out of a car on a California freeway and was not harmed more than this. We knew God had intervened and he was alive. Dad and Mom took Penny and Jim to our house for the night while we stayed in Stockton with Paul. We prayed and thanked our Lord that his life had been spared. Two weeks later the scabs had come off and it was difficult to imagine that he had so narrowly escaped death. I later told him that God had a special reason for saving him, but the results would come many years in the future.

CHAPTER 9

THE TAOS ADVENTURE

I was called by the seminary that a church in New Mexico was wanting a pastor and asked if they wanted my name to be submitted. I found out that it was First Baptist Church in Taos. I prayed, but not very hard and *in myself* I felt I wanted to submit my name. This decision is one that I have wrestled with in my soul. Did I believe God wanted me to leave Balboa Park Baptist for a church in my home state? I have often thought I had abandoned these good folks in California to pursue my own desires. What would my life have looked like had I stayed? What could God have done with me there? How would our family have turned out? I will never know. This church holds a sweet spot in my memory.

A deacon from First Baptist Taos invited us to come for an interview before the church. It was a chance to go back home and see everyone we had missed, and they would pay the expenses. Nice! Taos had been a place we as children liked to go. Fishing along the Rio Grande in the Gorge had been pleasant in my childhood and trips to the Taos Pueblo, probably the most famous Native American town in the world was fascinating.

We met with a group from the church who talked with us about our experiences in ministry and I was invited to preach. A meeting was held afterward and I was asked to come as pastor. The church itself was much different than any I had ever served. The building was mud adobe construction and had been built in 1932. There was no parking lot. The parsonage was attached to the sanctuary and the Sunday school rooms were in a building farther down the property. All of this was serviced by an alley winding alongside the buildings. There were cracks in the mud walls and some concern about the stability of the structure, but mostly the members were satisfied with their surroundings.

Across the street was Pueblo Drug Store and just to the south of that the Presbyterian Church adjacent to Kit Carson Park which holds the grave of the famed mountaineer and early statesman who was a part of that region's history. The National Forest near Taos bears his name as well. The mountains in the Carson National Forest are beautiful and Wheeler Peak, at an elevation of 13,159 feet, the highest peak in New Mexico, stands guard over Taos Pueblo as a sacred monument to the native people. Charles Bent, first Territorial Governor of New Mexico is immortalized in the history of Taos.

We returned to California, said good-bye to our Balboa Park church family, packed our belongings in a U-Haul truck and headed for New Mexico. We left California with mixed feelings. I had wrestled with the desire to make this my home and these people my people, but Taos took the lead in my thinking process and, whether it was God's will or mine, I don't know. I have often thought how my life and ministry would have been different if I had stayed there, but I didn't, so it doesn't matter what could have been. It matters what did happen. I am reminded of the scripture found in Romans 8:28 *And we know that God causes everything to work together for the good of those who love God and are called according to his purpose for them.* But I still wonder. God redeems past poor choices.

Driving back to New Mexico was a long hot trip. The truck didn't have air conditioning, most vehicles back then were lacking in this luxury that we consider essential now. We were nearing the New Mexico state line with Arizona, it was night and I had the radio on in the truck. The radio wasn't pulling the station in very well and I had a difficult time understanding what was going on. We were used to riots on the university campuses in California. Berkeley, San Francisco State and others. I was getting news broadcasts of a major riot going on somewhere, and finally I heard it well enough to make out that it was in Albuquerque, where we were headed on our way to Taos. The rioters were setting cars on fire at a major car dealer in Albuquerque, Galles

Cadillac! They were breaking out store windows along Central Avenue and I began to listen intently. Things were not good back home.

We arrived at my folk's house, quite a distance from where the riots were going on. I was too tired to really be concerned, and really there was no reason to worry unless you were around the conflagration, which we were not. We had no intention of going there either. Great visit with the family, but we were ready to go to our new destination, our new home. Taos. We were ready to pitch our tent and stay.

The people were diverse—and divided. The Native population mainly associates with other Natives. Those that belonged to the landed Spanish culture that began colonizing the area in the early 1600's were proud of their heritage and many had a disdain for those who had come in later, mainly the Anglos. The Anglos owned many of the businesses and service industries. Then there were the "artsy-craftsy" folks who painted, sculpted, wrote, acted and sang their way through life. Some of them had galleries and museums. Mable Dodge Luhan; D. H. Lawrence; Millicent Rogers, socialite, fashion icon, and art collector; Aldous Huxley, author; singer Lynn Anderson; R. C. Gorman, artist; Dennis Hopper, actor, director, artist; John Nichols, author of The Milagro Beanfield War; Julia Roberts, actress and many more have made Taos their home or have passed through on their way to wherever they went. There were also some of the same crowd I had seen in California: Hippies. They were everywhere. Taos had become a mecca for those seeking "spiritual" freedom and a counter culture that eschewed war. This was in the middle of the Viet Nam war and it was not popular. Instances of spitting on military personnel were hitting the newspapers and a backlash of those who were not so inclined ensued. Most "good" folks didn't understand the subculture, and the subculture didn't trust the others. Many of them, though were hooked on heroin, smoked pot and were reaping the results.

My training in seminary and my relationship with Christ told me that the "spiritual freedom" they sought could not be found in drugs or "free love." How was I going to pastor a church in such a diverse place as Taos? I would rely on the Holy Spirit of God to guide me. And that could get me into trouble.

Many of the church members were just plain, ordinary Christian people. They wanted to honor God, but they wanted to do it their way. Their way was pretty much like it had always been done before. They didn't like a lot of changes. On a good Sunday, we might have 75 to 100 people, Sunday night maybe 20 and on Wednesday night, 10 to 15. Not a lot of folks, but the community wasn't very big either. There was a Spanish Baptist Church, pastored by an Anglo family that spoke Spanish, and an Indian Baptist Church pastored by a Native American pastor.

There were others who were just "odd." One old fellow, claiming to be a starving artist came to our door one day and was acting like he was about to die. He couldn't speak full sentences, but with a look of panic in his eyes he asked me if I had any "sugar substitute. I didn't understand what he was asking and I kept asking him for clarification. He finally told me he wanted saccharin. We had that and I gave him the bottle. He took all the tablets in the container. He then tried to sell me a painting he had done. It wasn't a very good one and I didn't have money to buy it, so I begged off. He later gave it to me as a gift. He said he was diabetic and that was the explanation for his actions.

The church doing better than most in the community was a Reformed Church pastored by a Hispanic pastor. Many of the Hispanics that weren't Catholic attended that church and not First Baptist. We had no Hispanics or Indians. Only Anglos. Even though New Mexico had never been segregated, ethnic groups tended to flock together. Hispanics in northern New Mexico had some dislike for those who had usurped their territorial rights, but it was not an obtrusive issue, just personal. There was no outward disdain, just preferences. Such as "I prefer vanilla to chocolate ice cream."

Most people did not like the "hippies." They were at the bottom of the bottom. Many had come to Taos to find spiritual peace and that had little or nothing to do with organized religion. They were under the impression that Native Americana held the keys to real spirituality and tried to learn from the Taos Indian Pueblo people all they could to form their new way of life. They established communes that had names like *New Buffalo* and *Morning Star*. The desire of those who came to Taos was to escape the viciousness of the world with its wars, rules and rulers. Their intentions were admirable, but the methods led to more subjugation and broken lives. They wanted to establish brotherhood, but the underlying human nature of those who were drawn to the movement made this impossible. They brought with them their jealous natures, clashing visions for the future, pride and hurt feelings and without a system of governance the tribal unity disintegrated into disgruntled people who found it difficult to get along with each other. They expelled each other and became vindictive toward one another. The experiment ended. Going naked and natural got cold and addicted. What felt free became more chains around the feet of those who sought life without cares and snares.

A dentist moved from Texas into a building next to First Baptist and wanted to turn the adobe structure into a dental clinic. He enlisted hippies who helped him with the renovating and remodeling of the building in exchange for work on their drug-rotted teeth. It was very common to see both men and women scraping, painting—whatever on the building next door. I got acquainted with some of them and found out that they were struggling to get off the heroin addictions they had been struggling with. They needed a ride to a methadone clinic and I volunteered to take them. I began to share the freedom I had found in Jesus Christ and how he wanted relationship, not religion. They listened. I invited them to church, they came…and sat by themselves.

I got complaints that "those people" didn't smell good and some in the congregation would grumble about the fact that I had invited them. For me, I was following the admonition in James 2:1 which says, *"…How can you claim to have faith in our glorious Lord Jesus Christ if you favor some people over others?"* My Bible said that the gospel is for ALL people, not just those who are like us. At one meeting of our association, as we were filling our plates from pot luck dishes, the wife of the deacon who had asked me to come before the church in view of a call, a pillar of the church, said to me, "I wouldn't go to that dentist (meaning the one who had moved next door and used hippies to renovate his building) because his dental instruments are contaminated from working on *those hippies.!*"

My mind overloaded my emotions and my mouth exploded: "That's the most unchristian thing I have ever heard come out of anyone's mouth!" I was now *persona non-grata* in her book. I tried to smooth it over, but she was having none of it. I had crossed a line with her. She had her ideas about who Christ could save and it sure wasn't hippies. My Bible said otherwise… I was not forgiven for my culture clash.

Other things happened in Taos. At one point we were invaded by a battalion of "Brown Berets," Hispanic activists who had been stirred up by Reyes Lopez Tijerina and his quest to return lands grated by the King of Spain to their rightful owners. A Californian, David Sanchez had issues with farm workers being mistreated. Many of them felt that the state of New Mexico had not been treating Latinos with the respect they deserved. Many of the politicians of the state were Hispanic, as were most of the local jurisdictions that governed the daily affairs of the citizens, but this didn't make this group satisfied that they were being treated fairly. Most of the locals had little in common with this bunch that had come in mainly from other places to establish a pro-Chicano movement, they didn't live in Taos or Northern New Mexico for the most part. They finally left after marching up and down the main streets in brown uniforms while the populace ignored them.

The state Convention office called one day and said they had a group of college students who wanted to work in our area doing Bible studies and Vacation Bible School with local kids. I was happy to say yes to the offer, but we were to house and feed them. This posed some difficulty and I announced it to the congregation. A few offered to help, but for the most part my family had to provide food for the six students. Our salary at the time was six thousand dollars a year and a house. That was it. The economy was different, but we had little left at the end of the month after food and car payment. I rode a bicycle through town quite often for three reasons: the first was for economic reasons, foot power was much cheaper than gasoline. The second was because of the traffic problems caused by having tourists and others in a small town where most of the streets had been planned long before automobiles came on the scene; and I also needed exercise since I was gaining weight.

The initial meeting was great and the kids were terrific as well. But they soon began to complain that we served too much chicken, they wanted other things. My family was sharing our food with them and it wasn't what they wanted. We asked for more donations from the church members and we got a few cans of groceries, but no meat or money to buy meat. We did the best we could, but usually it was not enough.

It wasn't that the church members were stingy so much as I didn't want them to know how close to the edge our salary was from our being poor. Since Taos was a tourist town most everything was more expensive than it would be in larger cities.

One winter our family was invited to go skiing with an optometrist and a state police officer who were members of our church. We had never been on skis before and this was a new experience. We drove to Red River, one of the better ski areas in New Mexico and we were outfitted for our trip down the mountain. The state police officer was a member of the ski patrol and was very adept at the sport. The others were not amateurs like my family—and me!

I strapped on a pair of skis and practiced going down the beginner slope. I found it difficult to get back up after I had fallen. I was not a lightweight, but I kept trying and I finally had the "snowplow" movement down pretty well. I caught the chairlift and up the hill I went. I was told how to get on and off the chair properly, and I did it right! The first time.

I was in position to go down the hill and went from side to side as I had been instructed. Nearing the end of the run, I went into the snowplow position and stopped. Perfect! Amazing! I could now ski. So back up the hill I went on the chairlift. I got on right. As I got out of the chair at the top of the hill I fell squarely on my backside. Definitely not what I expected. I managed to get up and struggled down the slope. The optometrist said I looked like a "pregnant chicken" coming down the hill. A couple more times and I was done. I went to the lodge and sat out the rest of the day. That was my first and last time on skis. I didn't break anything, and only my pride was harmed in the process. My other family members had a great time, except Fern. She never got the hang of the snowplow and never went any farther than the practice slope. The kids were a little better, but none of them ever took up the sport.

The optometrist was also an avid bow hunter. He made his own arrows from scratch as well as the bows he used. For three years running he got an elk and did divide the meat with some of us in the church. It would have been nice had he given us meat during the time the summer missionary students were there. I asked him one day if he lassoed an elk and tied it to a tree when he went scouting prior to the hunt. I think he was a little insulted but he treated my comment as a joke the way I had intended it to be.

I often tell a not-so-true story about a funeral I once had at the church in Taos. The way I tell it is that the deceased died in the middle of winter after a snow. The street outside was icy and covered with snow. The funeral was held in the church and as the casket was being taken up the steps into the sanctuary it slipped off the gurney and slid across the street and down a hill into the Pueblo Drug Store. It was going so fast it went through the door, slammed up against the pharmacy counter, the lid opened, and the body sat up and said, "Do you have anything to stop this coffin?" Sometimes I get a laugh, but mostly I get a scowl.

I tried to get the church to buy land south of town at a time when it was affordable. I brought it up during a church business meeting and it was soundly voted down. Our building was historic. Adobe. It had character. But it didn't have parking nor could it grow larger as the town's population grew. I felt discouraged and defeated. This group of Baptists didn't want to reach lost people, unless they were like themselves. They had no heart for being on the cutting edge of helping those who struggled with life. They wanted members who could join the club.

The summer missionaries had discovered a group of people in Ojo Caliente who had been left without a pastor when the denomination it was from merged with the United Methodist Church. They were United Brethren. There were not enough pastors to go around and since they were smaller than some of the other churches they were left on their own. I began to go down there to hold services.

At this point I was becoming aware that while I was called to ministry, it was not to the pastorate. I began looking at the classified ads in the Santa Fe New Mexican and discovered the Corrections

Department was needing caseworkers at the Penitentiary in Santa Fe. I applied. I interviewed and was hired by the state, so I resigned from the church and went to work—at a higher salary that also had health insurance and retirement. The church had a small retirement plan that I paid into out of my salary.

CHAPTER 10

THE PRISON YEARS

We moved to Santa Fe, buying a mobile home that was placed in a mobile home park on Airport Road. I felt somewhat guilty for abandoning the pastorate and at the same time relieved to be away from the frustrations the church in Taos had put me through. I continued to serve the mission in Ojo Caliente while I was in Santa Fe and we met some great people there. Austin and Lucille Bonner from White Rock, near Los Alamos were great friends who drove the distance from their home to the small village. Lucille played the piano and Austin taught Sunday school. We remained friends for many years, I still get phone calls and Christmas cards from Lucille, although Austin went to be with the Lord many years ago. The town was home to a famous hot springs and spa that have a long history.

As a congregation, since nobody but the Bonners and my family were Baptist, we decided that baptism by immersion would not be a big deal. None of the others were convinced that adding water to their faith made any difference and that was how we decided to run the mission. Those in the Santa Fe Baptist Association did not like our diversion from "the faith once delivered to the saints." While we were not ostracized outwardly we were made to feel inferior and when churches were recognized at associational meetings, our congregation was not mentioned or introduced. Again, I was a failure at getting my congregation to comply with what was expected.

Moving to Santa Fe began a new chapter in our life as a family. I didn't just wake up one morning and say, "Gee, I really want to work in a prison." The position at the Penitentiary was a lifeline that I grabbed onto when I felt adrift in Taos. There were times I had thought about what would have happened if I had stayed in California. Would I have remained a pastor? Well, I was still the pastor of a mission church that wasn't recognized by the denominational authorities. And now I had a "real" job. But was I following my own desires and not allowing the Holy Spirit to guide me. I didn't know, and I didn't care at that point.

Working at the penitentiary was different. My first day there, November 16, 1972, I was outfitted with a uniform. Grey wool trousers, a wool jacket and a shiny billed cap with a badge pinned to the front of the cap. I looked like a bus driver. My picture was taken, and my training was to work as a Corrections officer for six weeks. I was hired as a caseworker, but this was the training. I was taken on a tour of the facility, shown the gas chamber, all of the cell blocks and dormitories, instructed how to put handcuffs on a person after patting that person down for weapons and told to be careful.

The next day I was assigned to the swing shift, handed a set of very large keys which I hung on my belt and was assigned to the "south side." This meant cell blocks 1 and 2 as well as the four dormitories south of the chow hall. There were no radios, only black rotary dial telephones at the end of each housing unit. When it was determined that the unit was to be released for chow, the phone would ring, and after answering it I would be advised to unlock the door to let the inmates out.

The first day went well. I had told Fern that there may be times when I would not be home at the regular time and for her not to worry. I had no way to call home in the event of an incident and I hoped she would not be concerned. My second day was different. I was assigned to Cell Block 3, the segregation unit. All of the inmates were locked down but let out of their cells to take a shower one by one, not in groups. Those who resisted the officer or had behavioral problems had to stay in his "stink" until his behavior warranted more civilized treatment.

The unit was usually noisy as they conversed with each other through the open bars. They made strings, called "fishing lines," from bedding or sheets, or their own clothing, whatever they could find, weighted at one end with a note or other item attached and flung down to another cell by the "sender." The "receiver" took the item off, and could attach an item to be retrieved by his cohort. What was sent could be anything from a note to a syringe or drug of choice. Notes were referred to as "kites." This even translated to communication with staff. An inmate would say, "Man, I sent you a kite," indicating that a written letter or note had been sent through regular channels to the person intended.

Using individual mirrors, they watched for correctional staff presence and when detected, the action quickly ceased. There were no surveillance cameras, only mirrors to help staff see around corners. Images were somewhat distorted by the curved glass.

I had been working all day since 6:00 a.m. and not long before I was to be relieved to go home, information came that there was a fight in the chow hall. Inmates were hitting each other with fists, dinner trays, salt and pepper shakers, anything they could get their hands on. At first I thought they were pulling my leg as the newbie, but when I got a chance to look out the window of the door to the cell block, I saw staff herding inmates down the corridor, some of them not cooperating, and the officers used billy clubs to force compliance. Some had bloody gashes on their heads, others just decided to forego the refusal to obey and go with less body pain.

The incident was put to rest and the institution locked down and at about 8 p.m. I was told I could go home. It had snowed most of the afternoon and I drove home over the slippery pavement. From our mobile home park in the southern part of Santa Fe on a good day the trip would have taken me 15 or 20 minutes. This evening it took longer and when I got home, Fern was frantic. "We've been looking for you all evening," she said. The neighbor next door had offered to drive the distance to the Penitentiary looking for me, expecting my car to be in a ditch because of the slick road conditions. I assured her I was okay and that we had had an incident at the prison that delayed my getting off work. I did remind her that I had mentioned this possibility, and she agreed I had.

At night, especially during the winter, it was cold in Santa Fe, at an altitude of about seven thousand feet. Sometimes, the temperature could get well below freezing, often below zero. Most of the posts weren't bad, but the one I hated was "outside perimeter patrol." This required walking around the building, checking for windows that may have been tampered with as an attempt to escape, or signs of other activity along the edge of the building. I was given a set of keys to padlocks that opened gates going from one area to another. I didn't have a jacket that was designed for the really cold weather, the Ike jacket barely kept me from freezing to death. I brought my own gloves to protect my hands, but when reaching for the right key, I had to take the gloves off. I once touched a fence pole and my finger stuck to it. I managed to get it unstuck without losing skin, and I was elated to get back inside the building.

Other night posts included Tower 2, located on the south side of the prison. For eight hours, I was stuck in the tower with a rifle, a mounted search light, a pair of binoculars, and a telephone. It was not easy to stay alert for that long, especially after dark. Occasionally I would get a call from a supervisor asking if I was still there, but for the most part I just stared out of the windows with the binoculars, looking for movement. The lighting wasn't great and in the shadows it wasn't hard to think I saw something move, but I never found anything and we never had an escape on my watch.

After my six weeks were over I was shown to my office above the institution's control center. My desk was overflowing with paperwork since they had no one to do the job while I was in training. The other caseworkers did what they could along with their own work, but usually that didn't accomplish everything that had to be done. I had no idea what to do with what I saw. It was an enormous task to sort through all of the objects, but the other caseworkers were helpful in showing me what went where, especially Johnny Vigil whom I shadowed for a week or so to get used to the routine. The other caseworker, J. B. Gonzales was an efficient person, but not quite as friendly as the others. My boss, Chief Classification Officer Joe Gutierrez, was half Polish and half Spanish descent. A decent guy who was a stickler for detail. He spoke some Spanish, but understood a lot more, which helped in the tasks around the prison. Many inmates had come from Latin American countries, mainly Mexico, and didn't speak English. I found my background from Spain and my degree from UNM to be helpful as well.

As I sat in my office working, I could hear the barred gates below me in the Control Center opening and closing with loud clinks and clanks all day long. At first it annoyed me, but then it faded into the daily routine and I became used to it, like living next to a railroad and having the noise of the trains blend into the environment. All the caseworkers got along well, each having his own personality. There were only men, since only males were hired for the men's side of the prison. It was a misogynistic culture, built up over eons. We did have some female teachers, but they were "different." I'm not sure how they were different, but we didn't have younger women, only those with a "motherly" countenance were chosen for the positions.

One of the caseworkers had the same name as the Psychologist, Tommy Thompson. The name was similar to mine, Thomas, so often the inmates called me, "Mr. Thompson." I got used to it, even though I had my name on my door. There were five of us who divided up the inmates by the last number of their assigned prison numeral. If they had numbers ending in 1 or 2, they went to the caseworker who was assigned those numbers and so on. I had the 9's and 0's. Between 564 and 800 inmates were in the facility during the time I was a caseworker, so that number, divided by 5 resulted in the approximate number of inmates on a caseload. That could be from about 112 to over 200, if the population got larger, and it did, that was a lot of people to have to be accounted for.

My tasks included all intake, which required writing backgrounds, referred to as "admission summaries," or brief histories of the inmate gleaned from the documents submitted by the courts, parole and probation Department, police agencies and others involved in the arrest and conviction of the individual. This information was supplemented by calling parents, schools and other institutions to get a better picture of who had been committed to the Penitentiary. These summaries could go from a page or two to fifteen or more, depending on the age and activity of the man.

Often, we were to do diagnostic evaluations of those sent by the courts when the judge didn't know what to do or to give the person a "taste" of prison life. These required more investigation and a suggestion as to the disposition the courts should take.

None of the caseworkers had ultimate authority to finish a summary or an evaluation without review by the Chief Classification Officer (CCO). Joe Gutierrez, our CCO, was thorough and if the summary didn't read well or had faulty reasoning, it was handed back with the notation: "Do it over." In which case, you went back to the beginning and redid the summary. All documents had to be duplicated and, this being the era before Xerox copiers had been invented and were available, we had to write out our summaries by hand on yellow legal pads and submit them to clerks in the records office to be typed on stencils. They were then placed on machine drums that rolled paper through a trough making copies of the document that was typed.

When the volume of documents became so large that the typing pool couldn't keep up (or they slacked off) the caseworkers had to do the stencils on their own. Any mistake had to be corrected with a piece of the stencil inserted between the typewriter key and the main part of the stencil and the correct letter retyped. The stencils were purple and, if you wore a white shirt, your shirt took on a purple hue at the end of the day.

Felix Ródriguez (center) and Howard Leach (left wearing hat) being escorted by New Mexico State Police, circa 1971.

Above Joe in the administrative hierarchy was the Deputy Warden, Horacio Herrera, a short, humorless fellow who loved giving others a hard path to follow and very little direction. I disliked going to his office for anything, but I found myself there more often than not, very seldom initiating the contact. He gave my boss, Joe Gutierrez, a hard time as well in matters of classification and decisions related to the placement of inmates within the Penitentiary and at minimum security as well. While we were pretty good at making judgements regarding the inmates, we were not perfect, and if Herrera wanted to take the responsibility, I learned to let that happen regardless of what I thought.

Warden Felix Rodríguez, on the other hand was a tall man, gregarious and not afraid of anyone or anything. He would often be found in the inmate's cell or sitting on his bunk in the dormitory talking with them about almost anything. Sometimes he was gleaning information from them about illegal or dangerous activities, but didn't let them know what he was fishing for most of the time. Sometimes he was just doing the job of keeping the institution from harm relying on personal relationships to accomplish this. I generally liked the man.

Much of the classification efforts went toward sending inmates to the "Honor Farm" located in the village of Los Lunas south of Albuquerque. It had been renamed the Los Lunas Correctional Center and actually had a working farm that grew crops, bought cattle at auction, fed the cattle and slaughtered them for food at both facilities. I got to know the caseworker, Buddy Ramirez, who was the recipient of the inmates we selected to go to his facility.

Adjacent to the main unit at the Penitentiary was the Women's Annex that housed up to 54 women who were convicted of felonies. The Superintendent was responsible for the classification duties at his facility. At the time I got there, a male administrator who had "matrons" handling the correctional officer duties was assigned. After a few visits to the annex, I was delighted to be working with men. The women were very demanding and often obnoxious. Sometimes as they worked outside the building they would "flash" the inmates living in Cell Blocks 4 and 5, to great outburst of pleasure from the male side.

The male inmates were starved for contact with the fairer sex. When women visitors or education staff were present in the main unit, they would be greeted with whistles and lewd comments from some of the inmates. I had major adjusting to do to my new environment. It was nothing like anything I had been a part of this far in my life.

I got along well with the inmates for the most part. I found that if I treated them like human beings I generally was treated with respect back. A sponsor was needed for the AA group and I was asked to volunteer my time to be with them. We met in an upstairs room above the security and psychological offices every Monday evening. The gate leading up to the room was usually locked after we entered, and I listened to their "drunkalogues" and really had no worries about my safety as the "sponsor" of the group, even though I couldn't get out or notify anyone if there was a problem. I had no radio or telephone.

The Secretary of Corrections, Howard Leach, asked to sit in on the group one evening and both he and I were at the mercy of whatever happened. Neither of us had a concern. I didn't realize it but at this time in the history of the Penitentiary the facility was pretty well run, even though there were problems; of course when you take troubled people and lock them up, there's bound to be trouble occasionally. Many of the issues centered around inmates jockeying for position and power, and often for control of the drugs that were available. There was little animosity against staff, although inmates held animosity toward those they believed treated them unfairly or were hard to get along with. One of the first clichés I learned was that we were to treat inmates "firmly, fairly, and consistently." Most staff did this well, but there were exceptions to the rule. I believe this was the reason the Secretary and I could be locked in an area with inmates and not have great concerns for our lives.

Howard Leach was only the second person placed in this position, created in the late 1960's. The first Secretary, John Sanchez was no longer involved in Corrections. During the years before the Department was established, each institution stood alone, the Penitentiary in Santa Fe was the prized possession of that city that was offered either the University or the prison by the Territorial Legislature in 1885. Santa Fe, known as the "City Different," chose the Penitentiary reasoning that "higher education would not be as viable in the future as the prison."

I'm sure Albuquerque, receiving the second choice has reaped a much better reward from that decision.

Juvenile facilities were placed under the Corrections Department located in Springer and Albuquerque. The Boys School at Springer was often used by parents and others to get wayward youth headed in the right direction. *"If you don't straighten out, you're going to find yourself in Springer,"* the admonition went. Stories of being beaten with links of garden hose and sprayed with fire hoses went along with the threat. As a teen, I had taken that threat seriously and didn't even come close to finding myself in that position.

The Girl's School in Albuquerque had become also the Youth Diagnostic and Development Center, housing both girls and boys in separate facilities. The Superintendent, Eloy Mondragón, became an acquaintance early in my employment. At Springer, Bob Marrs supervised the facility and I would get to know them both better as time went on.

I settled into my position and worked hard to prove myself. Seldom did I get home before 6:30 or 7:00 in the evening even though the work day ended at 4:30. Being a caseworker was not an hourly job, it was a "position" and an important one for the criminal justice system of New Mexico. It took dedication and an ability to make judgement calls on individuals who had not done well in society. I interacted with the Parole Board, making recommendations as to whether the person should be paroled or not. Each inmate had, at that time, an "indeterminate" sentence which was stated in terms like 1 to 5 years, 2 to 10 years, 10 to 50 years and so on. Sometimes they had a combination of terms. A parole hearing would be scheduled in a fraction of the minimum time. The Board could give a response to an inmate of "Parole Pending Parole Plan," "Review in ___ months" or, "Parole Denied," in which case the board would review the person in a year. During my first few appearances with inmates the Parole Board gave the decision to the inmate after the hearing, but because they might be subjected to harsh words, it became the duty of the caseworker to relay the decision a little later.

One inmate with the last name of Chapell, had mental health issues and I was his caseworker. After his hearing, I got the Parole Board's response to give to him. He was in Cell Block 3, segregation, since his behavior couldn't be predicted. During the hearing, he had to be restrained from coming at the Board from his seat behind a table, as they were questioning him. I was not looking forward to giving him the bad news. He didn't like bad news.

He had other quirks I had learned to deal with. One was that he didn't like being called by his real name. He wanted to be called "Sarge," or "Snow," or anything but Chapell—That was the name of his horse! As I walked up to his cell door, I prayed, "God, give me wisdom and strength." I was apprehensive and when I saw him, he was shaving his black skin with a single razor blade, mercurochrome had been wiped on his face. He looked gruesome.

"Sarge," I said quietly. "I'm sorry I have some bad news for you."

He looked at me, and asked what it was. "The Board didn't parole you," I said with as much sadness as I could muster.

"Why?" he shot back. Looking somewhat crazed with the razor blade in his hand and his face covered in mercurochrome.

I don't know what possessed me, but I calmly answered, "Maybe we have grown to like you."

"Aww, Mr. Thomas," he said. "I really 'preciate dat, but I do wants to go home."

I assured him that I realized that, and told him when his next review would be: In a year. He looked dejected and took the slip of paper from my hand and thanked me. *Whew!* I managed to get through that one unscathed. I got along with "Sarge" while I was his caseworker and I suspect it was because I had at least tried to sympathize with him and his plight.

Another inmate, "Barry," had been unable to stay in population and out of segregation for any length of time. His mother called me and asked why he was in Cell Block 3—again. I told her that when he was allowed in population he had a bad attitude toward both staff and inmates and needed to be there for his protection and others. He had serious mental issues that the psychologists were trying to work with, but they were not successful.

On my next trip to Segregation I walked down the tier talking to those on my caseload. When I got to Barry's cell, I looked at him semi awake on his bunk. "How's it going, Barry?" I asked. He looked up and saw me through the grille and sat up on the edge of his bed. After shuffling through some of the papers on his floor, he found one, picked it up and stood, saying angrily, "What do you mean telling my mother I have a bad attitude?"

"You don't think you have a bad attitude?" I asked him.

"HELL NO, I DON'T HAVE A BAD ATTITUDE!" he shouted while standing on the grill door. I stood back and said quietly, "I wish I had a camera right now." That set him off and he began cussing me and the others in the cell block took up the hurling of insults my way. "I'll see you later," I said as I walked down the tier to visit with the last inmate on my list.

As I finished and headed back toward the exit, I had to pass by Barry's cell again and he reached through the bars at me. It crossed my mind to break his arm by bending it against the iron bars he was holding it through, but the Holy Spirit of God restrained me. That's the only explanation I have for not doing what my mind was thinking. The only repercussions I would have had would be to write the incident up and notify medical, maybe not in that order. But as I later reflected, I would have gained an enemy for life. The following week I saw Barry again and it was as if the incident had never happened. Thankfully, I never had another call from his mother.

The inmates had an in-house "newspaper" that was printed for all inmates and staff. One of the inmate "reporters" for the newspaper wrote to Governor Bruce King and asked for an interview with him to put in the paper. Governor King graciously granted the interview and I was asked to escort him to the "Roundhouse" which is the nickname for the capital building in Santa Fe, where we were greeted by the governor as if we were from Associated Press or Reuters. We were ushered into the governor's conference room and sat at the very large round marble table in that room. Governor King leaned back and let the inmate ask any questions he wanted to, responding to him forthrightly. On the way back the inmate reporter commented on the interview. The governor would have had another voter, had he been able to vote.

Bruce King was an extraordinary individual who had a wonderful memory that served him well as a politician. He had served in the state legislature for many years and, as a rancher and cattleman, had an easy way about him; country, but definitely not a bumpkin. He talked with a country twang and wasn't beyond slapping someone on the back. A Christian, he was open about his faith and his wife, Alice, was an asset. He served three terms in office. I had a chance to experience his ability to remember. I attended a function at which he was present and seeing me he walked across the room, grabbed my hand and said, "Hello, Mr. Thomas. How are things at the prison?" I had only met him during the interview, but he knew me long after I had been in the conference room.

Years later, I was in a Santa Fe Restaurant when he walked in and meandered to every table introducing himself. When he saw me he said, "Well, Mr. Thomas, it's been a long time since we saw each other," as he grabbed my hand and pumped it. Fern was floored that her husband was remembered by the governor. Years later we saw him again at the retirement dinner of a friend I worked with who became the Superintendent of the Youth Diagnostic and Development Center. He gave me a copy of a book he wrote called, *Cowboy in the Roundhouse*, talking about his memories. He wrote in it, *"To our wonderful friends -- Jan and Fern. Thanks for all you do for the young people of NM. God bless you and your work."* And then he added, *"Enjoy the book."* I had told him of our work in the prisons with Crossings and Alice had championed better conditions for incarcerated youth. I guess he thought it was youth we were working with, but at that time he was in his 80's. He died in 2004 at the age of 84

Captain Gene Morgan and I were assigned to travel to California in 1974 to pick up some inmates who had absconded from parole. We drove a state car first to Salinas, where we stayed with his brother and his wife. The next day we went to San Francisco and picked up one of the absconders from the Jail. I reflected on my time at the Seminary, just to the north across the Golden Gate Bridge as we drove through the city.

We crossed the Oakland Bay Bridge and received our other passenger from the Alameda County Jail at Santa Rita. That name continues to ring a bell when I think of the place I was born, but it was not in California. This guy, when we got him in our car stunk! He smelled like he hadn't had a bath in like—ever. Gene and I looked at each other and, since we had no choice, we put up with the odor until we arrived in Bakersfield. We lodged him in their local jail and asked that they aid us in our quest for deodorization. They complied and the next morning we picked him up in different clothing and the car smelled like—well, not quite roses, but a lot better. His traveling mate was also pleased.

Nearing the Arizona border near Kingman, he asked for a pencil. We looked at each other and decided that we were well protected by the iron screen that separated the front seats from the back. I handed him my ball point pen and he immediately pulled out the lining from the Bugler Tobacco can he made cigarettes from. One side was tinfoil, the other was paper he could write on.

I glanced back to see what he was writing only to discover it was symbols of quarter moons, animals and things I couldn't decipher. I became concerned that he might try to get a message to the Arizona Agriculture inspectors that he was being kidnapped or something else, but that didn't happen and we drove on toward New Mexico without incident. That was my first and only long-distance escort of inmates. I got to know Gene Morgan well during that trip and we had a great relationship until he retired.

For amusement, I love practical jokes. I played one on people who came into my office. I got a mailing envelope, wrote on it the words in red ink: RATTLESNAKE EGGS—DO NOT OPEN! With two paper clips I fashioned a device that with a rubber band I could wind up one of the clips and put it in the envelope. Now here's something you may or may not know. Rattlesnakes lay live babies, not eggs. I learned that in my childhood in Española. Most people don't know that. If the envelope was opened, it allowed the wound-up clip to vibrate on the paper. If left alone, it just sat there. People, including inmates, would come into my office and ask: "Are those REAL rattlesnake eggs?" I would nod. Then they would get inquisitive, "Can I see them?" I would say, "Well, okay, just be careful."

The person would open the envelope and the device would buzz and the individual, with a frightened look on his face would throw the envelope away from himself, either screaming or cussing. "I told you to be careful, didn't I?" It was good for a few laughs, but most people caught on and the game was over. You have to keep some humor in a place that can be less than jovial.

The prison population kept growing, especially after the state legislature toughened sanctions on drugs and drug dealing. Joe Gutierrez was made the Administrative Assistant to the Warden and Sam Esquibel became the CCO. Our caseloads got heavier and, with a change in administrations as Jerry Apodaca was elected in place of Bruce King, we had a shakeup in Corrections. Horacio Herrera was fired, Joe Gutierrez, was named acting warden as Felix Rodriguez was moved to Central Office. I was promoted to CCO when Sam decided to retire. Another employee was for a short time Deputy Warden and another group was recruited from outside the NM Corrections Department to run the Penitentiary. They had experience in the federal Bureau of Prisons and had retired from federal service. Ralph "Lee" Aaron became Warden, Clyde Malley, Deputy Warden. Lee Aaron had mainly been the Corrections Industries Director for the federal maximum-security prison in Marion, Ohio. He assumed the duties as warden for a short, interim time before he retired, but he was on the list they selected from. My suspicion was that they picked the first name on the list. Aaron fits.

My family had moved from the mobile home park to one of the staff houses at the prison. That came with the promotion to Chief Classification Officer. When Aaron and Malley came to the prison we decided to get to know them better and invited them for dinner. As soon as Aaron came into our home, he noticed that one of our wall clocks was not set to the correct time and remarked something to the effect that he didn't like people who couldn't keep up with their clocks. I swallowed my pride and said nothing. He was a humorless person and definitely not one who had a lot of love for his fellow man. Clyde Malley was more gregarious and not as critical. He did crack a racist joke during the meal. I hoped he could learn to work with those in New Mexico who were not of Anglo-Saxon derivation.

Late one afternoon I was in Aaron's office discussing classification matters when he got a phone call. His face lost color and he began to stammer, "Gggggeeeetttt SaannCCHEEZ," he shouted over and over, referring to the Chief of Security whose name was Ernie Sanchez. We had tried to help him learn to pronounce Hispanic names, but this one always came out as San-CHEZ, rather than SAN-chez. His face paled as he continued to stammer.

Finally, he composed himself a little and said, "Get San-CHEZ, get a gun, get San-CHEZ..." He finally spewed out that a CO had a knife pulled on him by an inmate who had commandeered the car on the way back from the detail assigned to the Governor's Mansion. The officer was calling from somewhere down the highway from the prison and had the other inmates who were on the detail.

We armed ourselves and headed toward Cerrillos, a small town south of the Penitentiary. After driving for five or six hours, actually winding up in Albuquerque, we decided it was useless and we returned to the prison without the escapee. He was caught a few days later and the vehicle was found on a side road in the mountains that we had not traveled.

By this time, I had resigned my position with the Ojo Caliente mission church and we joined St. John's United Methodist Church in Santa Fe. I was disgusted with the attitude of the Baptist association that had shunned us as a "not so Baptist" congregation that had been resurrected and was Christian. Lucille Bonner was our pianist, travelling from White Rock near Los Alamos with her husband, Austin, also Baptists. We served this mission for a couple of years, but the workload at the prison became more than I could do along with getting sermons ready every week and attending the meetings I was to attend. Lucille had remained in contact with us even to the present day, having had a ministry at the Penitentiary.

The pastor of one of the major Baptist churches in Santa Fe paid a call on me at the prison one day to let me know they were displeased with me joining the Methodists. I found the visit to be one more chip in the armor I had built up and settled in to worship with the group that accepted me as I was. The church was friendly, honored Christ, and we felt accepted. I even considered doing what was necessary to be a Methodist pastor, but there were some practices I wouldn't be able to wrap myself around, the main thing being the mode of baptism. I was convinced that immersion was practiced in the New Testament and that it symbolized the death, burial and resurrection of Christ that we entered into at the time of our conversion. That has never changed. This was my period of rebellion and my attempt to find authentic faith that was grounded in really helping people to find life in Christ. But I would have to go deeper myself and I was not willing to do so at that point. So I drifted along being somewhat like the church in Laodicea "neither hot nor cold." I was burned out, mainly because of my own reluctance to engage with the Holy Spirit on His terms. I wanted to do it "my way."

I attended more of the social functions of the prison staff and on one night one of the other caseworkers got really drunk and his wife was even more inebriated. The party was not far from where I lived and I invited them to my house for breakfast. His wife refused to come in and stood out in the street yelling and cussing him. I didn't want them driving until there was a little more sobriety. They managed to get home on their own, though without killing themselves or anyone else.

Warden Aaron took a disliking to me and I'm not sure of the reason. It may have been my propensity toward the necessity of having programming and volunteer services in prison, or it may have been my lack of correct time on my clocks at my home, but I began having more disagreements with him. I can't remember the specific act, but something told me I needed a change in scenery.

CHAPTER 11

ALBUQUERQUE AND LOS LUNAS

It was 1975, and the population continued to climb at the prison. We knew we were going to have to find additional space for inmates. Thankfully I was recruited, along with Joe Gutierrez, to help renovate a former Air Force radar site west of Albuquerque. There were houses there as well as barracks that had been used by the airmen before the facility had been closed. I immediately felt at home since this had been a neighboring Aircraft Control and Warning unit we worked with when I was a radar operator and stationed about 75 miles to the west. I moved my family there and supervised inmate work details from the Farm to do the work of rehabilitating the buildings. There was even a swimming pool and a bowling alley intact, just needing some attention.

As we worked on the project the local news began to report on what we were doing and a "nimby" group formed to oppose us. For the uninitiated, the term stands for "Not In My Back Yard." They didn't want a prison anywhere near the sprawling development of the city that was moving westward. We worked on it regardless of the noise that had been created, until the cacophony reached the chambers of the Legislature and we were ordered to cease and desist. I had the lonely detail of staying and keeping watch over the place until we figured out what to do. My only job was to listen for the telephone to ring, which it seldom did. Fern had gotten a job at the University of Albuquerque in the business office. We started going to Wesley United Methodist Church in Albuquerque with my mom and dad, since Dad had committed his life to Christ as well. Dad's demeanor with others of different races changed and he mellowed in his obstinacy and bull-headed opinions.

The church was small, very friendly and the pastor, Clarence Stanfield, had become a great friend to my folks. The only thing that detracted from my experience of worship was the fact that the lady playing the organ played it like a piano, not the instrument it was intended to be. It sounded terrible. Clarence asked me to preach for him a number of times and I enjoyed the experience.

A decision was made in Santa Fe that we would pursue enlarging the living quarters of the Los Lunas Correctional Center. We determined to live in Albuquerque rather than move to Los Lunas and purchased our first real home. The mobile home we lived in when we moved to Santa Fe had been sold on a real estate contract to a couple who moved it east of the Capital. They were to have kept insurance on it and when it burned we found out that the policy had lapsed. Thankfully the insurance company backdated a policy that covered it.

The house we bought was in the Northeast Heights of Albuquerque, a brand-new one, and we saw as it was being built every aspect of the construction. We were allowed to live in the house we had moved into at the radar site until our home on Guadalajara Avenue was finished. At no cost. The purchase price for our new residence was $32,900. A three-bedroom two bath home with both a living room and a den. By then the kids were old enough to be in both the mid-high and elementary schools close-by. A very happy time.

Driving to work was easy since we had a state car issued to us and Joe Gutierrez lived not too far from our home. I would usually drive and pick Joe up on the way to work. Almost immediately he was named Warden of the facility and I was somewhere between Chief Classification Officer and caseworker. Another person was Director of Programs and I worked with him until he was fired. As part of our responsibility we assumed direction of the newly-formed women's minimum-security facility located in a former staff residence on the YDDC grounds in Albuquerque. The Programs Director couldn't keep his hands off the young ladies who were incarcerated and lost his position as a result. I was promoted to Director of Programs at that point.

On Thursday evenings, after a full day of working at "The Farm," I went to the women's minimum-security unit in Albuquerque and handled the caseworker duties. This was something I didn't like doing since it was fraught with pitfalls and innuendos. One of the ladies suggested I put her in my "stable," a term used for prostitutes handled by a pimp. No thank you! Most of them were nicer, but this was a long evening for me. The night a man jumped the fence and stuck his hand in through the window was even longer. I tried to follow him, but he was a lot faster and was down the street before I could get a look at him. A higher fence was requested and put in place a few days later.

There was no way I was going to be put in temptation's path like my predecessor. The facility had an office for the caseworker to talk to inmates and I made sure the door was open when the women were there. I never bit on any of their suggestive comments. The assignment lasted a few months, perhaps a year, but that was too long. Most of them were in for drug-related charges, some for dealing, some for stealing to support their habit, but a few for more violent crimes, many of which were domestically related. A few boyfriends or husbands lost their lives to the "weaker" sex after being killed for having abused or threatened by them.

Joe and I along with another staff member who was the business manager continued to carpool. One night, after I had let the business manager out at his house, Joe asked me to drive to another apartment building. He was now divorced from his wife and had a new love interest. He asked me not to say anything and I didn't. It was none of my business. Joe often brought up issues he had with his wife. She seemed nice enough when you talked to her, but according to Joe she was pretty good at nagging. She would complain about how he folded the toilet paper on a shelf by the toilet ready to be used, this was one of many problems he talked about. I have no idea what else went on, but Joe was not a happy husband and she was not a happy wife. Joe is no longer with us having died a few years ago.

The number of inmates grew to about 200 in a few months. We had converted an old cannery building into a dormitory. The cannery was no longer used to can vegetables grown on the farm as in the past. The old cannery had gone into disrepair and all of the equipment was removed. I was assigned to go with a Penitentiary captain, Gene Long, to gather mattresses, beds and other equipment to expand beds in newly created minimum-security facilities. Gene and I drove 1-ton trucks to military supply units at Ft. Bliss, Texas in El Paso, Holloman Air Force Base, near Alamogordo, and other places where these supplies could be located. At one point, we had to stop for the night in Alamogordo and Gene walked into the motel office asking, "Do you have trucker's rates?" They answered in the affirmative and he told them we "were truckers." Not exactly the truth, but we *were* driving trucks. One of the items we had loaded onto a truck was a commercial kitchen range that was extremely heavy. We were concerned about getting it off the truck, but with the assistance of some of the inmates at the Roswell Correctional Center we did it without dropping it or killing anyone.

Classification to minimum-security was less than scientific. It wound up being a discussion about "if the person escaped, would he hurt anyone." That's not very satisfying when you are trying to run an institution without public scorn. When an escape was reported, the television stations and newspapers made it top billing and it wasn't long before the citizens of New Mexico began to complain. I had been promoted to Deputy Warden of the facility and often I had to be the spokesman for the institution. I was placed in front of the cameras or questioned by reporters and asked to account for the problems.

Now, you must understand that at that time there were no fences around the minimum-security facilities to keep inmates in. A barbwire fence marked the boundaries, but these fences were easily scaled and in many places, there were gates or roads that weren't blocked. Some of the administration in Santa Fe, who were getting the political fallout, began to complain that we weren't doing our jobs. At one point, Capt. Gilbert Castillo, the Chief of Security, and I were ordered to work the swing shift—in addition to our regular duties, by Central Office. I would go to the facility at about 7:30 each morning and work one full week, Monday through Friday getting off at 11:30 p.m. On Saturday and Sunday, I would go to work from 3:30 until 11:30, coming back the next Monday to work from 7:30 a.m. until 5:00 p.m. through Friday. I got the next weekend off. As an administrator, I got no overtime pay or compensatory time. I "donated" this extra time to the State. Gilbert and I, while not liking the assignment did it. I chafed inside because during this time a Correctional Officer level 1, with some overtime, would take home a paycheck much larger than mine. I tried not to let it hurt my ability to do my job or to get along with my coworkers.

Finally, I was able to talk those in authority into letting myself and Bob Marrs, the former Superintendent of the Boy's School in Springer who had been transferred to the Farm, make the selections of inmates to come to minimum-security. We reasoned that if we were to be "responsible" for keeping them "down on the farm," we should have some say in who came. I had studied the records of those who escaped and discovered that most of them had behaviors that indicated the possibility of escape. These factors included: failure to appear in court; AWOL in the military, absconding from probation and parole authorities, crimes involving outward violence, and having to be separated from other inmates because of threats. These, in my mind were men who did not realistically face their problems, their situations, or take responsibility for consequences. They would act impulsively when conditions didn't meet their idea of reality and to escape became the means to avoid what they didn't like.

Bob and I would review files, "jackets," they were called, of inmates who had been referred to minimum-security. We didn't interview the person, because most of them could talk a good talk. We wanted to see the results of their "walk." For the most part, it worked. We were able to substantially reduce the number of those who escaped.

The state approved the construction of an administration building and, to accommodate the offices that had been housed in the caseworker's home, the superintendent's home was now used for this purpose. It was across a roadway from where the old building was being torn down and reconstructed. My office was in one of the bedrooms and inmates would come to me for various requests. One day I decided to have a little fun, again the practical joker in me came out. I found an advertisement that on one side, looked like a hundred-dollar bill. On the other side it had a comment, to the effect that if it had been a hundred dollar bill the recipient would have been happy, but would be happier with the product or service advertised. I rolled the advertisement up in a roll that showed the money side and laid it on the floor just inside my office.

Two inmates came in to ask me something and one of them spotted the fake money. One guy came up to my desk and began talking to me, the other leaned on the wall by the door, stooped down and scooped the object up and slid it in his pocked. I acted as if I hadn't seen the activity through the corner of my eye and had no idea what he was doing. They both left and I said nothing until a couple of days later when I asked, "Did you have fun spending that hundred-dollar bill." Looking embarrassed, the inmate tried to shake it off. I added, "Sometimes what you think you see, is not what you get." He broke out in a nervous smile. It is a major offense for inmates to have possession of money. Since it wasn't real money, he wasn't in trouble. Another practical joke gone right.

In February 1980 I was in the Penitentiary scanning files. I had occasion to walk through the Control Center and notice changes had been made in some of the security features. The window that looked out into the main corridor had been changed from small, thick, 8-inch glass that had a checkered steel framework preventing anyone from breaking into the sensitive area to a large, protruding sheet of Lexan® that was touted to be "bullet proof." As I walked along the corridor I began to feel tension and it felt like the hair on the back of my neck was standing up. I couldn't put my finger on my uneasiness, but I knew that the population at the prison was many more than it was designed to hold. I had never felt this sensation previously although I had walked this corridor for more than seven years. The date was Friday, February 1, 1980. I mentioned to some of those I talked to about the tension I felt. They told me it was the overcrowding that I was helping to alleviate by sending more of these men to minimum-security. I drove back to Albuquerque and tried to shake off the experience.

The next morning was Saturday and all three of the kids were on a field trip to Bosque del Apache National Wildlife Refuge, a wonderful place to watch sandhill cranes as they migrate from northern states and Canada to winter in the more moderate climate New Mexico affords. Fern and I decided we would have a quiet Saturday to ourselves with no television or other distractions. We had just finished a leisurely breakfast when I got a call from the probation-parole officer, Ralph Castner, who was assigned to the Farm to put together parole plans for the inmates who would be reviewed by the Parole Board. He asked a simple question, "Do you think the Farm is okay?" I was puzzled by the question and said, "Yes, why?"

"You haven't seen what's happening at the Pen," he asked.

"No, what's going on," I replied.

"Turn on your TV. The Pen is burning."

I turned it on and the first picture I saw was a view of the Penitentiary from a helicopter with smoke pouring up from the gymnasium and another two wings of the prison. I remembered my feelings from the previous day and it all came together. It was a major riot.

I thanked him for the call and immediately called the Farm to find out what the status of the inmates there was. I was told they were concerned, but they were not acting out or showing any kind of affinity for the actions of those in Santa Fe.

I tried calling Joe Gutierrez, but he wasn't answering his phone and I reasoned that he had probably gone to the Penitentiary. As I watched, I wondered if I should be there as well, but I saw on the TV many of the staff, State Police, National Guard, and politicians standing around with their arms crossed just watching as negotiations were going on. I decided they didn't need another person in the audience. My eyes were glued to the events as they were being reported live and I wanted to be available in case there were problems at the Farm.

This has been termed one of the most violent riots in American prison history. The cause of the riot, besides the obvious overcrowding of 1,136 inmates in a facility designed for 900, was the decision to terminate all volunteer, education, and rehabilitation programming. Prior to 1975 the facility was relatively calm. I like to compare what happened to any space in which some substance has been continually compacted with no outlet. An explosion occurs sooner or later.

Inmates in dormitory E-2 had made "hooch," an alcoholic concoction fashioned from bread or yeast, fruit, and whatever else they could get. Having found this before during shakedowns, I had been repelled by the smell. How they could drink it was beyond me.

They were drunk and had been looking for a weakness to take over the prison.

In the early morning of Saturday, February 2, 1980, two inmates in the dormitory overpowered a Corrections officer. They soon overpowered four more officers and used keys taken from one of them to unlock the grill between the north and south wings of the prison. A fire extinguisher was used to batter the newly constructed "bullet proof" glass window of the Control Center and when the officers there fled, they had control of the prison with keys, weapons and access to all parts of the institution.

The inmates involved had been housed in a more secure Cell Block 5, but when the construction ordered by Governor Bruce King began, the inmates were moved to the dormitory. Dormitories are designed for those whose behavior is not violent or disruptive. They were triple bunked, and some were sleeping on the floor. What has been termed "new breed" of inmates were in the mix. This group of inmates had little regard for human life and violence had become their mode of behavior.

Those interested in the gory details can find a plethora of books, papers and articles on the subject. In summary, in the words of one of the chroniclers, Mark Colvin, the New Mexico prison riot of 1980, "is without parallel in the penal history of the United States for its brutality, destruction, and disorganization among the rioters. In the 36 hours before order was forcefully restored by the New Mexico State Police and National Guard, 33 inmates were killed by other inmates; 12 were first tortured and mutilated. The exact number of inmates injured during the riot is not known." In another report, "…As many as 200 inmates were beaten and raped; the New Mexico attorney general reports that at least 90 inmates were treated at local hospitals for overdoses of prison pharmacy drugs and for injuries sustained in fighting among inmates. Seven of the 12 correctional officers who were taken hostage were beaten, stabbed, or sodomized, though none were killed. No inmates or hostages were killed or injured during the retaking of the institution by authorities."[1]

Most of the reporting mentions that prior to 1975, the Penitentiary was fairly well run, some stronger inmates kept the peace, there was illegal drug trafficking, some of it brought in by staff, although it was well known that if anyone was involved they would be prosecuted to the full extent of the law. The inmates keeping the peace used this as an incentive. When changes began to occur in 1975 and programming was shut down, the inmates who were holding things together found themselves in segregation and the "new breed" began to emerge. By this time Lee Aaron had been removed and Clyde Malley became warden. On December 9, 1979, there was a mass escape of 11 inmates who got out under Tower 1. This was the precipitation of the construction that moved the inmates from Cell Block 5 to Dorm E-2.

I was inwardly breathing a prayer of relief that I had been transferred from the Penitentiary before things fell apart. Construction had already begun on another medium-security prison on the grounds of the massive farm in Los Lunas. Santos Quintana, previously the Director of Probation and Parole was transferred to Los Lunas and no decision had been made as to who would be the warden. Some tension between Santos and Joe Gutierrez could be felt as both had eyes on the position. Since I wasn't in the running, I quietly hoped Joe would get it since he had much more experience in prison than Santos and was presently the Warden of the Los Lunas Correctional Center.

Efforts were made to get the new institution at Los Lunas on line as soon as possible because of the issues that remained after the riot. Inmates had been shipped all over the country to other states and federal prisons. The Farm took some of them that could be classified as minimum. At night, some of them who had been traumatized during the riot would scream out. We heard stories of the ones who wanted no part of what had happened. One man related that he and other inmates were in a dormitory above the security and psychological offices that had been set on fire, the same area that Secretary Howard Leach and I had been in that evening we were with the Alcoholics Anonymous group. The floor heated up and they were in an oven. The windows were steel frames and there was nothing to cut them with. They tried battering the wall, but the concrete fortifications were impenetrable. Finally, someone found a key that opened the padlocked chain on the door to the upstairs unit and they were able to escape the conflagration. None of them died or were seriously injured.

As the new prison began to take shape, we often drove over the back roads through the farm to see the progress. It would be named Central New Mexico Correctional Facility, the first to be built outside Santa Fe, other than the Honor Farm which at that time was officially Los Lunas Correctional Center. The farm had existed as a prison facility since 1939, the oldest existing prison in the state. The Farm and I share the same birth year.

Joe Gutierrez became the Warden of Central New Mexico Correctional Facility, and Santos his deputy warden. While Santos was not extremely pleased about this, he settled in and found out that Joe's experience in Santa Fe at the Penitentiary was useful in getting the prison off and running. I elected to stay where I was. I was content to be who I was and where I was at that time. Bob Marrs was selected as the warden at the farm, having had experience running the New Mexico Boy's School in Springer for several years. I was content with that and Bob and I got along well together. He was from West Texas, Andrews, and had married a Hispanic woman, Inez. His nickname for her was "Big I" and that referenced the newest interstate exchange in Albuquerque merging I-40 with I-25, which had been dubbed with that moniker. They soon moved to Belen, a short distance from Los Lunas. Bob had a way with words in a West Texas accent that added humor to our day's work.

Bob fancied himself as a cattleman and he would have loved to have been a rancher. It had become his job to buy cattle at the local cattle auction, have them transported to the farm to be fed out and slaughtered. I would accompany him sometimes and marvel at the ritualistic proceedings of the auctioneer, his assistant and the various means by which the cattle buyers would up the bid. Sometimes by a nod, sometimes by a flick of the thumb, sometimes just a look. The assistant knew the cattle buyers and what the motions they made meant. I was generally clueless, but it was an interesting experience.

New Mexico State University had an experimental farm carved from some of the land at the Correctional Center. Bob engineered an agreement with them to do an AI course for the inmates. AI, in aggie language is "artificial insemination." The instructor and any learning student put on a long latex glove that reached up to the shoulder. Taking a vial of bull semen, the objective was to place your hand and arm as far as it would go up the cow's vaginal tract and dispense the semen. It was quicker and more reliable than having the bull do the work. I didn't relish the hands-on experience, so I declined to participate in the actual act. That's probably a good thing for the cow. My arms are short…

Most Tuesdays were slaughtering days and a state meat inspector came to the slaughterhouse on the grounds of the farm and passed on the meat that was to be fed to inmates at the Penitentiary and the farm. Any cow that was diseased was immediately discarded and not used for food. The Penitentiary often complained that we kept the better beef for ourselves and shipped the tough meat to them. We discovered that instead of hanging the meat a couple of weeks to cure in their refrigeration unit, they served it almost immediately. It had no time to let the enzymes work and become more tender. They didn't realize that was how meat was processed.

Our farm manager, Bob Tagami, the son of a local Japanese farmer, was as good a farmer as his dad who owned a local farm and was well known for his produce. We continued to grow chile, and one year we had *ristras* hung all over the facility waiting to be used in our kitchen. We grew corn and milo for silage to feed the cattle. Silage allows the corn and grain to ferment and produces a better feed for the cows to eat and get fat on. Alfalfa fields for hay were producing well and we had inmates bucking hay after it was bailed.

One inmate, a big African-American man in his 40's put everyone else to shame as he threw bail after bail onto the trailer pulled by a tractor. He was affable and nearing parole. He expressed one day his anxiety about leaving the farm. I listened to him and really didn't understand why someone would not want to get out of prison and live whatever a normal life for him would be. He paroled but was back quickly. The police reported that he broke into a jewelry store window, smashing it and grabbing as much of the pretty stuff as his hands could hold. The alarm went off and they found him hiding behind a dumpster in back of the store, a trail of jewelry dropped along the way to mark his "escape." He had committed the crime so he could go back to the life he missed—prison. This is what happens when a person spends too many years in custody. It always amazed me that the objective of corrections is to take someone who has acted irresponsibly, put them in a place where they have no real responsibility to speak of, do nothing to help them understand what a responsible life is, and after months or years, let them out of prison, expecting them to be responsible citizens. I had begun to think that there must be a better way. But what was it?

For a number of years we had no medical personnel assigned to our facility. A staff member, in most cases myself, decided as to whether or not the inmate would be taken to a physician in the community. That duty fell to me since I had at least had Air Force First Aid training. That was my qualification for being "chief medical officer." If an inmate complained of a stuffy nose and congestion he got over the counter medication for the complaint. If there was a stomach issue and he was just throwing up, Kaopectate. If it couldn't be determined, we had a contract with a local doctor who would make the diagnosis. My position was more as a parent than anything else. We never had anyone die, so I guess it worked.

Food was good in those days. Inmates had steak, great hamburger, and from the pig farm we were able to provide pork. Bob went to Guymon, Oklahoma and purchased a boar used in breeding hogs. From this boar we grew the number of hogs from roughly 10 to about 700. Inmates worked with the sows that were giving birth to piglets in the farrowing rooms and often helped when the birthing became difficult. The ears of the piglets were notched to provide identity and to keep track of the individual pig. This job was one of the most sought out positions on the farm. The inmate often had to sleep in with the pigs and be there when needed. It gave them time away from the more confined parts of the farm and helped them to feel like human beings. Correctional staff drove out to check on inmates who had night duties. Once in a while someone would be missing. Sometimes it would be an inmate assigned to irrigation. Irrigation water was dispensed at various schedules to farmers along the Rio Grande and when you got it, you used it, regardless of the time of day. Bob remained at the farm until the Warden at Camp Sierra Blanca retired. He jumped at the chance to get farther away from the "politics" of Corrections and the mountains near Capitan gave him opportunity to do so.

I was named acting warden. It was again during a time of administrative change. Toney Anaya had become governor and named Michael Francke, a District Judge from Santa Fe, as his Secretary of Corrections. Francke brought in a former Corrections director from California, Ray Procunier as his deputy. The farm was in a financial deficit, not because of mismanagement, but because we had a lot of unfunded mandates

Michael Francke

to implement. Secretary Francke called a Departmental budget hearing in Santa Fe at the Roundhouse. The morning I was to be there to defend my budget, I woke up with a burning, painful urinary tract infection. I knew what I had since I had previously experienced the awful debilitation, but I had no choice other than to show up, calling in sick was not an option.

During the meeting I excused myself to go to the restroom frequently and by that time I was passing blood. Finally, the meeting was over and I drove back to Albuquerque and directly to the office of my family doctor. He was not in, so I called him and he told me to meet him at one of the hospitals not far away. I was able to get medication and begin to have the pain relieved. I have termed this the worst day of my life, bar none. Not even having loved ones die even came close.

Michael Francke worked hard at getting the Department out of a financial hole. At one point he ordered all of the facilities to document in detail the budgets we submitted. The first budget we sent to Santa Fe met with his disdain. We were ordered to put meat in the budget -- meaning to write absolutes as to what would happen if we did not receive the requested funds. We received the order on Friday afternoon. So, we took Saturday off, worked all day Sunday, all night Sunday night and had a state police escort take the document to Santa Fe so that it would be on his desk by eight on Monday morning as he had ordered. The legislature took one look at it, remarked that it was too much to read, and gave us what our budget was the year before.

Michael was somewhat known as a womanizer. He always had a new lady hanging around him. We have surmised that that may have been a reason for a later development, but probably not. He became the Corrections director in Oregon in May 1987 where he was murdered on the grounds of the Oregon Department of Corrections.

A person was convicted of the crime and there is much controversy that the person in prison for life without parole did not commit the crime. Some have speculated that he was killed because he was exposing corruption in the Department of Corrections and two officials have been cited as possibilities. Regardless, the convicted man stands convicted today and Michael Francke is no longer with us.

Ray Procunier paid us a visit at the farm one day and I was prepared for him. He was late, very late, and I made a comment to the effect that I thought he had forgotten us. He quickly let me know that was not something he wanted to hear. He was rude, making comments about how poorly the facility was run, what an abysmal state New Mexico was and a number of other unsavory remarks. I asked him about a memo I had sent him asking for help in a matter and he gave me a blank stare. "I didn't get a memo from you," he said gruffly. I had a log of the memos I had sent and referred to that. He told me, "Well, I get a lot of stuff on my desk. Most of it I just rake off into the trash can. If It's really important, I'll get another memo." He had been in California as director of Corrections, also Virginia, Utah and finally, Texas. After 11 months in Texas he called it quits remarking that it was a tougher job than he had thought it would be. He only lasted a few months in New Mexico before going to Texas. I was delighted when Dan Moriarty was appointed Warden of the farm.

The caseworker, Buddy Ramirez, who had been with the Department for about 20 years at that point and had not been promoted, mainly because he was unable to plan or execute new or different ways to do things and was not willing to work more than the minimum hours necessary. He went through Procunier to get a promotion that had been offered to me. I had elected not to take the additional pay in deference to the status of the budget. I had held off until we could get a little healthier, a move that was probably noble, but stupid on my part. His end run not only shocked me, but I found myself supervising someone who was paid at a higher classification than I was. It didn't sit well, although I continued to be civil toward him. He retired and was replaced by a person from Central Office who was brought into the position vacated by Buddy. They wanted to keep him in the Department and this was the only position available—the one I had been promised. A former FBI agent, Ken Rommel, got that position as his former post as investigator was eliminated, and I, technically, was his supervisor. He was moved from being an investigator for the Department to… Well, we weren't sure what he was to do.

Ken was over six feet tall and had chiseled facial features. He spoke with an eastern accent, I think he was raised around Boston. He was a second-cousin of the famed "Desert Fox," Erwin Rommel, who served as field marshal in the Wehrmacht of Nazi Germany during World War II. Ken's father and Erwin's father were first cousins. He had fascinating FBI stories to tell, which he did. I liked him, and he became an asset to those of us at the farm because he had the ability to think outside the box. I guess we could have given him the title: "Outside the Box Thinker."

As a minimum-security facility we had inmates going on work release, school release and furloughs to their homes. Most of the time they came back without incident, sometimes not. When they didn't we began looking for them if we had an idea where they might be. Now, picture this: I would go alone most of the time, sometimes with one other person, and knock on doors of people living in areas that were mostly high crime and vice. Unarmed. When the door was answered, I would ask: "Is Johnny here?" I would usually get a "no." "If he comes here, tell him he needs to call or get back to the Farm as soon as he can, or we will have to put him out on escape status." That was about as gutsy as I wanted to get. I sometimes got the "willies" thinking about what could happen, but nothing ever did.

One day one of the inmates who had been assigned to the dairy was missing. We searched all the places on the farm we could, and Captain Gilbert Castillo and I set out in one of the vehicles to look for him. We drove into town, then turned west on the main street leading up to I-25. Crossing an irrigation ditch that went under the roadway we decided on a hunch to drive the dirt trail along the ditch and about a quarter mile down the pathway we saw a man in jogging gear running toward us. He was about the same height and appearance as our runaway and pulled down his sweatband over his eyes as he approached and saw who we were. He didn't resist and willingly stopped, let us cuff him and put him in the back seat of the car. It was only a short drive to the Valencia County Detention Center where we placed him in their custody. Dan Moriarty wrote commendation letters to the Secretary regarding our capture of this person.

The State Fair in Albuquerque contracted to have our inmates clean the grounds during the yearly events which included days of racing. We had staff supervision, but it wasn't easy to keep up with those we placed there. Most of the time Dan, myself and other administrative staff would go to the fair grounds and help. One night we had an inmate we couldn't find. We were looking for him, me on foot, Dan in one of the golf carts we were allowed to use. Dan saw our guy running for his life and was able to get him into the cart before the "carnys" caught him. Carnys are those who work the carnival and often have parties after hours. The inmate had peeped into the carny tent and was watching what he described as a "strip show." They saw him and, since he was an outsider, they decided to teach him some "manners."

The event turned into a carny brawl and the police intervened. Dan had driven between the carnys and the police and was able to get the inmate into his vehicle and to safety. As he was talking to the inmate a State Police vehicle pulled in behind him and over the loudspeaker he was told: "Get the hell out of the way." Dan was about to tell the cop who he was and what he was doing but seeing the melee in front of him and from all sides, chose to do as requested. Good move. There were several injured that night.

When the fair was not in session we had inmates assigned to clean out the stalls of the racehorses since the racetrack was used for racing at other times. One of the inmates assigned one day was a former UNM basketball star who had gotten sideways with the law. It was early afternoon when Dan and I got to the fairgrounds and the officer assigned to supervise said he couldn't find two of those who were working there. We looked in all of the obvious places and were about to go and report the escape when we saw the two of them walking toward us. As they neared, we asked where they had been. They said they were working. "Take everything out of your pockets," Dan told them. The basketball player placed a large bag of marijuana on the hood of the car. Busted! But not as bad as being placed on escape. I then gave him a pat down. It seemed to me that he was nine feet tall, or maybe even taller. As I scooped my hands over his massive arms and down his legs, I felt like a grasshopper, but an "in charge" grasshopper. I put the handcuffs on him and off we went, straight to the Valencia County Detention Center where we placed all the inmates who had become involved in misconduct. We had to go through the proper procedures to have him transferred back to Santa Fe.

Another time Dan Moriarty and I went to an apartment together. Dan had been a Las Cruces police officer during the time he was getting his degree from NMSU in criminal justice. He told me, "if I don't get back in 10 minutes, come and check on me or get the police down here." The time came and went. I went to the door and hearing calm talking, I knocked. The door was opened and Dan was sitting there talking to the guy's mother and having a great time.

Dan was great to work with. A tall man, he had very black eyebrows and a bald head. He became our "chile barometer" since the heat of the chile we ate in restaurants would cause beads of sweat to appear on his head. If it was "better" chile, his upper lip would perspire. Tears indicated perfection.

He had a good understanding of Corrections although he had never directed a prison before. His experience came from being a cop and a probation-parole officer and had managed the Albuquerque district. His instincts were good about inmates and he had a great sense of humor, often cracking jokes. A Roman Catholic, he went to church regularly. His language was a little on the foul side, but he was ethical and let the others know he wasn't into treating people unfairly or cheating on his wife. A nurse one day came onto him and he set her straight.

Dan and I carpooled in the same state vehicle. We were allowed to do so since we were technically on call all the time. It was good for the Thomas travel budget, actually for all of us. We discussed almost everything. His viewpoints were conservative as were mine, although at that time we were both registered as Democrats. I was feeling uneasy as a Democrat because some of the platforms of the Party were becoming harder for me to support. I stayed registered because New Mexico was primarily Democrat and I wanted a chance to select candidates in the primary. I voted for Carter and Clinton the first time because they were Southern Baptists, but I soon learned that one's profession of faith and what they did with it politically could be diametrically opposed. One of these presidents I questioned his faith. I won't say who.

A man running for Congress called one day and said he would like to tour the facility. We readily accommodated him and took him for lunch in our chow hall. We talked about a lot of things and he asked a lot of questions. He won his seat and remained in Washington for a number of years. He was Ambassador to the United Nations, Secretary of the Interior under Bill Clinton, held a number of other positions as well as becoming a negotiator with North Korea, and came back as Governor of New Mexico. He ran for President of the United States. His name? Bill Richardson. So, I can say I had lunch with Bill Richardson, after I had tossed off his brand of politics I didn't vote for him.

On one occasion we were scheduled for a meeting in Las Cruces. We were late, but Dan was driving and we managed to make the trip in about two and a half hours. It is normally a three-hour drive going a little more than the speed limit. Somehow, we were not stopped by anyone. We made the meeting pretty much on time.

Several new people came on board from other states when Central New Mexico Correctional Facility finally opened. Don Dorsey came as a Captain, Dareld Kerby as the Major and a few others. They were good additions and helped the Department to grow better in the way we operated. Dareld Kerby began his correctional career in Iowa and later went to Arkansas being recruited to help straighten out the mess the prisons had gotten into. He became the Deputy Warden at the Cummins Unit, best known as the prison subject in the movie, *Brubaker*. The prison was corrupt, brutal and inhumane. He went on to become Warden of Central NM Correctional Center and later Director of Adult Prisons. After a few bouts with alcohol and being arrested in El Paso for being drunk in a state car and soliciting prostitutes, he was fired and went to work for Truly Nolen Pest Control as a district manager. Basically, he was a knowledgeable person, good to work with, but had personal issues that destroyed his ability to work in the correctional field. Most, along with me, felt it a great loss. As I understand it the charges against him were dropped, but his corrections career was finished.

Dareld told me of his introduction to the Cummins Unit in Arkansas. They gave him a side arm, a shotgun and a "sap," as his tools. A sap is a device made from leather, rounded on one end with a handle. The rounded end had buckshot between the layers of leather and was used to beat inmates who were not cooperative. He recalled a time one of the prison officials "interviewed" an inmate in an office. The inmate was hit so many times that blood came from under the door. He was horrified and helped to bring the operations of the department into a more humane way of incarceration.

Don Dorsey, on the other hand also had a career that started in Nebraska where he was recruited to work along with Kerby in Arkansas. He was personable, intelligent and stubborn as a mule, but became one of my favorite people. He also had the ability to run prisons as warden and worked for private prisons after he retired from New Mexico as Director of Adult Prisons. We will mention these people later on.

I was elected President of the New Mexico Correctional Association. I think it may have been because nobody else really wanted the position, but maybe not. We had yearly conferences, some in Las Cruces, our favorite place, some in Albuquerque, and Ruidoso. NMCA was an affiliate of the American Correctional Association which was established in 1870 to help bring correctional practices into a more humane and treatment-oriented profession. They have established national standards by which corrections facilities and other entities should be run. Following the 1980 riot in Santa Fe, a federal court Consent Decree was placed on New Mexico prisons. In essence, the federal courts took over the general operations of the New Mexico Corrections Department and ordered the state to provide certain elements in its operation.

A whole host of attorneys and others, along with the Plaintiff, Dwight Duran, popped into administrative offices or institutions sometimes barking orders. Many of them were rude and obnoxious, belittling staff and intimidating whomever they chose. Those law firms and their minions reaped millions from their efforts into their own coffers. Yes, the Department was improved, but not to the extent that their bank accounts were augmented. Led by Vincent Nathan from Ohio, local attorneys such as Peter Cubra and Mark Donatelli, Raymond Towhig, and Ralph Knowles began changes in such things as establishing a Corrections Academy, a good move, medical services made some improvements and more programming was available, along with educational classes, both basic courses as well as university level classes. These had been lost during the "change years," when Governor Jerry Apodaca brought in the federal corrections guys that wanted to get rid of programming.

Most of us bought into the need for change, but not those who were trying to whip us into shape. We weren't very affected at the farm, but other institutions were. A new classification system was implemented which was a great improvement over what we had which was really nothing. Our way of helping was to be involved with the ACA and promote standards by which the institutions would be operated. I joined the organization in 1981.

I was able to get some of the inmates at the farm interested in taking local college classes at the Valencia campus of the University of New Mexico. One of these I attended along with the inmates, a course in solar adobe construction, taught by a man from India, Dr. Job Ebenezer. This man was brilliant and was married to a woman who was a practicing pediatric physician. I promptly dubbed them with the title of "para docs" having a pair of doctor's degrees between them. His was in mechanical engineering.

The course was interesting, but full of mathematical formulas and equations. I had never been good in math, mainly algebra, because I didn't understand its purpose, as I explained in my analysis of the trains crashing earlier. I appreciated this math and aced the course because I grasped the principles and reasoning behind them. We learned about how to build houses, using adobe mud bricks that would hold in the heat during the winter and be a cooling agent in summer, a boon to those who don't want to spend a lot of money on electricity or gas.

During the class I got to know Job pretty well and when we were allowed to have an educational director at the farm, we talked and he agreed to come on board. We had GED courses and, along with that he helped inmates learn to build tamped earth structures and put in the electrical, plumbing and other items needed to make a house. Fern and I had the Ebenezer's to our home for dinner and we went to their home as well. They were Christians, from Christian families in the Tamil area of India. We had theological discussions and agreed on most points. At the time they were attending a conservative Presbyterian church in Albuquerque. It was his passion to try to develop mechanisms that would help people in third world countries enable themselves to farm, pump community water into water supply tanks, and process items grown by them without using fossil fuel. He developed ways to do these things using bicycles which they could also ride when unhooked from the devices.

He was recruited by the Hunger Committee of one of the Lutheran denominations and left New Mexico. I miss knowing him and being able to learn more about him and his ministry. I'm sure his ideas are being incorporated somewhere and God is continuing to use him.

Most of the time social interaction at the farm was pleasant. We often went out to dinner together, mainly in the Los Lunas area. Several restaurants offered great Mexican food, one of them Teófilos, which was directly across the street from the Luna Mansion, an antebellum mansion constructed of adobe, the only one in existence in the United States. It too, was turned into a popular restaurant known for its great steaks, hot chili, and great deserts. There's a history to this building and the town.

In 1692 Domingo de Luna was granted land by the King of Spain in what would later become Los Lunas, New Mexico. A few years later, Don Pedro Otero arrived under similar circumstances. Over the years, the two families added to their fortunes through livestock and additional land acquisitions. Both families became extremely powerful and were involved in politics. The marriages of Solomon Luna to Adelaida Otero, and Manuel A. Otero to Eloisa Luna in the late 1800's united these two families into what became known as the Luna-Otero Dynasty. The Spanish term *Los Lunas* means the Lunas, or the Luna family. That's what the name of the city means. There are other towns in the area, Los Chavez for the Chavez family, Los Trujillos, and so on… Much like family names anywhere else.

The Acheson, Topeka and Santa Fe Railroad wanted to build a track through the Luna property in 1880, but the right-of-way went through the Luna hacienda. A new home was proposed for Antonio Jose Luna and his family who decided on a southern colonial style mansion. Most buildings were from adobe and that became the material from which the mansion was constructed as they wanted it to be. The house was finished in 1881, the same year Antonio Jose died.

Over the years the mansion changed hands several times before it was purchased and renovated as a fine dining establishment in the late 1970s. It was then it is said that the ghost of Josefita began to appear. Perhaps she didn't like the renovations or maybe she just wanted to stick around to make sure they were doing a good job on the repairs. Staff suggests that other spirits also roam this historic building. True or not, it has an enthusiastic following.

When we first began to discover Los Lunas it was a sleepy little village near the Rio Grande. Not much going on. Only two places were available to eat on our side of the river, one with walls painted "Peptobismol pink," and a smaller Mexican café. As Albuquerque grew, so did it. It now has the appearance of maybe… Albuquerque south? Everything from Applebees to Chile's and a huge Walmart distribution center—and a Walmart store—now bring life to Los Lunas. More than the prison can be cited for the growth of Los Lunas' present size, but we were definitely a part of the health of the community. So much for the "nimby's."

One night I got a call from Myrna Brown that my college friend Ron, from "Pipesville" had been taken to the hospital he had had a heart attack and was in a coma. The medical staff had declared him brain dead. I was devastated. Myrna related the event telling me that Ron had been out for a jog, which he always had done to keep healthy. Coming in the house as Myrna was studying he went into the bedroom and she began to hear gasping sounds. She saw him lying there and tried to turn him over for CPR. His body fell on top of her. She managed to call 911 and EMT's came in an ambulance and tried to resuscitate him. He had been without oxygen for about 18 minutes.

By now the Browns had left the Methodist Church and were members of Hoffmantown Baptist Church. It was now in the larger megachurch building. I prayed with Myrna and she prayed that if Ron could not come out of the coma healed, she wanted God to take him home to be with Him.

Church members came and sat with him while he was in the coma, many of them praying, some talking to him, but this went on day after day. I took my place in the prayer lineup, praying for healing for Ron until weeks later he woke up. It took a little while for him to recover from the effects of being in a coma, but Ron did and regained all of his faculties—and maybe some additional ones. Myrna went on to become a Ph.D. in forensic accounting and Ron taught at a local Christian college. Ron is from August to November older than I am and continues to learn Italian so he can teach in seminaries in Italy to help the budding Evangelical Churches in that country. These churches are making a difference in the religious life of the people since many of them became cynical regarding the Roman Catholic Church and the nation has thrown off its reliance of Catholicism as the "official church." Ron's desire is to help the emerging Evangelical church bring people to the Lord Jesus Christ.

The position of warden opened up at Roswell Correctional Center and I put in for it. I had acted as warden on many occasions and I believed I was ready to assume the responsibility. I was interviewed by the deputy secretary and the conversation went like this: "Now, when you are there, these are the issues you will find, and we would like for you to correct them." I felt pretty good about my chances, although I knew that the move would be a big jump for my family. Penny and Jim had graduated high school. Scott was about to finish, and things looked good.

During his senior year Scott met a young lady at a church function. We knew she came from a difficult background, but they dated, and she became pregnant. What should we do? Her mother was absent, she was living in a foster home and that situation was tenuous. We turned the garage into a bedroom and she moved in, with him. As soon as it was able to be arranged they were married and as soon as he graduated from Eldorado High School, he went into the Air Force to be able to get medical attention that otherwise would not be affordable. Lisa turned out to be less than helpful in the relationship and became demanding on our time and resources. During basic training at Lackland Air Force Base, we did all we could to keep her healthy and somewhat happy, but it was not easy. Andrew was born at Kirtland Air Force Base in Albuquerque in 1986, Scott wasn't able to be there for the event.

Scott was transferred to Lowery Air Force Base in Denver and we made a trip up there to show his new son to him and he was able to get some time off to be with us. We got an unexpected call from my mother at the base entrance building. My dad had died. How she was able to find us there at that time, I never was able to understand, but she did. Our visit was cut short to return to Albuquerque and to my dad's funeral. The memorial service was held at Wesley United Methodist Church and he was cremated. Dad had been in poor health for many years, suffering from emphysema. He was attached to an oxygen tank for at least fifteen years, sometimes thinking he wasn't getting enough oxygen, he would turn the amount he was supposed to have up and have problems with too much in his system. Hospital visits were necessary to get his blood gasses back on track and he would experience something like bugs and other creatures around him until he was returned to normal.

While on leave Scott and I took the ashes up to a spot on the Rio Grande south of Taos where he loved to go fishing and let the river water take them downstream as he had requested. Even now as I cross this river, wherever I stand in the state of New Mexico, I think of my dad since this is his burial place along the river, from north to south. I know God will give him a new body and resurrect whatever is needed from wherever it has gone. My dad knew Jesus the last twenty years or so of his life and for that I am blessed. I never really got to know him well this side of heaven, but I am looking forward to getting to know him as he is when I get there.

We found out that Scott was being assigned to Holloman Air Force Base near Alamogordo and we took Lisa down there to find an apartment to live in. We had to find one they could afford and most of the ones that were affordable she didn't like for one reason or another, and we spent a lot of time looking. Finally, I had to put my foot down and say to her that we knew she wasn't going to find the perfect place, but she would have to live somewhere and the last place we looked was it. She grumbled, but accepted it. She often had strange thinking that clouded her viewpoint. On the way down to Alamogordo, we passed a point near where the first atomic bomb had been tested. Jokingly, I said to her, pointing to a cloud, "And there is the remains of it..." She got really serious and said, "Really, that's pretty cool that it's still there." I quickly explained that my comment was only a joke, and she still didn't get it.

I didn't hear anything about the position I had put in for at Roswell. I still, to this day, have not heard anything official as to why I was not selected, but I did find out that the man who was the Superintendent of the Youth Diagnostic and Development Center in Albuquerque was moved there because he was not working out well where he was. Roswell was out of the political arena and they wanted him as far out of that as they could place him, which pretty much describes Roswell Correctional Center. The YDDC was, at that time, still under the New Mexico Corrections Department and the Children, Youth and Families Department had not yet been created.

In 1987 Fern was working for Armstrong Pest Control in Albuquerque. The company was owned and operated by Warren Armstrong, gregarious fellow who knew his business. The advertisement line on TV was, "Take an APC... Armstrong Pest Control, that is." Warren was always promoting his company and urging his workers to do better.

One of the other workers was Judy Jacobs, a girl I had gone to high school with who married a guy who, as a kid, lived next door to us in Hurley at the end of World War II. They were no longer married, and she never remarried. She and Fern became friends and at one point, Warren put a challenge to his office workers who sold contracts for pest control. Each contract sold by the office staff and remained in effect for six months warranted a slip of paper with the name of the person selling the contract to be placed in a large jar. At the end of the period a drawing would be held to draw the name of the employee who would win an expense-paid trip to Hawaii. Fern worked hard and was excited to be challenged to sell contracts. She was concerned though that she might not win, even though she had sold more contracts than anyone else in the office. The time came, and the name was drawn... and she won! We were treated to a trip Warren had gotten through a radio station for purchasing a lot of commercial time with them. He said he and Millie, his wife, had been to Hawaii so many times, it was time someone else got a chance to go.

The day came, and we flew to LAX from ABQ and from there to the islands. Landing on Maui, we remained on the aircraft while some of the passengers deplaned and then flew over Honolulu on our way to Kawai. Neither of us had traveled much on airplanes, I more than she, but not that much. We both were excited about this trip together. The trip had taken about 6 hours and the sight of flying over the Big Island of Hawaii, and then over Honolulu was breathtaking. We landed at the airport at Lihue and were met by the traditional leis around our necks and a taxi to our hotel which was on the beach. The hotel was beautiful and had a large swimming pool with a waterfall in the middle of it. We met a former player for the Cleveland Browns and his wife on the trip. Although I can't remember their names since I'm not a great football fan, they were both Christians and we enjoyed their company. We rented a car and drove all over the island; then flew to Honolulu and toured the USS Arizona Memorial at Pearl Harbor, reflecting on the tragic events that began our involvement in the Second World War with the oil slick still seeping to the surface from the sunk war vessel. As our bound duty we went into the water at Waikiki. Somewhere I have heard it is illegal not to do so. After spending the afternoon at the largest city in Hawaii, we returned to Kauai, which was slower paced and better suited our time away from home.

A helicopter flight over the island took us up and over the "Grand Canyon of the Pacific," which covers much of the western half of the island. While it is much smaller than the one in Arizona, it was a huge rush to fly up and over Waimea Canyon having it spread out below us in all of its colors. One difference between Hawaii and Arizona's canyons—Hawaii has waterfalls in theirs. We also saw the inside of dormant volcanoes, the Na Pali Coast with its crags and cliffs draped in lush greenery. I wanted to stay, but economics being the rule, we had to return back to the Land of Enchantment because that's where our life was rooted.

We nearly missed our flight from LAX to ABQ because we arrived in the middle of the night and nothing was moving from terminal to terminal. We had to run to the next gate at a different terminal and barely got our seats before the doors closed.

CHAPTER 11

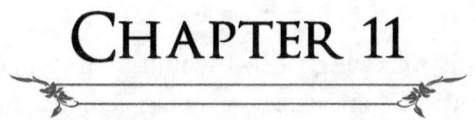

ROSWELL CORRECTIONAL CENTER

It would have been nice had someone talked to me about not getting the warden's job at Roswell, but they didn't, and I accepted the absence of news graciously, still thankful for my position in Los Lunas and the great folks I worked with there. A year or so passed. Another administration was put in place, and one Friday afternoon about three I got a call from the Administrative Assistant in Central Office.

"The Secretary of Corrections would like to talk to you on Sunday morning about going to Roswell as the Warden there. Can you be in his office at ten thirty?" he asked. I blinked a couple of times and said I would be there, knowing I would miss church, an event I have rarely missed since my faith in Jesus Christ began in 1961. The new secretary, Lane McCotter, was a Mormon and I wondered why he wasn't in church, but I didn't ask him. He had a background in the US Army and had been the Warden at the United States Disciplinary Barracks on the adjacent Fort Leavenworth Army base in Ft Leavenworth, Kansas, not far from the United States Prison. The USDB is the sole maximum-security penal facility for the entire United States Military.

Secretary McCotter was in conference with someone when I arrived. I sat down and waited and at about eleven o'clock he walked into the waiting room and saw me. "I'll be right with you," he said and finished the conversation with the other person. As I went into his office after he summoned me, we sat down, and he got right to the subject. The man who had been sent to Roswell when I thought I was going to be selected was not doing a good job and was being replaced. In state government, as in most government positions, it is almost impossible to fire somebody without gross negligence. Evidently whatever he had done or not done didn't rise to that level, so they were moving him again. We talked about my experience and he seemed satisfied. "I'll let you know next week," he said. I hadn't even applied for the position this time, but here I was being interviewed.

I told him the following week I would be in Omaha at a Deputy Warden's Association conference, so he agreed that he would let me know the week after I got back. As a member of the Deputy Warden's Association, we met in various places and exchanged ideas and had more training on what our positions required. It was a good way to get to know people from around the country and find out what the issues were that each of us faced. At least it got me out of New Mexico for a little bit. I had been to El Reno, Oklahoma and Cañon City, Colorado on other conferences.

I returned to New Mexico and was expecting a call from Central Office, but the week flew by and by Friday morning I had heard nothing. At about three-thirty in the afternoon I again got a call from the Administrative Assistant who told me I would report to Roswell and be ready for work at eight o'clock on Monday morning. I had Saturday and Sunday morning to prepare. Driving to Roswell on Sunday afternoon, I got a motel room for the night, and presented myself at the correctional center at the specified time. Secretary McCotter was already there and had been meeting with the person I was to replace, who was looking a bit frazzled at this point.

I was called into the warden's office by the Secretary and my replacement followed us in, but was told to wait outside by the Secretary. He nervously complied. We talked for a little bit about what had happened there and why the person was being transferred. I was then instructed to begin undoing some of the damage that had been done and after this discussion I was asked if I had any questions. I said I did, and began to talk about the fact that we had not discussed salary. At my previous assignment, I explained to him, I had been sidelined a couple of times with promotions I should have had, and my paycheck showed the results. What did I think my pay should be, he asked? I gave him a figure I had gleaned from others who had the same pay grade. These figures were made public and were easy to find. He said he would think about it, got in his car and left. The former warden cleaned out his personal effects and left the office. He would have to return to get his belongings from the house that went with the position later, since he had not been previously notified of the transfer. I remained in the hotel that week and allowed him until Friday to move. Returning to Albuquerque on Friday and spending the weekend at home, I loaded my small Isuzu pickup with what I needed to set up housekeeping and drove back to the Correctional center on Sunday afternoon.

Fern was still working at Armstrong Pest Control in Albuquerque and we needed to sell the house. She stayed while I made the round-trip each weekend. During the summer months the drive wasn't terrible, it was just longer than I wanted to spend commuting to work, just over 3 hours each way. In the winter, conditions were not good and at one point, after Penny had graduated from UNM with a degree in broadcast journalism, she got a job with a local radio station in Roswell and lived with me in the warden's house. We commuted to Albuquerque each Friday, returning on Sunday afternoon. On one particular winter Sunday afternoon we started out for Roswell, but the usual route, I-40, was already snowbound and slick and its closing was being reported on the news. We decided to go the southern route, down I-25 south of Socorro and then cross over through Carrizozo to Capitan and then to Roswell. We didn't make it.

Traveling east on Highway 380 from I-25 we were met with a near-blizzard and, at one point, nobody traveling that way could make it up to the top of a hill. We helped each other turn around after we were told by a vehicle traveling from that direction that the road had been closed from Carrizozo eastward. It was nightfall when we arrived home. The wind, in some places recorded over 75 miles per hour, was blowing the snow on the interstate and we had difficulty driving. We were unable to make it to Roswell until Tuesday, and Penny was in trouble with her bosses. I wasn't in trouble, I *was* the boss. At the prison, they had to ask the National Guard to help take the shift change to work in Army vehicles more designed to handle the snow. There was a dip midway up the access road to the prison that had been completely filled with blowing snow so that no car or regular vehicle could come or go. The

Eastern Plains of New Mexico have no barriers to block the Canadian air masses that flow down the center of the country and the weather in these areas can change from warm to blizzard within minutes. I was in telephone communication with those at the prison and authorized contact with the National Guard to use military vehicles to get staff in and out. One shift was on duty a full 24 hours without a break.

The National Guard bailed us out another time, shortly after I arrived as warden. A 26-stage pump brought water out of the ground and pumped it up into a water tower, about two hundred feet high. When the pump broke, we were in a predicament. We had to have water. The National Guard brought water for drinking and cooking out in "water buffalos." The inmates and staff living at the facility took water in whatever containers could be found to where it was used and only flushed the toilets when necessary and the stink was so bad a person couldn't stand it. We executed an "emergency purchase," from the state and located a suitable pump to replace the one that had broken. I'm sure the one that had failed was the one originally installed when the facility was built as a missile site that guarded Walker Air Force Base until it was decommissioned in 1967.

Opened in 1941 as an Army Air Corps flying school, Walker Air Force Base was active during World War II and the postwar era as Roswell Army Air Field. During the early years of the Cold War, it became the largest base of the Strategic Air Command. It is also known for the Roswell UFO incident, an event that supposedly happened on July 4, 1947. It is alleged that a "flying disc" crashed during a severe thunderstorm near Corona, New Mexico a number of miles from Roswell. This is still a matter of speculation and many theories have arisen as to what it may have been, but Roswell is now capitalizing on the notoriety it brings since "aliens" were supposedly found inside the craft and taken to somewhere secretly where they were placed in a secure area. The base is now home to airliners that have been taken out of service and need to be flown occasionally to maintain their airworthiness. Some airlines use the facility to train pilots and an occasional Lufthansa aircraft will be seen flying over the area or Air Force bombers will use the facility for training. It has one of the longest runways in the United States.

The house in Albuquerque sold and Fern moved to the facility in 1988. We genuinely loved living there. Located south of the city of Roswell, north of Artesia and about 5 ½ miles west of highway 265, it was quiet. We could hear vehicles coming up the access road long before we could see them. The porch on our house looked eastward toward the Pecos Valley and the small towns that grew up around the small river; Dexter, Hagerman and Lake Arthur. A farming area, lots of crops were grown and later dairies relocated from California, making the most of the water that was available. Farther to the east was the Llano Estacado, "staked plains," that included the "Caprock," a geological formation that hid oil beneath the surface of the earth. Oil wells dot the entire southeast quadrant of New Mexico, reaching east and south into Texas.

We went a few times to the Methodist Church in Roswell but found it not very friendly. I learned that a fellow student from Golden Gate Seminary in California was now pastoring the First Baptist Church in Hagerman, so we started going back to a Baptist church. Spiritually and professionally this was a good move for me. Willis and Rebekah Blair became good friends. He had graduated in 1968. It took me until 1971 to finish. There were times I was asked to preach and that was refreshing. I also had opportunities to preach in other Baptist churches in the area and, in 1989 I volunteered for a mission trip to Yucatán, Mexico.

Since it was known that I had a degree in Spanish and I had been teaching English as Second Language classes at the Spanish Baptist Church in Dexter, I was asked to prepare six sermons in that language to be delivered in Yucatán. Google translator had not yet been invented, or at least made available to ordinary people like myself, so I painstakingly wrote the sermons, trying to make sure my vocabulary and verb tenses weren't too bizarre. This took a lot of time since I had not been using the language that much in conversation or in reading.

The missions team had several meetings in Artesia and Roswell and I was immediately accepted by the group. Led by the Pecos Valley Baptist Association Director of Missions, Ken Robinson, we drove to Lubbock, Texas to board an American Airlines flight to Mérida, Yucatán by way of DFW. Several Spanish-speaking pastors were along, one from Mexico, one from Colombia and another from Guatemala. Most of those on the trip didn't speak the language, but we were assured that there would be translators enough to go around.

Landing in Mérida we were having some difficulty in getting some of the items, like Bibles, through customs. That changed when Pastor Armando Mandujano showed up. He was well known in the city and elsewhere and highly respected. Things moved through customs smoothly and we were soon on our way to the hotel. Local Christians had volunteered to drive us to our lodging in downtown Mérida. Some of them spoke English, some did not. I managed to get along either way.

The team leadership met with the local Catholic bishop and explained our purpose there; not to undermine those in the Catholic faith, but to reach out to those who were not involved in any expression of Christianity. Blessing received, we were assigned to churches throughout the Peninsula, from Progreso on the Gulf of Mexico on the north to Chetumal on the southeast Caribbean coast bordering Belize. Many of the names were difficult to pronounce coming from the Mayan culture.

I wasn't assigned anyone to translate for me. I sometimes felt like I was on the edge of a cliff about ready to fall off, but I adjusted and was able to get along pretty well even though my thinking processes didn't keep up with the pace of the conversations as I would have liked. I had to rely on faith and the Holy Spirit brought me through it nearly unscathed. My mind has a jumbled memory of four years going to the Mexican peninsula and, almost thirty years later, I can't sort out what happened when, but there were many memorable events.

During one service in a Colonia outside Mérida I was to preach an evening service and after about a half hour of praise and worship a man came into the church with a live chicken. I thought to myself, *"I'm a Baptist, not Santeria..."* he reached into his right pants pocket and took out a string, tying one end of the string to the chicken's foot. He walked behind the pulpit to a post that was holding up what was somewhat functioning as a roof and tied the other end to a nail at the bottom of the pillar. When I got up to preach, I made a lame comment about the chicken and its purpose, saying something about if I made a mistake in my Spanish would the chicken peck my leg. They laughed, and I prayed.

The chicken remained through the sermon and we left for the night, going back to our hotel in downtown Mérida for the night. After breakfast at the hotel we returned to the Colonia and visited in the neighborhood sharing Christ with those who would listen. We were instructed that when going up to a house, we were not to knock, but call out from the front, "*hola*." Most of the time the people were friendly and invited us to talk; sometimes asking us to come into their homes. Once in a while someone would ask us if we were *Testigos*, meaning Jehovah's Witnesses, and we assured them we were not. Most seemed pleased we were Christians and Baptists didn't have a bad reputation in the area.

We were fed lunch in the church and returned to the hotel for the afternoon. Siesta, especially in this part of Mexico is sacred. Afternoons are hot, and nobody goes about any business. It's nap time and they take advantage of it. We did too. Returning to the church that evening I mentioned that the chicken was missing from the post behind the pulpit. I was told that we ate it for lunch… The man who had tied it to the post was giving an offering that became our meal. It wasn't a weird religious sacrifice after all.

At the hotel in downtown Mérida, we ate from the buffet they served. The food was plentiful and, even though I wasn't always sure what I was eating, it tasted good. In one large bowl there appeared to be chocolate pudding, which I adore. I got a bowl and filled it, taking it to my table. My first bite was a shocker! It wasn't chocolate pudding—it was whipped black beans that had spices in it. After the first disillusionment, I took a second bite with a more discerning tongue and, throwing aside my disappointment at not getting pudding, I began to enjoy this new dish. It was actually very good. But there was no chocolate pudding to help my former desire.

On one of our trips we were taken to the famous *Chichen Itza* to tour this famous Mayan ruin. It was magnificent! One of our guides said he had played all over the grounds when he was a boy and ran barefoot up and down the structure known as *El Castillo*. It is a pyramid rising almost a hundred feet off the main grounds. Our guide may have had little trouble going up and down the steps, but at fifty years old I had a much more difficult time ascending the steep climb. A chain was available to hold on to, but the steps were narrow, about 5 to 6 inches wide.

Standing on the top of the ancient temple huffing and puffing, I looked down and immediately my acrophobia kicked in. *How was I going to get down?* I had visions of the rest of my life being lived there, not a thought that thrilled me. At the apex of this structure was an altar and we could see the rock which was stained with a red color along with the carved image of the Mayan god, Chac Mool. The color, said the guide, was the deep stain of blood from those who had been sacrificed by having their hearts cut out on the altar. Children, adults and animals were sacrificed in this manner. The more he talked about the blood sacrifices, the more I decided to overcome my fear of heights and I descended, holding on to the chain, not looking down, facing the steep stairway and stepping backward. I made it and vowed never to climb this or any other pyramid in the future. So far, I have kept my promise to myself. I believe with all my heart that blood sacrifices were ended with the sacrificial death of Jesus Christ on the Cross, and that sustains my life.

The modern Mayan people have a distinctive look, short, big noses, and maintain their language as well as Spanish. They have been termed "The Little Smart People" and have surnames like Ek Puc or something else harder to pronounce. Many are Christian and have come to know Christ through the ministry of Pastor Armando Mandujano, who was pastor of *Primera Iglesia Bautista* in Mérida. He is credited with establishing over 100 missions up and down the peninsula. I am sure he is no longer living and has gone to be with the Lord. He was old then and walked with a cane. The culture is different than in other parts of Mexico. They call people from Mexico City *gringos*.

On one of these mission trips Fern joined us. We were assigned to the church in Tekax (pronounced Tay-KASH) and stayed in a local hotel that had air conditioning. Those with us were assigned to two other towns, Oxkutzcab (Osh-koots-cob) and Ticum (Tee-koom). Fern had a great time with the children at Tekax. During the afternoons we went to Oxkutzcab where the team had lunch with a doctor and his family. His wife was the pharmacist and the pharmacy was located next to their house. With no air conditioning at the home, we were treated to napping in hammocks with fans blowing on us and the youth gently swung us back and forth as we rested. Ahhh, the bliss. I'd do it again in a heartbeat.

On the back fence made from cinder blocks a huge iguana peered into the house through a window as it clung to the structure. We admired it, but it seemed to ignore our attention. We had seen many iguanas and other critters on the trip from Mérida through the jungle. At one point we nearly ran over a large snake that appeared to be at least 8 feet long as it slithered across the road in front of us. Poisonous or not, I wouldn't want to meet one of those guys anywhere.

One afternoon Fern and I decided to go into town and buy flowers for the family to show our appreciation for their hospitality. It was hot. Very hot… and humid. One of the younger men accompanied us as we walked along. We found no businesses open. At one point we were thirsty and asked if the guy with us could find us some water. He said he had something even better and led us to a downed palm branch with coconuts still attached. Getting a machete, he cut the tops of the coconuts off and told us to drink the water from the shell. We did, and it *was* much better than water. It even relieved the headache I was experiencing from heat and dehydration. We returned to the house and prepared to get ready to go to our assigned churches for the evening, minus the flowers which we managed to get another time during another morning.

After services were over each evening, our hosts picked us up at the churches we were assigned to and we all gathered at the hotel where the restaurant had agreed to stay open as long as necessary to feed us. The food was native faire, sometimes plantains with a syrup on them after they were fried, sometimes the local variety of tamales, minus the chile, but usually sweet to the taste. I could live on this food, often served with rice and black beans.

Mornings were a treat as we were awakened by one of the Spanish-speaking pastors playing a guitar and singing *Las Mañanitas*. Primarily a birthday song, it fits well with waking up to a new day. He would go from door to door of those of us on the team. We went to breakfast and then were driven out to the churches we were assigned to. Visiting in the neighborhoods of the churches were special and we used beads on a leather bracelet to get across the gospel message. Black for the sin in our lives, red is the blood of Jesus that was shed for our sin, white displays the forgiveness and purification of our sin by the blood of Jesus, purple tells of our adoption into God's family and the royalty we become by that relationship. The blue bead is for water baptism that testifies to our faith in what Jesus did for us, and green for our growing in our knowledge and understanding of what he wants our lives to be. And, yes, yellow for our home in heaven, paved with gold. The message, as always, is simple and easy to understand and was well received by the people we talked to. Some would not pray with us, but we invited them to the service in the evening, many of them coming to real faith in Christ.

One lady we visited lived in a hut made from tree trunk poles with palm fronds making the roof. The only piece of furniture she had was a hammock that served as bed, couch and chair. Her two children clung to her legs as we talked with her. I had never seen poverty like this before. We were told by those who knew her that her "husband" was an alcoholic who was seldom there. She did have some food to eat and we brought her more. She cooked over a fire just outside the hut.

The evening services were usually well-attended. The church I served borrowed electricity from the home across the street, stringing a long extension cord from a house next door to light the interior of the church structure and to power the loudspeaker that broadcast the singing and message throughout the neighborhood. One evening after our services were over, we were invited to go to Ticum. The people listening to the translated message from one of our team spilled from the church building out into the street. It was packed! And the message was still being spoken when we got there. The next day we visited in that town and enjoyed a fellowship with the people who were wanting to know more about Christ. I had never seen such a reception of the gospel message before. It not only changed lives there, but my life was renewed as well.

Until this time I had been putting my spiritual life on low burner. Not antagonistic, just not terribly involved. My experience with the Baptist association not accepting my little mission at Ojo Caliente and the recalcitrant attitude in Taos still bothered me. I was now back in the Baptist fold and there was a better atmosphere and outreach to people who needed the ministry and love of Christ. As an ESL teacher I had groups of Mexican immigrants who wanted to learn English and the Spanish Baptist Church in Dexter opened their doors to me and welcomed this ministry. I had a chance to share the gospel with the participants in an informal setting and some of them began attending the church.

The Correctional Center was generally a great place to work. I got to know the business manager, Paul Haberling, who had previously served under the other warden. He and I both had weight issues and we began to take walks along a long-forgotten air strip built by the Air Force in a by-gone era. He was full of ideas and had an ability to handle budget issues with skill, something I lacked in my own set of abilities. He had a fiancé and I agreed to perform the wedding which was held in the New Mexico Military Institute chapel in Roswell, since he was a graduate of the program and was commissioned as an Army officer following his graduation.

I often tried to help him see his need for Christ, but that was not something he saw any value in, or at least he didn't show any interest. His background was not very family oriented, and he wanted to have a family of his own. His first great help to me was in getting the paperwork done for the well pump that had gone down. An emergency purchase must be well-documented, and he did it with enthusiasm.

Several of the other staff enjoyed getting together for events. One year we had a party with no booze at our home and shot fireworks from our back yard. This wasn't exactly legal since no explosives were to be brought into a corrections facility, but—hey! It was the Fourth. Besides we were on the opposite side of the prison from the inmate quarters.

For Halloween, we dressed up for a party in Roswell at the home of a caseworker, Liz Caloor. Her husband was simply called "Caloor" because no one could pronounce his first name. An Iranian, he had come to America and was a nurse working on his Nurse Practitioners' Degree. He was a Muslim, but not a practicing one. His parents were still in Iran and he was doing all he could to get them to the States, since things were not good back home. We set out on a scavenger hunt that night dressed in our Halloween costumes. Caloor was dressed in a red turban, curly-toed shoes, green flared pants, a red shirt, and at one point, in downtown Roswell, some of the participants riding with me got out and did a "Chinese fire drill" walk around the car while we were stopped at a traffic signal. Not very dignified, but it was fun, and we were sober.

The Chief Maintenance officer, Jim Bass, was an intelligent fellow with a lot of ideas about how to do things, sometimes not exactly kosher, but it got the job done. During one of our health inspections we failed to pass water health tests, *e coli* was found in a sample. He climbed the water tower and had a rope lowered down to bring jugs of chlorine bleach up to the top of the tower and he poured them in until the sample came out clean. We were never sure how the sample got contaminated, but some suggested he tainted the vial of water just to see if they would catch it. They did, we're not sure if he did contaminate the sample or not. He was the only one who knew for sure.

He and I went out in his boat on a new lake that had been made by a dam constructed on the Pecos River just north of the city of Carlsbad. The Brantley Lake State Park had not yet opened, but we were sure we were the first to put a boat on these waters. If we weren't we were close. We later saw signs saying that boats were not permitted at that time, but no one made a complaint. Fish had not yet been planted, so we didn't put a line in the water, just skimmed over the choppy waters. Jim had come from a Jehovah's Witness family and his sister had at one time been the Warden at Roswell Correctional Center. He was not open to any conversations about religion and was not impressed with his sister's faith.

One year we were invaded by skunks. They were carriers of rabies and were hard on our dogs. We kept large cans of tomato juice, the only substance known by us to reduce the stink of a skunk that we were aware of. We went through many cans of the stuff until we decided to do something about the presence of the black and white critters. I called the county animal control office and they agreed to send over something to help. We got one trap. It was quickly occupied, and it took two weeks to get someone out to dispose of the varmint. There had to be a better way. With the two "idea guys" on my staff we decided that we would spotlight them at night and shoot them (off grounds of the prison, of course). It wasn't exactly legal, but our experience with the "legal" way was not a real solution. Thirty small, smelly animals lost their lives in our onslaught. There was no mourning. No graves were dug. No one challenged us. And the dogs no longer stunk.

In the mail I received a communication from the Criminal Justice Committee of the Presbyterian Church, USA. The tone of the article was that real justice was not being served by the corrections system in the United States and that there should be more done to reconcile the offender with the offended. I responded to them in a letter I sent to the address listed.

I received a phone call asking me if I would like to be in a symposium to discuss issues relating to corrections that would be compiled into a format that would be published by the church. They offered to pay my way to Covington, Kentucky, just across the Ohio River from Cincinnati and I agreed to go. The meeting was congenial, about six or seven of us, some of whom were experts in a concept called "Restorative Justice." Among the experts were Howard Zeher, Daniel Van Ness and Mark Umbreit. All of these have published studies on the concept. Daniel Van Ness was the Special Advisor on Restorative Justice at Prison Fellowship International in Washington, D.C. until his retirement recently.

Prison Fellowship International has been instrumental in changing the way the Christian Church approaches justice. I had the privilege of meeting Chuck Colson during a meeting in Albuquerque in 1976, at a "meet and greet" event held at a large hotel. I met him again much later in Toronto and again in Albuquerque just before he went to be with the Lord.

He was known as President Nixon's "hatchet man," and was one of the Watergate Seven, who pleaded guilty to obstruction of justice in 1974. He served seven months in a federal Prison in Alabama as the first member of the Nixon administration to be incarcerated for Watergate-related charges.

Colson became a Christian in 1973 and had a radical life change that led to the founding of his non-profit ministry Prison Fellowship and, three years later, Prison Fellowship International. His keen intelligence led him to focus on a Christian worldview that has affected not only criminal justice issues, but the Evangelical and Catholic relationships around the world. He authored more than 30 books and was the founder and chairman of The Chuck Colson Center for Christian Worldview, which is "a research, study, and networking center for growing in a Christian worldview," and includes Colson's daily radio commentary, BreakPoint, heard on more than 1,400 outlets across the United States (and continues to be broadcast with an alternating panel from the Colson Center). Colson was a principal signer of the 1994 Evangelicals and Catholics Together ecumenical document signed by leading Evangelical Protestants and Roman Catholic leaders in the United States.

Colson received 15 honorary doctorates, and in 1993 was awarded the Templeton Prize for Progress in Religion, the world's largest annual award (over US$1 million) in the field of religion, given to a person who "has made an exceptional contribution to affirming life's spiritual dimension". He donated this prize to further the work of Prison Fellowship, as he did all his speaking fees and royalties. In 2008, he was awarded the Presidential Citizens Medal by President George W. Bush. This man had and still has a great influence on my life.

Getting back to the meeting in Kentucky, I felt like a bumpkin in the midst of these intellectuals and some of the concepts sounded good, but in my experience, would not work very well unless the person was a fairly decent sort and had a Christian experience to begin with. Zehr was a Mennonite and Van Ness, a Christian also. Most of the discussion was around restoration as resolution for crime and they were not in favor of imprisonment as justice. The concept was to bring the offender and the offended together and hold the offender responsible to do what was necessary to make restitution to the victim. Much of this I could agree with. Most of the time the victim gets a raw deal and the offender is, well, a con man or woman who has manipulated their way through life just getting by. I believed and still do, that prison is the place for many offenders to go to and most of them would not be open for restitution or reconciliation without a major change in character brought on by a commitment to Jesus Christ. I received a copy of the book published by the group which somehow, I have misplaced.

I got a call from my daughter-in-law. She and Scott were at Holloman AFB, and she said in no uncertain terms that we should come and get our grandson Andy, since she couldn't handle him any longer. Scott was on temporary duty out of state at the time, so we went over and brought him to our house at the Correctional Center. Her behavior had been less than helpful to either us or Scott. She moaned and groaned about the living conditions, spent money like it was free and had strange quirks that were hard to anticipate. One afternoon she invited us to come over to Alamogordo for dinner. We got there and waited. No dinner was prepared, none was in preparation and it became evident that if we were to eat, we would have to go get something from a local eatery. Scott told us later that he had no idea she had invited us and was surprised that we showed up. They had been having financial problems, we knew of that. Exactly what, we didn't know.

Andy settled in at our house and we got him in school in Hagerman. He had a cute way of talking and especially as he saw horses along the routes we took. He called them "worses." He wasn't especially hard to manage. He was a boy with typical boyish traits. Not long after that we were told they were moving to Albuquerque, since their financial condition had become a problem and the Air Force was giving him a general discharge under honorable conditions and had us take Sarah as well. Chelsea was still small, and Lisa wanted to keep her.

Transportation was an issue and we loaned them our Isuzu pickup. After a while it became obvious that this was not a "loan" and I signed the pickup over to Scott. He promptly sold it. Their finances got worse and they were arrested for check forgery. Not something I wanted to have happen. Scott needed work and I told him the Corrections Department was looking for correctional officers. He applied and went to the corrections academy and graduated with a high mark. That didn't help. Their marriage was over. She called me and told me she was leaving, and she wasn't taking Chelsea. I called Penny and had her go and get her. We drove up to Albuquerque and brought Chelsea back to the Roswell Correctional Center with us. We now had the three of them. Scott was left with nothing in the apartment. He had to get a mattress to throw on the floor. There was no other furniture for him to use.

One funny incident happened when we took the kids in for their vaccinations. Andy was very vocal about not wanting a needle poked in his arm. The girls were not thrilled about the prospect either. The nurse was all ready and Andy spoke up, "You go first, Sarah, then I'll go." Sarah mustered all of the courage she could get and let the deed be done in her arm. "Okay, Chelsea next," he said. Chelsea was still small and not terribly afraid, and she got hers. Andy began to holler, "No… no… no… NO!" I had to hold him while he shed tears to get the shot that was inevitable.

Generally, the kids were well behaved. Normal, whatever that is. They played in the yard, got to know some of the neighborhood kids that also lived at the correctional center. They were the Padilla kids and their dad, A.J., worked at the facility. It came time for Vacation Bible School and all of the children were part of it, the Padillas even went to church at First Baptist Hagerman. It was a pretty happy time for the grandkids and for Fern and me. We had no idea where Lisa had gone, and the children didn't seem particularly concerned about it. Scott had entered the ranks of corrections officers and worked at the Penitentiary along with Jim. Somehow the arrest for forging checks and his receiving probation never made it to any place where it was noticed, and it didn't affect his employment.

One summer evening I was playing in the yard with the grandkids, swinging them around when I looked up and noticed a small airplane circling above us without an engine driving it. I continued to watch as the single engine airplane silently made a dead stick landing on a dirt road just outside our yard. The pilot took a little while getting out of the craft and I went over to meet him. He explained that the engine sputtered and died in flight and he was trying to make it to the airport at Roswell but had to land in the prairie instead. He said he needed to call his company and tell them of his predicament. I led him toward the house and let him use the telephone. He said he was on a courier flight from Hobbs on his way to Albuquerque and he believed he had gotten gas with water in it at Hobbs. His company was not pleased and said they were flying down to Roswell to check the aircraft out and asked me to take the pilot there to meet them, which I agreed to do. I also brought the two men from Albuquerque down to the downed airplane where they tried to get it started. They drained out gas and finally the engine turned over and they needed to get it on the roadway to fly it out, but they would have to wait until morning to do so. Would I take them back into Roswell? I would, and I did. I got home after midnight.

The following morning, I drove into town and picked them up and brought them back to the airplane. We opened a part of a barbed wire fence and one of them taxied the plane onto the road. I drove down about a mile or so to stop traffic if anyone was coming our direction and the airplane lifted off and they were gone. There was no word of thanks from either man, but the pilot called me a few weeks later, thanked me and asked if I would testify on his behalf. He was being fired for negligence. I was a witness to the dead stick landing and the fact that the engine was not running, but the company men thought he should have brought the plane into the Roswell Airport. My efforts to help were not important to them either. I hope the pilot got better than they were trying to give him.

I returned to my duties at the "Little Prison on the Prairie," and enjoyed my time there. The Department wanted to get all the facilities in New Mexico accredited by the American Correctional Association under national standards. It would help in fighting lawsuits that were always being filed by inmates, many of whom were always disgruntled about something.

Additionally, the Department was still under the Duran Consent Decree and under the thumb of the federal courts. Accreditation was a way out. Roswell Correctional Center made the grade while I was there, and I was pleased that others in the department were pleased.

I was sent to training along with other wardens in New Mexico by the National Institute of Corrections on several occasions. Once in Phoenix we were placed in a hotel with training conducted by national trainers. My roommate was Eloy Mondragón, then warden of the newly opened Southern New Mexico Correctional Facility in Las Cruces. The first night I rolled over and went to sleep and the lamp came on between my bed and Eloy's. I turned it off rolled back over and went to sleep. It came on again. I turned it off. This went on a few times and finally I saw Eloy awake and mentioned it to him.

"Yes," he replied. "You keep snoring and I turned it on to stop you…"

I had no idea I snored. No one had ever told me.

CHAPTER 12

RETURN TO SANTA FE

At one point the administration in Santa Fe changed and old friends of mine were appointed to positions of authority. Eloy Mondragón became Secretary of Corrections, Dareld Kerby Director of Adult Prisons, and a new warden and deputy warden were appointed at the Penitentiary. During one visit to RCC, I was asked if I had any interest in coming back to Santa Fe as an associate warden. It would be a promotion and I thought about it and, since it came with a house on the Penitentiary grounds, I said yes. This decision nearly killed me as you will find out later.

The move back to Santa Fe was more difficult than the move to the correctional center. We had a lot more beds, clothes and "stuff" than we brought down from Albuquerque. The only house available on the Penitentiary grounds was a two-bedroom home that was very cramped for my now large family. We decided to make do until a three-bedroom unit became available.

My new position was as the associate warden at the "South Facility," a medium security prison that housed up to 288 inmates. I was there a couple of months and then was told I would be moving to the Minimum Restrict Unit (MRU) or "Murf," so that I could get it accredited because I now had that experience behind me. After a couple of months more I was placed in the position of "Central Services" a position that included maintenance, food service, medical services, psychological services, education, construction projects, chaplains and volunteer programs, and anything else they wanted to throw in the mix. I called it "things nobody else wanted to mess with."

One day the Catholic Chaplain came to me with a problem: The warden would not let him order wine for Communion. I was aware that there was a state law requiring the Penitentiary to allow wine for Catholic Communion, so I got the statute book, marked the page, and took it into the warden's office. Being convinced he had no choice, he agreed to have the wine stored in the walk-in safe located in his office.

I got a call a few days later inquiring as to whether white wine, a Sauterne, was proper for Communion. Being a Baptist and only used to Welch's concord grape juice which resembled the blood of Christ, I called the Catholic Chaplain and asked the question. He simply said: "The Catholic Church prescribes wine and doesn't say that one wine is required over any other. I like white wine better than red wine." I sat back in my chair, trying to be as ecumenical as I could be, called the Warden and gave him the answer to his question. He was as taken aback as I was.

After a particularly hard snow, I got a call about 7:30 a.m. from the Deputy Warden chewing me out that I hadn't gotten an inmate crew out in the middle of the night to clear his driveway. I had not been informed that this was a requirement of my job, but I decided to stuff my anger and apologize.

I was scheduled as Duty Officer over the New Year's holiday and, on New Year's Eve, I got a call that an inmate had been stabbed in Cell Block 4. I saw them taking him out in a gurney as I walked into the Administration Building. The prognosis was not good, his bile duct had been nicked by the shank poked into his side and I kept getting reports from the hospital that his family needed to be notified.

I informed the family, but in addition I was to call my administrative superiors as well. I called their homes. No answer. I called a number of times but still got no response. After working all night, I finally got in contact with the Warden who had been partying. They both had gotten drunk but were upset that I had not sent someone to their homes to knock on their doors. Again, I stuffed it. It seemed that I had a lot of stuff stuffed in my stuffer.

One night I got a call that an escape plot might have been in the making. I went to the Main Unit and down to Cell Block 6. A hole that was exactly two floor tiles wide had been chipped through the floor under a bunk in a cell. It went under the facility, down into a series of tunnels. Various items had been taken into the area including lights on a string of wire, fans, a refrigerator, and there were syringes scattered here and there.

We conducted interrogation of all inmates to find out more about who had been involved and what the purpose was. We got nothing. Equipment was brought in to see if additional tunnels going outside the fenced perimeter were there. Nothing. The cell where the breach was through the floor had been vacated and the inmate had been paroled.

That day I worked 36 straight hours helping with the interviews. The facility was on lockdown and a fellow associate warden was actually cooking in the kitchen to feed the population. The obvious conclusion was that the area below the floor of the prison was a clandestine "recreation" facility unknown to most of the inmates and, of course to the staff. Ingenious, but not an escape plan.

Moving to Santa Fe brought my family and myself additional ministry involvement. We joined Rodeo Road Baptist Church, a really loving bunch of Christians who no longer sang from hymnbooks but had the words to the songs and hymns projected on a screen. There were people there who literally raised their hands in praise to God, something I had not experienced in Baptist churches before.

The Santa Fe Baptist Association had changed leadership and I was asked if I would be willing to pastor a mission at Peñasco, a town south of Taos on Sundays. It was kinda-sorta Baptist, but not quite. That didn't stop the association from adopting it unlike the mission I had served in Ojo Caliente a few years earlier. It felt like a breath of fresh air to me, so I took the mission on.

To get to Peñasco from Santa Fe, there were two main routes. One was through Española to Dixon and across a low mountain range, the other was by traveling north from Santa Fe, turning at Pojoaque, driving through Nambé, through Truchas, Las Trampas and then to Peñasco. A beautiful mountainous drive. The Christian singer, Fernando Ortega's family comes from Chimayó not far from this area and he wrote *Road Song,* a beautiful reminiscence of thinking about friends and this beautiful country as he drives along. I get teary when I hear him sing it. The area was settled by Spaniards during the days of the Conquistadores. They had mingled with native pueblo people and had developed a culture all their own. Not exactly like Spain, definitely not like Mexico. The language had become "Spanglish" mixed with some French words. "Pues, you know, my abuelita, she no hace na(da)." The book and movie, *Milagro Beanfield War,* by John Nichols was set in the area around Truchas ("trout" in Spanish).

The mission was called simply, Peñasco Christian Fellowship. There were a few in the church who came from Pentecostal backgrounds and some from other denominations, even Catholic, but the experience for me was a good one and my spirit soared as I served.

My Uncle Gene Peper had moved back to New Mexico after his wife, Merri, died of a stroke in Illinois. He was devastated by the loss and his consumption of alcohol increased to the point that he lost his driver's license in that state for DUI. He had been a state highway engineer and took the money he had in his retirement account and headed for Silver City to be with his mom, my Grandma Peper who was getting very old at this point. He bought a house and Grandma moved into a bedroom of the home. Gene was a great son and took care of his mother well. When she died at age 98 he was again into the alcohol addiction and also lost his driver's license in New Mexico. He called me one day at my home in Santa Fe and told me that he was in jail in Mora and that he had wrecked his car.

I went to Mora, New Mexico, to pick him up from jail and paid his bail. I asked him where his car was, and he told me it was in Wagon Mound, but it was not drivable. We drove there and found his Mercury sedan parked at a gas station with the windows down, his check book in the front seat, and his Boston Bull dog tied to a light pole next to the car. The keys were in the ignition and I turned the ignition on and started the car. It may have run off the road, but it was not wrecked. He paid the gas station owner what he was told he was owed for the time his car was parked there. The owner had also taken care of his dog and fed her. He drove on to Albuquerque but didn't go immediately to my mother's house. He later said he wanted to get a hotel room and clean up first.

When he was open to help, we tried to help him as much as we could, and he agreed to go to the treatment center at the New Mexico State Hospital in Las Vegas, NM. I got another call from him that he wanted to leave the hospital, but that he would first complete the treatment. I brought him to Albuquerque to stay with my mother and he mentioned that he never wanted to go back to the treatment center in Las Vegas. He related that the other patients and what they were going through and the screams at night were enough to keep him sober for the rest of his life. He returned to Silver City and found a job with an engineering firm that was working on local highways. This helped him to find some purpose in his life and he began to become more active in the United Methodist Church in Silver City.

During my time in Santa Fe, I began to experience being very tired all the time. I went to a doctor who put me through a sleep study and found out I had OSA, obstructive sleep apnea. I couldn't get a good night's sleep because I would snore, my throat would close, and I would stop breathing, wake myself up and then drift off only to keep on doing this, never getting into REM sleep cycles. I should have listened to Eloy when he was my roommate in Phoenix. Now he was the Secretary of Corrections for New Mexico. This added to my issues with the Penitentiary warden and deputy warden, but with the diagnosis and the help of a CPAP, a continuous positive airway pressure machine I began to feel better almost immediately.

The insanity at the prison continued, especially the deputy warden's poor administrative skills, as he ran "power trips" on those he supervised. For instance, I would be called to immediately report to the deputy warden's office, which meant I would have to leave the facility I was in, get in my car, drive to the main unit, go in and present myself at his office. I would be told to sit and wait until he was ready to see me. The wait could be half an hour, an hour or more. Sometimes I would be told to come back later. When I thought of all the tasks I had to do that day, this was a difficult way to approach my work.

But the time came when this ended and another chapter in my life began. My son, Scott, who was a sergeant working in the control center of the Penitentiary called me one day and said, "I hear you're going to Las Cruces."

I asked him where he heard it, and he said it was the "buzz" at work. I thought about it and when I heard an inmate porter also say he had heard that rumor, I thought back to a conversation I had had with those in Central Office. While there one day, I saw Secretary Mondragón, who asked me how things were going. I told him I wasn't going to say anything, but since he asked, I mentioned that I had been through Management by Objectives and Management by Responsibility classes, but I had never had "Management by Shakemup" explained to me.

He asked what "Management by Shakemup" was and I told him it was like taking a gallon jar of water, putting a scoop of dirt in it and shaking it up, trying to see through it. Since nothing could be seen, the jar is shaken up again, and again, with the same result. It reminded me of the definition of insanity.

How was that so, I was asked. I explained that every time I was put in a position of authority I was moved somewhere else before I could analyze the situation and work with it. I had been moved to three different positions within the facility within a few months and the experience was not pleasant. I also mentioned that both the Warden and the Deputy Warden couldn't agree on what needed to be done and that made working in that environment very difficult. I was told to speak with Dareld Kerby, Director of Adult Prisons, and let him know how I was responding to the management style. I did, and that's what got me moved.

CHAPTER 13

LAS CRUCES: AH, THE BLISS...

I got a call from Ron Lytle, the Deputy Warden at Southern New Mexico Correctional Facility who said he had heard that he and I were being switched. I told him that's what I had heard as well. He was not pleased. In fact, he was moved moaning and groaning. I was sorry he was put in the switch, but inwardly I was relieved to be getting out of the "jar of mud."

The move came on July 4, 1993. The day was hot, very hot and when we arrived in "Cruces." The mobile home we bought wasn't set up for living yet. No electrical hookup, no "swamp cooler" to cool the home, so we got a hotel room. It was a Sunday, and Monday was the observed Independence Day, so nothing happened then. It was mid-week before we could move into our house located in a pretty nice mobile home park located about two blocks from Mesilla Park Baptist Church. I had been aware of the history of that church and knew it was pastorless and that maybe I could be of some help. We joined the following Sunday. I was wondering why, but I just knew this was where we were to serve.

About thirty-five old people were the congregation and a deacon, Warren King, was moderating the service. A young man had been asked to preach and most of us were less than impressed with his over-the-top delivery of a very shallow message. I found out that they were in the process of calling a pastor and a man had been on their hearts since he had preached a "youth revival" earlier that year. I never have understood why he was preaching a revival for the youth since there were none. The former pastor had resigned, he was not in good health. The church declined in recent years, to the point that the deacons had recommended that it be closed, and the keys given to the Association and be disbanded. Our grandkids were the first children in Sunday school in a long time.

A group of people in the church were convinced that God was not done with this congregation that had been in the building since 1923. So they began to pray and ask God for a leader who would help put the ministry of these people back on track.

Dennis Diaz, a graduate of New Mexico State University and a very recent graduate of Southwestern Baptist Theological Seminary in Ft. Worth, Texas was reluctant to move from where he was in Texas as a youth pastor. He said he wasn't convinced that God wanted him as a senior pastor and was not sure he wanted to come back to Las Cruces. We joined the church about two weeks before he came to talk to the church.

They asked him to come and at least talk with them about it. He did. He shared his reluctance. Later he said he didn't want to preside at the "funeral" of a dying church. After they told him how much they wanted him to consider coming, he began to ask questions.

"Evidently what was being done in this church was not helping people to find a relationship to Christ, so, If I come, what are you willing to do to change things?" he asked. He mentioned that he didn't mean doctrine or basic beliefs of Baptists, but the way church was being done. Would they be willing to change?

What did he mean? "I'm talking about the way you do worship songs. Would you be willing to change the music style?"

They said they would.

"Would you be willing to take the word 'Baptist' out of the name of the church?" They gulped a little and he went on. "Sometimes the name 'Baptist' is a stumbling block for some people. Do you want to do what it takes to win people to Jesus Christ? It's hard enough for people just to not stumble over Christ." They thought about it and agreed, "Yes, we would be willing to do that. We will do whatever it takes." They were willing to get tradition out of the way, so people could be saved and plugged into the ministry of the church. Tradition has a way of working its way in the form of how we sing, how we pray, how we make people do what we think they should do. It's something like, "I don't smoke, and I don't chew, and I don't go with girls that do." Or something similar. We impose rules on people that are not biblical but act like they are. Baptists have been known for the things they weren't supposed to do, like drinking, dancing, and in some places not allowing boys and girls to swim together. It was amazing to learn that in the Southeastern U.S. it was improper for teens to swim together in Southern Baptist Churches while during the same time SBC churches in California had beach parties… Legalism creeps in and steals the real relationship with Christ and his Bride, the church.

Dennis and his family went back to Texas with the meeting on his mind and heart. "I will pray about it and I will let you know in a couple of weeks." He said he and his wife, TJ (Tamera Jean) prayed and fasted that two weeks. He reported that he lost 15 pounds in the process. I had never heard of a Baptist preacher ever really fasting for anything. He was the first. I knew it was biblical and Christian to the core, but it just wasn't done in my experience. As a special "kicker" the church offered him salary ten thousand dollars *less* than he was being paid in Texas.

I agreed to preach until the decision was made and I tried to prepare the church for change. I had seen some of the change that could happen at Rodeo Road Baptist in Santa Fe, and I was tired of the old same old… It should be a joy and a challenge to be in the presence of the Lord of the Universe and I sensed that this man could bring it on, with the power of Christ in him. The decision was made, and his family moved. A house was made available by a couple in the church, Greg and Paula Moran. They had one next to their house and gave it freely to the Diaz family. Jessica, Tiffany and Ryan were about the age of our grandkids and now there was a "real" Sunday School at Mesilla Park Baptist.

Dennis brought fresh air into the old church and it began to become alive. We quickly grew to over 300. We still had a "choir" modeled on the old way choirs were done traditionally. A lady who was a music teacher was the "choir director" and music leader. She was somewhat challenged to begin to use more contemporary Christian music but made a stab at it.

Slowly, Dennis began to lead toward more changes. The organ went, and a guitar came in. The piano followed the organ and drums took its place. Over time a trumpet, a violin, a mandolin and other instruments began to change the atmosphere. We projected words to songs on a screen from an overhead projector. The church continued to grow. We went to two services after we got rid of the "pews" and replaced them with chairs. That got a few of the "old" members upset. Many of them remembered "buying those pews in memory of...." But it made the "sanctuary" into a useable space where we were able to have dinners and Harvest Festivals (not Halloween) and other events. The church was alive.

Other changes happened, we came to the place where we needed more space and a "commons" area was constructed along with a hallway and classrooms adjacent to the west side of the worship center. The children's program, SonTown, became a viable program and we had kids everywhere along with young parents, and university students. Dennis had a reputation at the University as a record-holding track and field athlete. His picture hangs in the NMSU Hall of Fame at the Pan-Am Center where he set records for the shot put and discus. He offered himself as an unpaid coach for the NMSU track team.

Work at the prison was much more enjoyable and the warden, Don Dorsey, the one who had originally started his corrections career in Nebraska, continued in Arkansas and was the Major at Central NM Correctional Facility after it opened had been there since Eloy Mondragón was tapped to be Secretary of Corrections. He was easy to work with, but stubborn as a mule when he didn't want to do something he detested or was anxious about. He genuinely liked people, even most inmates, but he could take stern action when necessary.

I was his second in command and we got along well. Not long after I came to Southern a couple of men came out and talked to me about having a Kairos program at the prison. I had helped get this program into the Penitentiary when I was in Santa Fe. We talked, I got Lupe Marshall, the Associate Warden of Programs involved in the conversation and she was also open to the idea. We presented the idea to Warden Dorsey who was generally in favor of it until we explained that they required a signed agreement with the institution for certain continuity of the program beyond the major weekend event. Don said, "I like the program, I think it is something good, but I won't sign anything." And he stuck to his decision. The Kairos people backed off and said, "It's just not the right time." Two of those making the presentation were Tom Zornes and John Pickett, pastor of the University Presbyterian Church.

In January 1994 I was at the institution and Don was at a meeting somewhere else in the state. I felt pretty good during the morning and called Fern who was working on the west side of Las Cruces at the Children, Youth and Family Department of the State to have lunch with her. We ate, and I drove back to the facility. I began to feel weak and thirsty. I don't know how many times I went to the water fountain located in the building but not close to my office. Each trip felt like a ten-mile hike. I had a stack of forms that had to be signed as acting warden, giving good time to inmates for extra efforts put in to running the operation. The stack of papers seemed higher than my head and when people would come into my office they would remark that I looked awful and should go home. I knew that was the case, but I needed to finish the paperwork.

At about 4:00 p.m. I finished and drove home. Fern was just arriving after picking up the kids from school and told me I needed to go to the doctor. I told her I didn't feel like it and that I probably had the flu and needed to go to bed. I got in bed and immediately had to go to the bathroom. I had diarrhea and looking at the results which were black, I concluded that maybe she was right.

A neighbor of ours was a physician and our kids played with their kids. She told me that Dr. Cash Duhigg was on duty at the Lovelace Clinic across the street from Memorial Hospital, the only one in town at that time. We presented ourselves at the clinic and Cash took a look at me, asked a couple of questions and did a couple of tests. He told Fern to take the kids home, he was taking me to the hospital across the street.

He made room for me in his black pickup truck after moving some of the stuff on the seats. We drove across the street and he checked me into the emergency room. The diagnosis? A G.I. Bleed. I was bleeding internally from something in my gut. Cash later told me that if he hadn't driven me himself, he would have had to call an ambulance.

They put me on some kind of medication that would hopefully help the duodenum heal. The next morning Fern came to see me after she took the kids to school. I wasn't feeling any better and a nurse had put a bedpan under my rear end and left me. I told Fern how I was feeling and she called for medical attention. A doctor took a look at me and said something like: *"We've got to get him to ER, stat!"*

I felt myself being rolled quickly into an elevator and being prepped for surgery. They had bags of blood that they were pushing through the plastic tubes into my arms and the cold blood hurt. A nurse got some damp towels and heated them in a microwave to help relieve the pain, but it still hurt. Shortly after that they gave me the knock-out meds and I didn't wake up until long after the surgery was over. I remember seeing my sleep doctor, Paul Feil, involved in the mix of people who were rushed to my aid.

I was later told that a blood vein in my duodenum had ruptured and was bleeding into my intestines. A total of 9 units of blood plus plasma and platelets were dripped into my system to keep me from bleeding to death. Pastor Dennis came to see me and prayed for me as did Don Dorsey who didn't pray but let me know he was concerned for me. Even the hospital administrator came and talked to me. He was a member of our church and I hadn't realized his position in the community until then.

A lady psychologist was sent to interview me, and she asked a couple of questions, one of which was, "Have you been under any stress lately." I said I worked in prison, and she seemed satisfied that indeed, that was probably the reason I had begun to bleed internally. I didn't tell her about all of the events that had happened in the previous year and a half. They had taken their toll on my body and I wasn't handling it well. All of the stuffing I had stuffed had worked its way into causing my system to spew acid across the blood vein and it ruptured. I knew that even though the stress had stopped, my body was still reacting. I was in the hospital for nearly two weeks and when I left I was given instructions to walk short distances each day, increasing my strength.

The day I walked around the block was a milestone and I was on my way to healing. The scar left on my stomach ruined the modeling career I was planning for my retirement, but my life was spared.

Getting back to work was a good thing. The kids were in school and Noah's Arc—a pre-school and kindergarten program of First Assembly of God Church. Things were going well until Uncle Gene was diagnosed with prostate cancer. We traveled to Silver City numerous times when he was in the hospital. The pain became more pronounced as the disease took over. The doctors prescribed what I believe was a modern form of laudanum to kill the pain. He carried the bottle with him and took a swig as he needed it, or maybe a little more. We were going to take him to Albuquerque to live with mom and he decided he would drive down from Silver City to Las Cruces, but he didn't show up at our house. I went looking for him and saw him sail through a red light on a major thoroughfare not too far from where we lived. I followed and finally caught up to him and got him to park the car and go with me to the house. He had no idea he had driven through an intersection when he should have stopped.

He wasn't very happy about having to go to Albuquerque, but he did, and he was dying. I hated seeing him in this state. Gene had always been the "good uncle" whom I liked. Aside from the alcohol problem, he was a very bright man and kind to everyone he met. His wife, Merri was an avowed atheist and had thrown off anything resembling religion although she had been brought up Episcopalian. It was later learned that her father had been abusive which may have led to the break with God. I never learned any more about it. Mom called and said Gene had been placed in a hospice in Albuquerque, but before I could get up there he died. His burial was in Albuquerque.

I was nearing the end of my twenty-five years in Corrections and I was "ready for retirement. My plan at the time was to move to Grant County and serve a church that needed a pastor. I made myself available to preach and I got a number of calls to fill the pulpit in a number of churches. Truth or Consequences, Hatch, Rio Mimbres and several churches in the local area including Anthony were on the list of those who called me. Fern and I talked it over and we purchased land near San Lorenzo, in the Mimbres Valley. It was a beautiful place, an acre of land that had water on the property and would allow mobile homes. I was considering moving my double-wide there. It was less than ten miles from where I was born, and I had a lot of nostalgia about that area.

The owner and developer had subdivided the property left to her by her father, a rancher in that area. She knew my grandparents and that sealed the deal. We thought, dreamed and planned where things would go and how it would look. With a hillside to the west, a view of Cook's Peak to the south, the Black Range to the east and the Gila to the north—it seemed perfect. A school, San Lorenzo Elementary, was about a quarter mile to the south, great for the kids. And, when they were of age, they could graduate from the same high school as I did. Oh, the dreams we had.

Well, the time came when the kid's mother decided she wanted them back. We had legal custody and a battle was soon started by her and her boyfriend. A decision was made by the court that the mother could have the children every other weekend.

We would drive them to Socorro and the mother and her boyfriend would meet us there. It was less than what was good for the children and we definitely disliked the arrangements. We began to get reports from the kids that they were being abused; physically, Andy was thrown into a glass door which broke; and the two girls were reporting sexual molestations. Scott transferred from Santa Fe and filed a counter-suit against his former wife and we were in a battle. Child Protective Services were notified and documented what the kids had said.

A counter-charge was filed against me for similar behavior and they found none. The animosity got so bad that I put a recording device on my phone and recorded the boyfriend threatening to blow up our home. Copies were given to the attorneys.

Fern became frightened and told me I needed to do something about the situation. Don't think that only good thoughts were going through my mind. I was issued a Smith and Wesson .357 with ammunition which I had in the trunk of my state car. I knew where they lived in Santa Fe and, if I had not been restrained by the Holy Spirit of God, I would have done something that could have changed my status from deputy warden to convict.

Not long after this a girlfriend of Scott's also a correctional officer, came down and they asked to be married. I did the honors, or dishonors, as it turned out. She was less than a good mother or person, for that matter. Her mother lived in Las Cruces as well. She left Scott for a friend of a couple of years after they were married. He was devastated, and the kids were further traumatized.

At one point we were going to be held in contempt of court if the children were not turned over to the mother and we needed to not be available in the event that anyone went looking for them. A court appearance in Santa Fe on Monday had been scheduled. We went camping for the weekend in the Gila at Lake Roberts, planning on making the trip to Santa Fe to be at the hearing.

The outing was not fun, although we tried to make it as nice for the children as we could. On Monday, we drove to Santa Fe, where the court was held and entered a counter plea with the judge in that district. The kids were placed in a foster home until the evidence could be presented and the case was referred to a judge in Las Cruces. Scott acted as his own attorney and won custody of the children. They went to live with him and we helped buy a mobile home for them to live in. A decision I would later regret. We wound up trying to rent and then sell the home, a process that would take years and a loss of money to get out from under.

CHAPTER 14

BECOMING WHO I AM

I was ready to retire and do something completely different than corrections. The reality though was that God had a different plan. I received a cashier's check in the mail at my office at the Correctional Facility sometime in 1996. It was from a lady I didn't know. She had a note in the envelope that read, *"I am moving to Oregon, I had a yard sale and God told me to send you this check for a hundred dollars so that you can go on a Walk to Emmaus. But you don't have to do that, it is between you and God what you do with the money."*

I was stunned. I had heard about this retreat, "Walk to Emmaus," and had been asked to consider going on one. I thought about it. I hadn't made up my mind, but after receiving the check and putting it in my desk drawer at work I thought about it more. Two people, Jeff Dennis at Mesilla Park Church, and Tom Zornes, a person who had tried to get the Kairos program into Southern offered to sponsor me. After a couple weeks I prayed and said, "Okay, God! I'll go." And on October 24, 1996, I attended an Emmaus retreat at the Methodist Conference Center in the Sacramento Mountains of New Mexico, one of the most beautiful places in the southern part of the state. I was overwhelmed by the love of Christ poured over me during that time in the mountains. I had never experienced anything like it. All of those who were a part of the Emmaus Walk were from various denominations, mostly Methodist, some Presbyterian, some Baptist and others. This gave me a whole new perspective about the way Christ loves his Church—all of it!

Tom brought me back to Las Cruces and we talked about some of the things God was challenging him with regarding the incarcerated. I was also invited to be present at a "closing" of a Kairos Weekend at the federal prison at La Tuna, located between Las Cruces and El Paso. I attended. The Kairos team was working out of the United Methodist Church in Anthony, NM. The town is divided between Anthony, NM and Anthony, TX, both have post offices. The prison is located south of Anthony in Texas, but the mailing address is Anthony, NM.

The Kairos weekend is similar to the Walk to Emmaus, both of them developed from the *Cursillo* program that emerged from the Roman Catholic Church when men on the Spanish island of Mallorca wanted to help other Catholic men understand the Christian teachings in the Church, since most men in that country had looked upon the Church as being for women and children, the general understanding was that "real" men didn't need it. The Spanish word *cursillo* literally means "short course." It is designed to be presented over a long weekend, usually beginning on Thursday evening, all day Friday, Saturday and Sunday. In the words of the Kairos Prison Ministry history page, "Volunteers hold an Introductory Kairos Weekend, where they lead the participants through a carefully structured series of talks, discussions, chapel meditations, and music. The program takes the participants on a journey of self-discovery and relating with one another through the love and forgiveness of Jesus Christ. Following the weekend experience, Kairos Inside and Kairos Outside participants or guests gather regularly for accountability, support and prayer."

For many people, this is a life-changing encounter with God and the people of God. Through this experience, I began to see my own life in a different way. I no longer wanted to do the rest of my life "my way," but to go back to my encounter with Christ when I was in Spain in 1961 when I told Him, "my life is yours." I had gotten away from that original commitment, I had mainly been serving myself and doing some of the things God placed in my path, but I had not really made my life a *"living sacrifice, holy and pleasing to the Lord."* (Romans 12:1) One of the human problems with this is that a "living sacrifice" can crawl off the altar after the offering. I had done that too often.

Mesilla Park Community Church (we took the name "Baptist" out) was growing and we were changing the way churches did things, at least back then. Contemporary music was introduced, we stopped looking down at hymnbooks and started looking up to words projected on a screen and we were free to worship as we sang. It made the worship leader uncomfortable and she went to another church where her talents were more appreciated.

Many kinds of people joined the church, many of them needing help in specific ways. One man, Richard Morgan, was blind from a macular degeneration problem and he needed help especially when his wife, Hazel, was diagnosed with cancer. They lived on the other side of the Rio Grande in a mobile home and I and another man who worked at the prison with me, Jerry Wisdom, also a member of Mesilla Park, began to take them to doctor's appointments and grocery shopping. We all became good friends. I was teaching a Sunday school class at the church and they were all members of the class. Jerry's wife, Lorraine, worked at the White Sands Missile Range as a photographer shooting film of missiles that had been launched. Richard had to go to the New Mexico School for the Blind in Alamogordo to learn to read Braille. He also got a dog guide to help him go from place to place. After Hazel died, he needed companionship and Jerry and I did what we could to help.

My retirement was nearing. I was ready. I had a calendar and had begun "Xing" off the days until *that* day, December 26, 1997. I was still gearing up to move to Grant County, become the pastor of a small church, and serve "in my own way." Looking back that was a pretty self-centered plan. I'm sure God laughed. He knew what was ahead, even if I didn't have a clue. I was *so* done with prisons! I would be happy to find a "normal" life for myself and my family. No more doors, gates and "rigmarole." At one point I accepted the pastorate of two churches in the "Bootheel" of the state. The small towns of Animas and Rodeo were both small. I drove to Rodeo first, then back to Animas. Most of the people who came to church in Rodeo lived in Arizona, the town borders the state line. During the summer Arizona and New Mexico are in different time zones, Arizona electing to stay with standard time. Following services there, I drove to Animas, a little bit larger. The folks at Animas wanted us to become permanent and had a trailer home for the pastor to live in. We seriously thought about it… but not for long. I was still in my last days with the Department.

I got a request to attend a meeting for Corrections administrators at my old stomping grounds, the Los Lunas Correctional Center. It was August 1997. Dona Wilpolt was the Deputy Secretary of Corrections who called the group together. All I knew was that the Department wanted to go in a different direction with programming for inmates. When I arrived, I found out that she had invited representatives from Prison Fellowship to be there for a presentation.

Prison Fellowship had established a faith-based prison in Texas, the first in the United States. It was modeled after a program in Brazil called APAC, Associação de Proteção e Assistencia aos Condenados. In English it is translated as: Association for Protection and Assistance of Convicts. Chuck Colson had visited a Brazilian prison and was impressed with the Christian principles being used to help prisoners become productive in their communities after release and to help establish a prison that reduced the amount of violence and criminal behavior that is a part of incarceration everywhere. Their program named InnerChange Freedom Initiative Program started in April of that year in the Jester II unit near Sugar Land, Texas. The unit's name was later changed to the Carol S. Vance Unit, named for a Christian District Attorney in Harris County Texas who had proposed the Christian approach to rehabilitation. He continues to volunteer in the program.

After the meeting Dona and I continued to talk. She had been asked by Governor Gary Johnson to return to New Mexico and assume the position of Secretary of Corrections. She was living in California and related that she had been walking along a beach in Southern California and believed God was telling her that she should go, assume the position and that one thing that was needed in Criminal Justice was the element of a commitment to God and the change that would bring to an incarcerated individual. She was not confirmed by the State Senate; another person was selected who was and she became Deputy Secretary. She asked me if I would be interested in helping to get such a program started. After a brief moment I prayed silently and told her I knew "people" who would get this started. I related my experience with the team that had done the Kairos program at La Tuna Prison. She became animated as we talked, and I could see the excitement in her eyes. It was my understanding that we might be able to get such a program through Prison Fellowship.

A few days later we talked on the phone she told me that Prison Fellowship's program would not work in New Mexico and that we would be on our own if we began anything. I relayed all of this information to Tom Zornes and he began to get excited. We called a meeting of the Kairos volunteers to tell them of the possibilities we were being presented with. Without exception the group said it sounded good, but we had no plan. We had no curriculum and we really had no resources. How would this be possible? We had no clue…

After I retired, Tom and I decided to visit the Texas prison and see for ourselves what was being done. We call that day "The Day we Did Texas." We boarded a plane in El Paso early one morning and flew to Dallas, caught another flight for Houston, got off the plane and went to the prison for the afternoon. We left late in the afternoon, got a flight to San Antonio, and then another back to El Paso, landing late that evening. Our impression of the program was that there was no way we could handle a full-time program such as they were doing. First, we didn't have resources for the curricula, the full-time staff or the transitional services that were being set up. In fact, we had nothing but a God inspired dream. We knew how the Israelites felt when the spies went into the Promised Land: *like grasshoppers.*

It was obvious that we would have to scale back enormous amounts of what they were doing in Texas. Maybe we could get some churches to help us. So, we began to pray… Well, that's what we did a lot of. We prayed, and we met. Our group met with Dona, Homer Gonzales, the Prison Fellowship Director for New Mexico, Ike Griffin the Executive Director of Kairos Prison Ministries and others.

Early in 1998 Mesilla Park Church sent me to Saddleback Community Church in California for a *Purpose Driven Church* Conference with Rick Warren. Our church wanted to implement this model for our church structure. I also attended a workshop held during the conference called Celebrate Recovery. I had never heard of this program. John Baker and several of those at Saddleback made the presentation and I bought the kit to take back with me. The more I read it, the more I believed we needed this in whatever program we were developing for the Corrections Department. There were four participant's guides and a leader's guide in the kit.

I shared the curriculum with the committee and they were as impressed as I was. We still didn't have a handle on what else to do or how to do it. As we talked, the design for the program was that it should be in medium security, start in one pod and grow to at least 3 pods.

Southern New Mexico Correctional Facility had a change in wardens before I retired. Ron Lytle, the deputy warden I replaced who went into the "fiery furnace" at the Penitentiary, was now warden. He and I got along well. He had an "old country" manner about him and could tell hilarious stories one after another. We presented him with the Kairos program and he said, "Well, I don't think it'll do any good, but I'll give it a shot." I believe it was in April after I retired that I did my first Kairos at SNMCF. We asked for the most difficult of inmates to begin. Lytle selected the leaders of the major gangs: Black, Latino, White Supremist, and Native American. He said, "If you can do something with these guys, I'll be surprised."

We met in an auto shop bay in the education department. We put all the equipment in the center of the bay, wrapped it with cloth and one side became our community room and the other the chapel. Neither looked like what we had designated it to be. We didn't know how it was going to work, but we followed the program and the first night, a Thursday, the guys were eyeballing each other thinking, *"What's that _____ doing here?"* I don't think any of them had great expectations for the rest of the weekend. As we went through the talks, sang, ate and began to have a good time together, the barriers came down. They talked with each other and began to treat each other differently than they had in the past.

During the closing on Sunday, Warden Lytle came in to see what had been done. We gave each inmate a chance to speak for himself as to what the weekend had meant to him. One of the participants, a "skinhead" who had been extremely violent both inside and outside the prison got up and almost with tears in his eyes said, "I came to this weekend with a heart of stone, and I am leaving with a heart of flesh." I watched Ron Lytle who was leaning up against a wall in the visitation room. When the inmate said those words, he looked amazed and slumped down against the wall. This was an inmate who had killed people on the street as well as two inmates at the Penitentiary in Santa Fe. Ron was one of the correctional officers who had to wrestle him in and out of his cell there. They were not on friendly terms. But the inmate had really had a change in heart during that weekend. All of those leaders stood up and claimed that they would have each other's backs if anyone tried to harm them after the weekend. A more peaceful atmosphere had descended on the prison. Lytle didn't understand it. He had a King James Bible on his desk but claimed he really didn't believe it all. I had tried to be a good witness to him, but his mind was made up and he continued to resist.

Crossings was the name we chose to give to our new program. We developed a logo and a strategy; we would present the course in three 6-month sessions. As we added more inmates we would go from Phase 1 to Phase 2 and then Phase 3, simultaneously. We termed these: *Upward, Inward* and *Outward. Upward* would be learning about and appreciating who God is. *Inward* focused on who the individual is in relationship to God and *Outward,* how do I get restored to my family, my community and become involved in the church and community. Tom wrote a study called *Lifestyles* which describes how people live: in the flesh, without Christ; in the Spirit, with Christ's Holy Spirit directing and guiding one's life; and the carnal lifestyle that Christians are living in and becoming sanctified by following Christ and growing in His grace.

I got the materials I had put together to teach at the Corrections Academy regarding communications skills. I redirected these notes and wrote a study called, *How to Say What You Mean—Without Being Mean.* Originally most of the sources came from Christian authors, John C. Maxwell, Kenneth Blanchard, and Ziz Ziglar among them. I added a Holy Spirit-directed attitude of learning how to "love (*agape*) others as you want to be loved," as the basis of the course. I also found a book I had originally bought at Sam's Club called, *The Message in Your Emotions,* by Wayne McDill, a professor at Southeastern Baptist Theological Seminary. I manualized the book and developed a participant's guide with a lot of blanks for fill-ins. I had learned that most teaching is easier if the learner is engaged in the process. We used fill-in notes for the sermons at church which gave me the idea for doing this.

In December 1998, we had everything we needed to begin—except the inmates. We had asked for and gotten approved a pod of 16 inmates to begin, but no inmates wanted to be the first "guinea pigs." This was a problem, so we prayed. Tom, John Pickett the pastor of University Presbyterian Church and I went to visit with some of the inmates who had shown an interest and who had been a part of the first Kairos. Most of them were working in Corrections Industries, an inmate factory that made wooden furniture, uniforms and shoes. We asked to see them during their lunch break and talked with them. We found out that some of the Christians working in the Industries area had a prayer group earlier that morning and had been guided by God to abandon their "honor unit" where they had more privileges in favor of beginning the first Crossings Unit. Like us, they had no clue how this would work or if it would, but they felt they should give it a chance.

Just before Christmas they moved into the pod, had a "spiritual cleansing" of the unit, praying that any demonic influences would not be present in their new home. Tom and I showed up the first night for class. I pulled a "sneaky" on him. I failed to tell him that I was going to teach *The Message in Your Emotions*. "You're what?" He said as we walked into the facility. As we were beginning, a sergeant told the inmates to "lock it down." We tried to explain that the inmates were to be on outcount and that we would be having our class in the unit. The warden had signed the memorandum and the shift captain had a copy of it. "I said lock it down," was his response, so we picked up our books and left.

We got off to a rocky start. We were a little discouraged and made a trip out to the facility the next day. The warden was emphatic that the program would begin. We made the trip out again that next evening and the sergeant said, "Now what is it you are you doing?" We told him, and he let it happen. Finally, we were off and running. Christmas came and went. That year it was on Friday. On Monday when we met with the Crossings inmates they reported that they had their own Christmas feast, pooling their canteen items and making it a good time. They even invited the sergeant to have dinner with them—and he did! He became a proponent of the program after he understood the purpose. Not everyone gets it. Correctional officers usually do what they have always done—good or bad. For them, security is the name of the game, for obvious reasons.

Crossings went well, until two weeks before we were to have our first graduation. The Corrections Department sent 14 of the 16 inmates to a new facility that was being opened in the southeastern part of the state at Hobbs. A private prison known as Lea County Correctional Facility had been constructed by Wackenhut Corporation and the department needed to fill the beds. The Director of Adult Prisons at the time, John Shanks, told me, "Well, you did a good job on those guys. Let's see if you can do it again." Our plan had been to continue to build the program one phase at a time, now we had a do-over.

We got another group of inmates who wanted to become part of the program and we started again. We still hadn't developed the second phase. From Hobbs we got a message: "What did you do to these guys?" We said we hadn't done anything.

"Well, these inmates are exceptional, whatever your program is about, we want it here." We contacted a group of Kairos volunteers in that area and asked them if they would be willing to help in the program. Tom and I spent some time in Hobbs training the new volunteers—as well as working with those at Las Cruces.

Shortly after that we got another call, this time from the private prison at Santa Rosa. They wanted a program. We trained some Kairos volunteers there and they began the program. Then the women's prison at Grants wanted the same thing and we went there. Then Roswell and Los Lunas. We had no idea that the program would take off like it did.

In the summer of 1999 I took my family to California on vacation. The grandkids and my son, Paul, whom we had called Scott for so many years, were happy to get to go to Disneyland and, on Sunday we went to church at Saddleback. After the service I went to the ministry booth on the patio that had the sign, "Celebrate Recovery" on it. Behind a table John Baker was talking with people about the program and I went up to him, introduced myself and told him we were using the Celebrate Recovery materials in our prison program. He gave me a puzzled look, didn't say much, and I took his reaction to mean that it was of no particular importance to him. I was wrong! As I turned to walk away he handed me his business card and asked me to email him which I did as soon as I returned to New Mexico.

He called me on the phone and we talked about what was happening in Crossings and he asked to come and see for himself what was going on. He flew into El Paso and I had cleared him to come into the prison. Evidently, he was impressed and he came back a number of other times and through him, I became more involved that I had thought I would be.

I, in addition to all of this, was asked by a Christian state senator, Lee Rawson, if I would be willing to run for state representative. I was stunned by the call and I think my prideful self kicked in and, although I wasn't that political, I agreed to run on the Republican ticket. I was guided through the process by Lee and there were those who helped me as I gathered signatures to be placed on the ballot and began my campaign. The county Republican Party, including the chairman became involved with me as we went about running for office. It was 2000 and Bush was running against Gore. I was pitted against Dolores Wright from Chaparral; a land developer and the owner of the water system that supplies that area. She was the Democrat incumbent and I was in an area dominated by her party. My district went from where I lived just outside the city on the northeast side of I-25, east to Organ, excluding any of the incorporated city, south of Las Cruces to Chaparral, and Anthony, New Mexico right on the Texas state line.

I went to functions that put me in positions where I felt I was on the auction block. Questions were thrown at me and my response often made the difference between a yes and a no vote. I knocked on doors, did interviews for radio, had yard signs and mail-out advertising for my campaign. I solicited donations and received funding from the Republican National Committee. One rally at the town of Mesilla featured George W. Bush himself, another at the Dickerson Barn, an events center that looked more like a barn than a place to have meetings, where I met Laura and her daughters. My yard signs read:

"Jan 'The Man' Thomas for State Representative, District 52." There were radio ads and I was busy.

Came election day and I was with those in my Party at what was then the Hilton Hotel (now Hotel Encanto) watching the results on a TV projected onto a screen. At one point it looked like I was winning—big! Then the results from the southern part of the county came in. I lost by 53 votes. I found out later that Dolores was paying people to go vote. One of those people asked me to pay for votes and I refused. She won, and two weeks after the Legislature went into session, she died. Her health had not been good, she was on oxygen and had to have 2 canes to walk. I got a call from the chairman of the County Commission that he would push for me to get the seat which she had won, but he didn't think the full commission would make that decision since most of them were Democrats. One of the commissioners put his name in the pot and they selected him for the position. I was offered the county commission post, but I turned it down. Bush won by a "chad" in that election. Florida had a hard time deciding whether the punches in their ballots were valid or not. The Electoral College went for Bush. As I thought about it, I was happy I had lost. I had other things happening that were much more important.

In August 2000 John Baker asked me and Dona Wilpolt to share about Celebrate Recovery in the Crossings program during the summit held at Saddleback. Several others from the New Mexico Corrections Department also went, including the Director of Substance Abuse Programming, Charles King, and Homer Gonzales, who had become the Religious and Volunteer Coordinator for the department. Dona Spoke to those attending and got a great response from the CR people.

Shortly after that John called me and asked me if I would be willing to travel and share about CR in prisons wherever I was asked to go. He gave me a credit card with nearly a blank check to do that. Not long after, John said they would pay me "quarter time" to be on staff, then after a few months, "half time" and soon "full time." I told John I would be willing to do it for nothing, but now I was on the payroll at Saddleback Church. I was travelling throughout the United States and Canada meeting with wardens, doing workshops in churches, speaking at CR Summits during the main session, and began doing workshop breakouts at the summit. Most of my travel was during weekends, so I continued to take part in Crossings that met Monday through Thursday evenings.

Inmates changed. Some started in the Kairos weekends and then continued in the Crossings program. One man, a Marine Corps vet who had been in battle in Viet Nam was known as a cross-dresser and figured out ways to smuggle women's underwear and lipstick into the facility. He was a tall man, not very good looking, and had a scar on one of his cheeks from shrapnel that had torn his face during the conflict. As a man he was, well... not exactly ugly, but headed in that direction. As a cross-dressed woman he was downright frightening. He had filed in court to have his name changed to "Carol," (not the name he selected) even changing his last name.

"Carol" participated in a Kairos weekend, and then joined the program. One of the support team, a woman, wrote him a letter he received during the Kairos on Saturday afternoon. She told him how much God loved him and that he was loved just as he was. He began to reassess his status as a woman as the program took him into realms he had never thought of before and the Holy Spirit worked in his life. He came to a decision that his desire to be a woman was based on the fact he had never been loved before, especially by men and he thought the only kind of love available was sexual. Discovering that love was experienced on different levels he finally made the statement: "My name is John." He had come to terms with who he was and that he was loved.

In April of 2001, I was selected to attend a Faith-Based Initiative emphasis of the Bush Administration. I suspect my selection was on the advice of the Deputy Secretary, but I have not had that confirmed. My way was paid to Washington, D.C., but I would have to get a hotel. I elected to call my cousin, Vance Saige, and they offered to put me up for the time I was in the D.C. area since they lived in nearby Fairfax, Virginia. Two persons were selected from each state, Miles Culberson and myself were chosen from New Mexico. Miles was on our Kairos teams early on and helped with the planning and implementing Crossings.

The meetings were held in the Capitol building and Senate and Congressional buildings in the Capitol complex. We got a great tour of the Capitol from some of the U.S. Representatives. Zack Wamp from Tennessee was one who spoke to us the most. At one point, in the Rotunda of the building Congressman Wamp knelt down and prayed for the group, the United States and led us all in the Doxology as we walked into the Senate Chambers. The event brought tears to my eyes, and it was heartwarming to know that at least some of our lawmakers are Christians. They talked about some of the Bible study and prayer groups that met on a regular basis. A luncheon was held in the Library of Congress for us and a special dinner at a downtown hotel featured speeches by Attorney General John Ashcroft and Vice President Dick Chaney.

I got to the hotel for the dinner with Ashcroft and Chaney early, having ridden the Metro train into the City from Fairfax, exiting at the station under the hotel. I went up and found the room the event was to be held in and walked around until I was challenged by Secret Service agents who were sweeping the area. I was told in no uncertain terms not to come back until I could be properly admitted. I, having been a law enforcement person myself, quickly complied and got out of the room.

Meetings in the office buildings and hearing rooms included Bishop T. D. Jakes and other well-known preachers as well as Christian politicians. My impression of the Bush Administration's desire to implement faith-based programming wherever possible is that they really tried, but because of the anti-Christian bias in many government agencies and political opponents they were beaten back. I enjoyed myself immensely during this event.

Rick Warren and Chuck Colson announced a partnership with each other's organizations in a meeting held at Angels Stadium. Celebrate Recovery and Prison Fellowship would help each other as we endeavored to minister to the incarcerated and their families. I had great admiration for Colson and had read many of his books, some of which are great works of theological value in our generation. I remembered first meeting him in Albuquerque in about 1976 or so at a function of which I was a part.

I was invited to attend the Prison Fellowship International meeting in Toronto, Ontario, Canada. There I again met Chuck Colson and for the first time Ron Nikkel, the president and CEO of Prison Fellowship International, as well as a host of others, including the Christian author Phillip Yancy. Mary Kay Beard, the founder of Angel Tree was there, and I got to talk to her. It was during the Fourth of July events in the country to the south, but Canada had nothing for Americans, so we had our own celebration. I was invited to go on a boat ride on Lake Ontario to an island in the harbor on that overcast and somewhat drizzly day. There was a structure there that accommodated our group and we grilled hamburgers and hotdogs, sang American songs and then headed back to the city. My trips to Canada have messed with my head a little. While everything looks American, they speak… well, almost American, but the metric system always throws me off. In British Colombia I saw a sign written on cardboard and placed on a roadside that said: "Apples 300 Yards." It was probably for those who had been alive during the "olden days," when a different measuring system was in effect in Canada.

I sat up my Celebrate Recovery Inside information table next to the display from the Prison Fellowship of Fiji. I got to know these guys during the event and we had a lot of fun. Many of the PF'ers from Fiji were correctional officers. It seems that is not a problem in Fiji. I was given a piece of cloth that, when wrapped around a man's waist is his "pants." I later got in contact with the PF Director in Fiji, Dan Savou, and helped get some CR books to him. Prison Fellowship used the program there until another group began to do it in their prisons that had better resources to get the materials to Fiji.

I traveled to places I had been before as well as places I had no idea were there. In the Air Force I had gone to New Orleans on a weekend pass with some buddies. We took in the sights as well as the French Quarter back then, but now I had been asked to come to New Orleans for a different reason. A chaplain at the Jefferson Parish Correctional Center wanted to get Celebrate Recovery into the facility, but first we had to meet with Sheriff Harry Lee. The sheriff was one of the most powerful politicians in the New Orleans area. Jefferson Parish and Orleans Parish bisect the city. Sherriff Lee no longer had to run a campaign. Any donations he got went to projects within the parish and no one ran against him. Anyone running for office, local or state, had better check in with Harry to get his blessing; we had an appointment with him in his office. We sat outside and the chaplain pointed out people who were ushered into his office. One was running for the US Representative slot for Louisiana.

Once inside the office we sat in chairs in front of his massive desk. He was a large man, well over four hundred pounds and I noticed shelves, about five feet in height surrounding the rectangular office, all filled with carved duck decoys. Hundreds of them. I commented on the craftsmanship that went into each one and the sheriff told duck hunting stories and how these decoys had been used in his favorite recreational sport. After a little introduction by the chaplain we talked about using the CR curriculum in the jail, of which he was the head. He asked some questions, looked at the books and told the chaplain she had full reign to do the program.

On another occasion in the same location I was also invited to go with a couple of men who were attempting to get CR into the prison now known as the Rayburn Correctional Center. We met at their church in Slidell and drove north through Bogalusa. Once inside the prison we were given a tour of the facility and at one point an inmate came up to me and asked what we were doing. I replied, "We've come to try to get Celebrate Recovery started here."

"What's that," he asked.

"It's a Christian recovery program." I told him.

"You a Christian," he asked.

"Yes," I said.

He put his arm around my neck and said, "I love you, brother!" I smiled and he let me go. The prison began using CR.

Most of my time was given to our New Mexico prisons, mainly the one in Las Cruces. One morning I got a call from Dona Wilpolt telling me that the Secretary wanted to see me in Santa Fe, could I come up? Of course, I said yes. Arriving at Central Office I was met by Dona and she told me to follow her into downtown Santa Fe since the Secretary was there. I followed. She pulled into the parking lot of the Capitol building, "the Round House" as it is known. We walked into the building, got on an elevator and went to the third floor. We were standing in the lobby of the Governor's office when Rob Perry, the Secretary of Corrections, came up and started chatting. Nothing substantive, just normal chit-chat. I thought that was strange since he was the one who wanted to see me, and now here we were in front of the Governor's office.

Soon the door opened, and Governor Gary Johnson came out, shoved his hand toward me and said: "Congratulations!"

I asked him, "For what?"

"Oh," he said, "I guess they didn't tell you that you have been named Corrections Volunteer of the Year." I gulped and said, "Well, no."

"Let's go into the conference room." He ushered us into the same room I had been in with Governor Bruce King years before. I was handed a certificate with the congratulatory wording, pictures were taken, and I was blessed! I had no idea that this was being planned. I had thoughts that maybe the program was in jeopardy, or I was in trouble somehow. This was a pleasant surprise. Gary Johnson later ran for president as a Libertarian, I didn't vote for him, but I remember this event fondly.

In 2005 I had a gastric bypass operation to lose weight. I had reached over 300 pounds on my five-foot seven frame and my knees and back hurt. The surgery required an abdominal laparoscopic procedure with less than a week recovery in a hospital in El Paso. I healed very well and kept to my diet rigorously. My weight fell off to the point I was 170 pounds and I was feeling good. My energy level was up, and my knees no longer bothered me. I did have some emotional and psychological issues, though. I would often get frustrated with myself for very minor things and, of all things, I cried occasionally. But this was only a minor problem, or so I thought.

CHAPTER 15

MISSION TRIPS TO EXOTIC PLACES

In 2006, Mesilla Park entered an agreement with missionaries in East Asia to bring some of our teens to China for an English Camp. I began to feel a leading to be one of the sponsors and I agreed to join the team. We had several months of preparation and prayer. Derek Mitchell, our youth pastor at the time, along with Deborah and Lupe Cuellar, and several other adults helped the youth get ready for our trip. I had never been to China, and after our pastor, Dennis Diaz, had previously been to the area we would be going to, I was excited to go with them. Dennis told us what he had experienced in Inner Mongolia and the fact that they weren't riding horses and drinking yak milk and really had modern cities, made me more desirous to go. We had a lot of preparation to get ready. Everyone had to have a passport, I had never had one. There was no need for one to go to either Canada or Mexico. We had to get a special visa from China and our passports were sent to Houston for this purpose. Tickets were purchased and all of us had to contribute although the church would be helping with some of the expenses.

We flew from El Paso to San Francisco and boarded a Delta 747 to Beijing, a trip of about 12 hours. In my mind we would be travelling over the Pacific most of the way. After several hours in the air I had to use the restroom on the plane and as I was going to one of the stalls, I looked out a window and saw—mountains! That's Mt. McKinley," someone remarked. I was taken aback at this one. I wasn't thinking we would be going this route. We were still over land. The name of the mountain has changed to Denali, but it is the highest land-based mountain on the earth and we were flying over it.

I continued to look at the landscape below and the scenery changed little as we crossed the Bering Strait and continued over Siberia. Rugged mountains with snowcaps were still showing even though it was July. I had traveled quite a bit since I joined the Celebrate Recovery team and had flown all over the United States, but this was the longest single trip I had been on since I flew to Spain on the military transport years earlier.

The kids were great to work with and very well behaved. Their parents had done well and they followed suit. Two of them were Pastor Dennis' kids, Ryan and Tiffany. We arrived in Beijing and caught another flight to the city we would be living in for about three weeks. The Chinese name was, at least in my ability with the language, unpronounceable. Our Air China flight was much shorter, a couple of hours or so and we landed. It was evening and were met by the missionary who spoke Chinese fluently. She arranged our transportation to the hotel we were to stay and got us checked in. Our ability with the language was nonexistent for the most part although some had been practicing for a few weeks and the English spoken at the hotel was not good either. The hotel was six stories high, with no elevators and we had to walk on our own up the stairs to the top floor—with our luggage. I was happy I had lost the weight. I was old, at the time 66 and I was still recovering from the surgery. The exercise helped somehow in that endeavor.

The next morning, we ate in the restaurant at the hotel and discovered that the fare for almost all meals was about the same. The only difference in the breakfast menu was boiled eggs and—chicken feet! Boiled eggs and the rest of the food was fine for me, but I couldn't quite get to the point in my mind to discover anything good from the feet of chickens. I had seen too many of them and what they walked in. I was not going to eat them! I don't eat pig's feet either, for the same reason.

We met with the students we would be working with at the school which was about two blocks away, after adjusting to our home away from home. We had to cross a couple of busy streets that had both motorized vehicles and bicycles in special lanes on the outside. We were shown how to cross, waiting for a break in traffic, then standing on the painted dividing line, again waiting for a break and going to the next line until we were finally across. The first few times were very uncomfortable, but we got used to it and watched the local folks as they maneuvered through traffic. None of us lost our lives and we didn't see anyone else struck down because they misjudged the speed of the vehicles.

The Chinese students ranged in age from elementary school through high school and one of the young ladies in my group was in training to be a police officer. They all knew some English, but they wanted to practice and to learn more. Most of them had been programed by their culture to be very serious about education and they were allowed little in the way of entertainment or enjoyment. We tried to involve them in some activities that they could enjoy as well as learning English. We weren't allowed to preach or to teach them from the Bible, but we had other things we could do to witness to them, like telling about the holidays in America. Holidays, like Christmas when Jesus was born, Easter when he was crucified, and St. Patrick's Day celebrating the missionary who brought Christianity to Ireland. We could explain the history behind the holidays and talk about our faith. For those who were more interested the kids could sit with them and share over a Bible if they wanted to. Some of them did as relationships developed during our time together.

We caught busses all over the city of about two and a half million people, and sometimes taxis. Taxis were inexpensive, but busses were downright cheap. They were powered by natural gas and two huge dark green cylinders, each about 50 feet in diameter and about 150 feet high supplied the city and were located across the street from the school where we taught. It entered my mind that if those two tanks exploded the city would be obliterated.

We were given only a small amount of money to spend on a daily basis, so we were diligent in what we spent it on. There were ATM machines at banks that would accept credit cards and give us the local currency at whatever rate it was that day, but we seldom went there. We did have to exchange some US dollars by going to a bank and going through a process to get Yuan. A corner grocery store across the street and at the end of the block sold bottled water and other snacks we would need during our stay there. US currency was not legal tender, so we learned to buy things in Chinese Yuan.

The students were a delight and eager to learn. They asked questions and entered into the discussion in English, sometimes in trying to understand what we said and how we said it. Many of the students were Mongolian, as was one of the Christian leaders who was assigned to us as helpers. The school had posters in both Chinese and Mongolian languages telling about the school and its origin.

After the Communist takeover after World War II, the Party set about making changes in regions that weren't exactly on board with Communist principles. They moved many people from region to region to break up any backlash against the regime and Mao Se Dung ruled with an iron fist, along with his little book called *The Sayings of Mao* which became the bible of the people who were officially atheist. Millions were killed as they set about making a "utopia" from the nation that had been. Christianity still was not open, and no one could preach on the streets without arrest and harsh treatment. Churches that exist are required to register with the government and what is said is regulated by the state. Even we were required to be less than open with what we could talk about, although private conversations could be conducted without any problems. Most Christian churches growing in China are in homes, House Churches, they are called. Watchman Nee and those who followed him made personal relationship with Christ primary in their teachings which helped to expand the number of Christians in China estimated at over three hundred million and growing.

We were careful not to speak against the government, but we did take "prayer walks" and prayed specifically for government offices. I liked to stop by the outside perimeter of the Communist Party complex and pray for those in the party, especially the ones who were influenced by the house churches. I would pray specifically for the guard at the entrance to the compound. I walked a lot and enjoyed walking, but I prayed a lot that God would continue to bless His work in this vast nation.

The downtown area of our city was very modern and sported two McDonald's restaurants, a Kentucky Fried Chicken and a Dairy Queen. We didn't lack for a taste of America. Derek discovered a massage therapy clinic and recommended we go there. A full body massage cost roughly eight US dollars. I thought about this. Sometimes massage parlors have not been an endeavor Christians should be involved in and I didn't want to be sidetracked into anything like that. After several of the others had gone, I decided to try it. I was sore from all the walking and went to experience a massage for the first time in my life. I did, and it did what I hoped it would. From my feet to my head I was pounded, rubbed and relaxed. There were no innuendos or anything other than what was advertised. I went back several times during our stay. I have not had the pleasure since.

Eating was pretty good. Except for chicken feet at breakfast, all other meals we had were excellent in my opinion. I even found a grocery store that had fresh green chile—like the New Mexico kind, only big, plump and hot. Preparation of chile in China was not like Mexican food, but rather used in salads or other ways. I took several of them to the hotel with me. Several restaurants stood out as excellent, including one that featured a Mongolian grill. Charcoal was lighted in the middle of the table and a curved screen was placed over that. We were brought various pieces of raw meat: pork, beef and chicken that were cooked over the grill in the table. Other items were added, and we ate well.

At another restaurant we entered, there wasn't a table large enough to seat our group, which was about fifteen. They saw us walk in and motioned for us to stay. Two waiters rolled out a round table approximately 9 feet in diameter and placed it on a stand which held it. We ordered from the menu and they brought out the food in large quantities, placing them on lazy susans which we wheeled around to fill our plates. Rice, chicken, all kinds of meats, vegetables were displayed.

One night, three of the girls with us came back with another delicacy. Roasted scorpions. They were eager to show off and waited until cameras were pointed at them to place the strange concoction in their mouths. They chewed them and afterward remarked how good they tasted. I'm guessing the stinger on the end of the tail had been removed. I don't remember them getting more scorpions to eat any other time.

We had to get used to "squatty potties" which were mostly what we found outside the hotel. There were no seats to sit on, one squatted to do one's business. Often the restrooms were more than the nose could bear, even at the school we were teaching at. I usually waited to do what I had to do after I got back to the hotel. Sometimes it wasn't possible, but mostly I was able to judge the timing.

We were offered the opportunity to travel to the Grasslands of Inner Mongolia and our van took us through the countryside, much of it arid like many parts of New Mexico. As we went up in elevation, the grass got greener, but at one rest stop where we were to relieve ourselves, the stench was enough to gag a maggot, or make a vulture puke. It was awful! I'm glad I only had to make a "quickie" because I got sick to my stomach. We began to see wind generators first one, then many. They provided much of the electricity for the local region and the city we were in prided itself in being the "City of Lights." This was the ancient land of Genghis Khan, modern version.

Arriving at our destination, we were greeted by Mongolian people dressed in native clothing who performed a ritual with a fermented drink, *airag*, made from horse milk, not yak milk. In fact, I never saw a yak anywhere. We were to dip our finger in the liquid, splash some here, splash some there and drink some if we so desired. None of us "so desired." We were escorted to solidly built yurts, which, when constructed of animal skins and sticks look much like the Navajo hogans that are part of the culture of the people on the Reservation that straddles New Mexico, Colorado, Arizona and Utah. In fact, I found many of the features and customs similar to the Native American tribe.

The solid yurts were a place we could lie down and rest and we did. We discovered that the domed roof conducted sounds from one side of the structure to the other. At about 30 feet in diameter this became great sport for the kids—I enjoyed it as well. It was as if we could whisper into another person's ear from 30 feet away. We were prepared to stay the night, but plans changed later in the day. Most of the kids found the place "boring" and elected to travel back to our hotel in the city.

The noon meal was served in the restaurant in the middle of the compound and we were entertained by a group of singers who danced in beautiful traditional dress. One of the girls, Megan, had stomach problems and was unable to eat. She looked as miserable as she felt. She later became the sister-in-law to Derek Mitchell who some time later went to seminary and is now on staff at Mesilla Park Community Church as pastor of community groups.

That afternoon we were invited to ride horses to a more traditional yurt to engage in a traditional tea ceremony. We weren't allowed to control our own horse, it was led by a person by the bridle. As we approached the area at some distance from the compound, we got off our horses and presented with an opportunity to buy some of the trinkets that were offered to take back with us. I didn't buy anything, since I saw nothing I would want to take back.

The floor of the yurt was dirt covered by a rug. Those who participated in the tea ceremony sat on the floor and the tea was sipped as our guide described the significance. We were a long distance from "civilization" and the Grasslands were vast. I could envision Genghis Khan and his bunch of warriors coming over the green slopes headed for another victory. After we returned to the compound the decision was made to go back to the hotel.

In the city we saw many instances of construction, some of it in preparation for the Beijing Olympics in 2008, other buildings were being raised so something else could be built in its place. A row of buildings across the street from our hotel was raised right before our eyes. By the end of our stay, they were gone. Much of the labor by sledge hammer, other work by mechanized tools. These folks were serious about changing their surroundings.

One section of the city was inhabited by the Hui Muslims and the architecture reflected this influence. Meat markets owned by Muslims had a sign that the products were *halal* and these markets were accepted as being a better supplier of good meat products, even by other Chinese people. Often we would grab a snack from a street vendor, mainly looking for those whose products had just been taken off the grill. Only

Megan came down with any stomach problems on the trip. I made the trip without gastric incident; however, I have had much experience with foreign cuisine and probably have some immunity. One Chinese man who spoke English fairly well decided he would hang with us for a while and we got to know him. He wanted to be called Peter and we shared our faith in Jesus with him. He seemed interested but declined to really accept Christ as Savior. That was the experience we had with many of the people there. Some of the students said they had more faith in Genghis Kahn and still venerated him.

Peter joined us as we went to some of the finer eating establishments in the city, McDonalds being one of them.

Most afternoons were given to exploring the city. I found the Museum of Natural History that had dinosaur bones and other artifacts on display. Some of our group went to other sections of the city, but I was the only one who wanted to see "old stuff."

Another discovery was made: there was a Christian book store in the city. It didn't sell Bibles, but many Christian books could be

purchased that had a lot of Bible teaching in them. One lady brought out a copy of Rick Warren's *Purpose Driven Life* in Chinese. My picture was taken with her and the copy of the book. I emailed the photo to Saddleback. One of my objectives on the trip was to bring a draft copy of the Celebrate Recovery materials in Chinese to the missionaries and to tell them to get ready as the program would be coming into the country. It does. Many Chinese Christians living in the US take copies of CR materials with them when they visit. We know it is being used now in China.

We were nearing the end of our time in Inner Mongolia and getting ready to return to Beijing. We went to the airline office to pick up our boarding passes and also asked for the boarding passes to get us from Beijing to the US. We were given the first set of boarding passes but were told we would not get the others until we got to Beijing. There was a problem. Not knowing what that was we flew Air China back to Beijing and checked at the airport. They also said there was a problem and we should come back later. We did. The problem, we were informed, was that not enough had been paid for the tickets when we bought them. How much more would we have to pay? The answer stunned us: Twenty-three thousand dollars! We were flabbergasted. We had to pay that much if we wanted to return home. It was the beginning of the weekend in the US, so we called the US Embassy in Beijing and explained the problem. They wanted to talk to the airline officials, the airline officials didn't want to talk to them. We argued with them, they were adamant. We even noticed some of the Chinese passengers were having arguments with the airline for one reason or another. One man tried to jump the counter he was so angry.

Monday came, and we notified Lynette Muncrief, the administrative assistant at Mesilla Park Church. She contacted the American Automobile Association office where we had purchased our tickets. We aren't sure what arrangements were made, but we finally got our boarding passes to fly home. I suspect Triple A had to ante up the difference.

A couple more days in Beijing gave us opportunity to go places that are tourist attractions: The Grasslands were a little boring to our group, but the Great Wall of China was very interesting, and we enjoyed going up about a quarter of a mile or so. At that point a sign advertised a "Hero Card" that could be purchased for a few dollars which would sport a picture and the information that the bearer had traversed the Wall, at least to that point. Another sign, in English warned visitors: "Speaking cellphone is strictly prohibited when thunderstorm." It was understood, but probably written by the same person who gives directions to assemble items purchased in the US that were made in China.

We also went to a silk factory, well, at least a "demonstration factory." The process of making items from the cocoons of silk worms was demonstrated which gave the visitor an appreciation for the process. The finale was the presentation of those items that had been made from silk. I bought a comforter that had been filled with silk and a couple of pillow cases made from the cloth to bring home.

The most important part of the Beijing tour was Tiananmen Square and the Forbidden City. We stood on the spot that the unknown person stood on in 1989, when the Chinese military put down a protest by force. The man, known only as "Tank Man" stood in front of a tank and repeatedly shifted his position to block the tank's advance. The incident was filmed and shown worldwide.

As we walked under the picture of Mao and entered the Forbidden City, our guide, holding an umbrella and talking through a megaphone explained what we were seeing. The complex served as the home of emperors and their households as well as the ceremonial and political center of Chinese government for almost 500 years until 1912. Millions of visitors tour every year and until recently were greeted at the end by a Starbucks. We ate our last couple of meals at "American" styled restaurants, one of them the Hard Rock Café and the other at Peter's Tex-Mex where we ate what appeared to be enchiladas but tasted like something else. Good, but not like home.

Returning on the airliner was another experience. We got our boarding passes and the issue of not paying enough was cleared up, but after backing away from the gate we were informed that a storm was approaching and that we would have to wait until it passed to continue on. The storm lasted about three hours, pouring rain down and rocking the airliner with heavy winds. We ate one meal while waiting for the storm to end and, when it subsided, we again began to back away, but were stopped with the admonition that we would have to wait until a plane could be removed from the runway that had lost a wheel. That took another four hours. We had another meal on the tarmac before going into the air. This made the trip back to San Francisco on the Air China airliner more than 19 hours. We were ready to deplane… Thankful to be back in the "good ole' US of A."

My long-distance travel was not ended. In 2007 I was invited to join a team from Saddleback to present CRI training in Kenya, leaving Los Angeles on August 20 after the Summit that year.

We flew out of LAX overnight to Amsterdam, Netherlands, on a Delta flight and had a layover there early in the morning. My impression of the terminal was that I was in a United States facility. Almost everything was in English even though most of the workers there were Dutch. The only difference was that all prices were in euros, but dollars were good. Change was given back in euros.

The flight from Amsterdam to Nairobi was on a KLM Royal Dutch airliner. It was dark when we landed at Jomo Kenyatta International Airport. I was tired of sitting in the airplane and happy to be on the ground. We were met at the airport by a driver Jana had arranged to meet us and take us to the Methodist Guest House where we were able to sleep for a while before being awakened at 5:30 a.m., given breakfast and taken to the airport for a short flight from Nairobi to Eldoret and then driven in a car to Kitale. The road from Eldoret was extremely rough and I wondered how the trip would have been had we not been flown as far as we did.

The highway often had pits instead of potholes. Our driver pointed out where a person had been killed the night before, being run over. As we traveled we saw many maize fields (we call them cornfields) traveling through the small villages. The fields were reddish in color for the most part. Kenya was strongly influenced by Great Britain and drives on the left lane of highways. I silently felt happy we had a driver who was used to these roads and that I was not the driver. He was congenial and talked nearly the entire trip.

We arrived in Kitale at midday and were taken to the hotel located on a golf course. The presence of a golf course in this small, rural town of western Kenya seemed out of place. There were few who were actually playing the game and monkeys were all over the place. I wondered if monkeys playing with the balls were any excuse for a poor score on the part of a player. I'm sure there were local rules for "mulligans."

The food at the hotel was good. Our rooms were acceptable, but the showers were, in my opinion, a little dangerous. Heating water in many places in the world is not as easy as in the United States and heating elements are placed on the shower heads hooked to a power source so that only that water used for the shower is heated. What made it dangerous, in my mind was the uncovered wires that, if touched, could electrocute the person in the shower since the voltage was higher than in the US at 220 volts. I had no reason to reach up and touch the connection, so I didn't. Joe Clark and I were rooming together and got to know each other over the three weeks we were in Kenya.

Our first encounter with people at Kitale began at Deliverance Church that had in bold lettering, "Purpose Driven" on the front. It was a compound where some people lived, a school had been built, and there were happy kids that seemed very anxious to get to know us. Jana had been here before and was greeted as an old friend by everyone. The church and school were very important to the community and sheltered many of the children who had no parents. The AIDS epidemic has decimated much of the population of many nations on the African continent, leaving children orphans. As street orphans they were fair game for all kinds of abuse, the greatest of which was an activity called "huffing." Glue with toluene as a component that caused a "high" and euphoria that is addictive. The manufacturers had been asked to put within the substance a deterrent that would repel one from sniffing the glue, but they refused to do so based on "economic" reasons. The main reason is that not so much of the glue would be purchased if people were not buying it for this purpose.

Back at the hotel, we found that some of the buildings near the golf course were old slave quarters where African people captured other Africans to sell them to slave traders who would take them to America and other places where slaves were used. This dampened my opinion of the historical value of the place. The restaurant had a veranda overlooking the golf course and westward toward Mt. Elgon that straddled the countries of Kenya and Uganda. I took a beautiful picture of the sunset as it filtered through the clouds as the sun sank behind the mountain. We were told that a tribal war was still being fought in that area, but we saw no evidence of any conflict. Kitale was peaceful and friendly.

One morning we got up early and took a walk around the golf course, watching the monkeys scurrying from tree to tree and sneaking into a maize field that bordered the fairways to steal the ears of corn. It was beautiful, a little cool, but pleasant. I had always thought that anywhere in Africa it was steamy hot all the time. It is amazing how movies affect your mind and give stereotypes to people and places. This changed my whole opinion of this beautiful place on our planet earth. We were near the equator, but it was not hot, even though we were in the latter part of August. Kitale was just north of the equator, Nairobi just south. Both were a little cool in the morning. Most of Kenya is high in elevation, Kitale was a little more than six thousand feet and Nairobi just under.

We visited with a nurse, Sister Frieda, who was the only medically trained person in that area. As a nurse, she performed the duties that a physician would have elsewhere. She was born into very poor conditions but had friends who went to school who would let her study with them. Having no formal education, only reading the books of her friends, she was urged to take the entrance examination to enter a university in Kenya and she was accepted. Becoming a nurse was her dream and God used it for His glory. She, a black woman, married a white man from Uganda and they had been married for many years when I met them.

Her husband was a bit of a farmer and grew a variety of produce to help with the expenses of the clinic. He had a field of pineapple, a large stand of bananas, and grew coffee beans. Saddleback Church helped equip the clinic and Sister Frieda was having rooms built so she could train nurses at the clinic. As they invited us in for lunch, we were delighted to do so as we were in the presence of people who loved Christ and who had dedicated their lives in serving others in His name. The meal was delicious, and we chased it down with finger bananas, thusly named because they were approximately as long as a person's finger.

Sister Frieda said she triaged as many as a thousand patients a day, using those she had trained to help her. The clinic had equipment for dental work as well as most medical examinations, but not much in the way of medical equipment we are used to in Western countries. At noontime local children lined up to get a meal, maybe the only one they would have all day, and Sister Frieda reminded them to wash their hands before eating, most of them complying with a smile.

I was impressed by how many smiles I saw everywhere. These people were very poor compared to our standards, but for the most part, they were happy. The food they were eating was mainly rice and something else, I couldn't tell what, but they ate it with relish… and mostly clean hands.

We toured the grounds; the quarters being constructed for the nursing students a particular place of pride. Pineapples in the field and coffee beans on the plants were displayed and the process to turn the produce into funds for the clinic were described with a great amount

of satisfaction. The next day we drove to the prison, sections for both men and women were in the same compound. A Christian chapel and a Muslim mosque were on the grounds, but neither were being used during our visit. Entering the prison itself we met Abraham, the Christian Chaplain, who took us around and translated for me as I told the men in the yard about Celebrate Recovery. They stood around, in a variety of clothing, no uniforms, with two of the prisoners sitting in a tree on a limb watching the proceedings. I thought of Zacchaeus in the Bible sitting in a tree watching as Jesus spoke below. I was not Jesus, but I saw how that situation happened, or at least as I perceived it. It was enlightening, at least to me. I don't know how much the prisoners learned. None of them invited us to eat with them.

Going inside, we saw the dormitories where the inmates lived. There were no toilets or beds. They slept on mats on the floor and the "toilet" was a hole in the ground, with pipes leading to a… well, I am assuming… a septic pit below. Since there was no water in the prison, it had to be hauled from elsewhere, mainly in washtubs with handles welded on them carried by prisoners. A bit of water was poured down the toilet hole after the stench got so bad it was needed. An engineer had been working on getting a well dug and we met him and his wife at the clinic. They too were from Saddleback.

We went into the room where Celebrate Recovery met and heard from the inmates how CR was helping them. Over a hundred men were already participating in Celebrate Recovery in Kitale. Since they had no books, a chalk board was used to write the questions found in the participant guides. They would copy the questions and answer them, coming to their groups prepared to share their responses with each other.

On the women's side, some of them had their children with them and they also were doing CR in their unit. The guards were friendly, as were the women in the prison. It was not in the least part threatening. Linda, Jana, Joe and I felt very much at home with these people, even if they were felons in another country. As a former warden, I didn't think the security was as tight as we are used to in the United States, but nonetheless there was order and, perhaps a more humane attitude toward the incarcerated.

Returning to Nairobi, we were again at the Methodist Guest House. The accommodations were adequate, but not overly comfortable. The food in the restaurant was good, but the meat was sometimes tough.

One morning as we were eating, there were some other Americans there and we began to learn something about them.

Several of the men were Anglicans who had split off from the Episcopal Church in America since an openly gay priest had been consecrated as a bishop in the church, violating their understanding of Scripture. Because they were opposed to the legitimacy of gay leadership based on biblical grounds, they were seeking to be consecrated under African archbishops who also were not open to this kind of behavior in the church. One of them was from Virginia and knew my cousin, Vance, and his wife Patti, members of a church that was caught in the struggle. He was to be consecrated under a Ugandan archbishop and would head their faction of the split. I personally prayed for the man, John Guernsey, who also prayed for me and for our mission to the prisons in Kenya and that the country would more completely utilize Celebrate Recovery in the prisons.

Our first day of training at the West Nairobi Prison began with a formal visit to the office of the prison warden, a very tall woman who was all business. Dressed in a green uniform, she had a military manner that commanded respect, which we were there to do. She greeted us and motioned for us to sit. We had brought copies of all the Celebrate Recovery materials that were used in the program and gave them to her which she cursorily inspected. We explained how our training would be conducted, although this had been worked out in advance by Jana. This was the formal beginning of the training week and required this customary introduction and respect for the office of warden. I thought how our wardens were treated in the United States and selfishly wished this could rub off on our sometimes abrupt and rude treatment of people and positions in America. She thanked us for our willingness to provide such training and assured us that the program would be appreciated.

On to the conference room where we were to meet with those who had come from all over Kenya and as far away as Rwanda. The two who came from Rwanda had to travel by automobile over very poor roads taking over a twenty-four-hour period. The chaplain spoke Swahili and French, but no English. His companion spoke Swahili and English. Most of those from Kenya spoke Swahili and English, so everyone was able to understand. Our Swahili-French speaker had the English that we conducted the classes in translated to him as we went along. Rick Warren had already had a great influence in Rwanda through a relationship initiated by President Paul Kagame. Kagame wanted his broken nation to be based on the principles of "Purpose Driven," both Church and Life.

About 60 prison chaplains and others attended the 5 days of training in Nairobi representing 10 prisons in addition to the prison

commissioner's staff. CR was growing and helping people from across Kenya, Uganda and Sudan. Jana O'Guin, who led our team had been working with CR in these countries and had official status in the Kenyan prisons.

The week of training went smoothly. Our sessions began with singing like I have never sung before. Africans can sing! They can also jump as they sing, and they did. After singing we had training on understanding the CR model and its application to prisons.

Both at mid-morning and mid-afternoon it was time for chai. They mixed tea and milk with sugar, placing it in a large dispensing canister and provided varieties of bread that for all intents and purposes looked and tasted like tortillas and sopaipillas served with New Mexican food.

The flat bread is called chapati and the fried bread mandazi. These were "my people," although there was no chile in their food.

We formed groups to give them practice with open-share and step study experience and many of them shared from their own brokenness and sinful attitudes that they previously had been reluctant to share elsewhere; abuse, alcohol use, violence, broken homes and families. Most of the groups met outside on a grassy area. The prison was located within the city of Nairobi and traffic could be heard in the distance, but the nearby traffic was not a problem. I realized that their issues were no different than those experienced elsewhere. Some men were always in their best suit and tie, others more casual. We were always casual.

Daily we were driven from the Methodist Guest House to the prison and back by a driver who was skillful in handling the sometimes-chaotic local traffic. He would point out various buildings or areas of the city or the slums and showing us many modern conveniences, just as in any city. There are vast stretches of densely populated shanty towns, most of which are constructed of poles holding up corrugated roofing tin or whatever they can find to help keep the weather out. More than half of Nairobi's population live in these slums. Those who live there struggle to find just the necessities. Clean water is hard to come by and employment even harder. HIV and AIDS among the people is rampant

Almost a quarter of the four million population live in an area called Mathare. Many come in search of jobs or a better life, leaving the rural, agriculture-based life they had once known. There are no jobs and when the migrants run out of money they end up in the slums. When they find no other way to live, they come to accept this as their way of life, living from hand to mouth. They learn to scavenge for what they eat, and life becomes routine. With no electricity, running water or sewers, the place has a horrible stench. In order to get drinking water some have learned to tap into the city water supply and sell water by the plastic jug. It is illegal, but it is done without punishment.

Once becoming infected with HIV or AIDS the average life span of an adult is five years. No medical attention can be given to them, there is not enough to go around. Amazingly most children are born free of the infection and those that are infected usually die within months of childbirth. With the high rate of death of the parents who die of AIDS, there are thousands of orphaned children living in the slums. Many live with the oldest child, some as young as perhaps 10 years old, who take on the parental responsibility for their siblings. There are no beds, little furniture and they sleep on cardboard or mats they have found.

Those who are lucky enough to find work are usually paid $1.00 to $1.50 per day. Housing, such as it is, costs $5 to $10 per month to rent. The stench is horrendous, mainly because of human waste. Slum inhabitants deposit their waste into plastic bags when they can and throw them either into the ditch in the alley or the ink-black Nairobi River which runs through the middle of the slum. The bags have earned the nickname of "flying toilets." Even as bad as this is, farm animals, including pigs, cows, chickens and goats, also leave their droppings adding to the smell. Most cooking is done by burning wood charcoal. Somehow this helps ameliorate some of the smells that are more objectionable.

Seeing this kind of poverty overwhelms the Christian compassion in me that says: "Something must be done." But I am at a loss as to how to help. Some are trying and work among the people, but the task is more than anyone, including the government, can overcome. Another thought crosses my mind: "This is only one city in one country, there are thousands of cities in hundreds of countries that endure the same or worse conditions." I vowed to do what I can, but it isn't much. I thought about them as I swam in the pool at the Guest House. The water was a little cool, but it was water and many in this city had to do whatever was necessary to get even this simple need for their lives.

Graduation day came for those in the CR training and we had not expected the pomp that went with it. The Warden showed up and presented the certificates to the participants. As each of them came forward they came to attention, marched up to the Warden with a foot-stomping march step, bowed their heads and held out their right hand which was placed on their left. An act of respect. The graduation document was handed to the graduate who promptly stood at attention, about-faced and marched back into the group and the next graduate did the same until all had been graduated. We celebrated with more chai and bread.

Jana had planned a couple of days in the Masai Mara after we finished the CR training. How could we come to this part of Africa and not see the animals? Nearby in Nairobi we had visited an elephant sanctuary where orphaned elephants were taken when their mothers were killed or unable to care for them. We visited the park where this was located and saw baby elephants being tended by caretakers who even got down on the ground and rolled around with them. The ground was a reddish color and the animals had taken on a reddish hue from the dust left on them. Baboons made themselves visible scampering around and hooting at the people. But we had not yet seen the northern end of the Serengeti Plains that flow through Kenya and Tanzania. This would be the grand finale of our trip to Africa.

Our guides picked us up early in the morning at the Guest House and placed our luggage on board for the trip to Keekorok Lodge, our base for our visit to the Masai Mara. As we drove along, the highways became less smooth and in places pretty rough. Some work had been done on the roadways, but in order to keep traffic off the shoulders, rocks had been placed on them. At one point our guides stopped at a lookout and commented on the topography of the region. Below us was the Great Rift Valley that had extensions that went all the way north to the Jordan Valley and south through East Africa to Mozambique. The Masai Mara was along the Rift and we descended toward it as we travelled along.

At one point we could see giraffes running in the distance. That and communications towers that reminded us that we were, after all, in the twenty-first century. We traveled through small villages and past people walking from place to place. As we entered the National Park, more animals could be seen and as we pulled up into the lodge compound we had to pass water buffalo and hyenas who watched our arrival. We were checked into our rooms, Joe Clark and I in one room, and Jana and Linda Messner in the other. A cursory reminder was made that we should not leave our doors unlocked since the monkeys were curious and would visit with malicious intent… We would find out later what that meant.

We arrived in the late afternoon and before eating dinner we decided to walk along a plank walkway toward a pond. As we approached a shack built at the end of the walkway, we could see something in the water. Several hippopotamuses (or is it hippopotami?) were in the pond with their heads above water. They would snort and twirl their ears, looking at us without a lot of curiosity. I had seen hippos in zoos, but never in places that weren't contained. These guys weren't contained; they could go anywhere they wanted.

From time to time we could see monkeys scurrying around the ground and jumping to and from the trees in the compound. There were no fences or other barriers to prevent the animals from coming close to the lodge and we felt we were in the zoo, they were the ones who watched us with curious eyes. We ate dinner in the restaurant at the lodge, the food was good and the company pleasant.

The next morning, we went for a "game drive." This is the best way for a safari to take place. No animals are killed, they are only "shot" from cameras and the pictures taken home as reminders of the wonderful time spent in the Masai Mara. As we were driven along the sometimes-rutty roads in our Toyota vans, we were shown that the top popped up and was hinged so that about a foot of space was available to observe the animals without getting dangerously close to them and not having to look at them through glass.

One of our guides, Paul, had been a game warden in the Masai Mara and was very familiar with the area and the best places to watch the various animals from. He would drive off the road where we could get up close to see lions eating the remains of a wildebeest or some unlucky gazelle. We saw a leopard sleeping in a tree with a gazelle carcass cached in the fork of a limb below, and he drove us up to the bank of the Mara River to an excellent viewpoint to see the wildebeests gathering up on an embankment ready to cross the muddy water below that they knew crocodiles and hippos were waiting in. The hippos wouldn't eat them, but they provided a barrier that was helpful to the amphibious gluttons that were mainly unseen. Everywhere there were vultures and storks that picked the carcasses clean after other animals had had their fill, even sitting on dead wildebeests in the river.

As the herd gathered, you could almost see their courage wane and then flow and wane again. When would they cross? Only as their numbers grew would they attempt to get from one side of the river to the other. Finally, the rush began and they all plummeted down the bank into the water, many of them doing endos over the others. Occasionally we could see the rushing animals, one by one, being pulled into the water and disappear for a time. Paul told us that those that were pulled under by the crocs would be wounded. They were able to crawl up on the opposite bank but couldn't make it up the hill with the others. The amphibians had their meal later at their leisure after the herd had dissipated. Several of the wounded horned animals were seen later as the crocodiles licked their chops in anticipation of the meal ahead. There were so many wildebeests killed that not all of them were eaten by the crocodiles, and they floated belly-up in eddies and just off the banks.

As we waited for the herd to cross we saw monkeys scurrying around acting as if they were enjoying the spectacle. I may be wrong, but again It occurred to me that we were the animals in the zoo and they were the spectators. Monkeys are curious animals. I mentioned that we were warned to keep our doors locked in our rooms. Well, that afternoon we had gone back to the lodge for lunch and after eating, it was suggested we take a nap. I don't usually nap during the daytime, but since everyone else was sure this was a good activity, I went with Joe to our room and we pulled the curtain closed around the door and windows. The door was not quite shut, but I didn't think we would be bothered.

After a few minutes of laying down, the curtain began to move. *A puff of wind*, I thought. It moved again—and in bounded a monkey that sat on our dresser top! I raised up, the monkey looked at me, I looked at the monkey and he scurried out under the curtain. Well, I have never been surer of good advice as I was at that moment. Yes, check your doors. The monkeys are curious, and they *will* come into your room if you give them a slight opening to do so. I wonder who was the more surprised, the monkey or me.

That afternoon Joe and I went out on the patio for a time to reflect and look at the wonder around us. Joe was sitting under an umbrella and it began to rain. It seemed he didn't notice. I went into the lobby of the lodge. He kept writing in his journal as if nothing was happening around him. Joe had learned to journal and enjoyed doing so. This was something I always thought I should do, but never had the discipline to sit down and do consistently.

Joe's story appears in the book by John Baker, *Life's Healing Choices.* He had a chaotic childhood, alcohol and bipolar disorder inflicted his parents, his father deserted the family when Joe was in kindergarten, his mother had five marriages and many boyfriends, he was in seventeen different schools and lived in twenty-eight places by the time he graduated high school. His mother often was either absent, hospitalized, or confined to her room because of the depression. Joe blamed himself for his abandonment and his mother's disorder.

In 1976, his little sister, Jody, drowned in a canoeing accident, he blamed himself for not being able to save her. He also blamed God, wondering how He could have let this happen. He tried to deal with his feelings with alcohol and drugs using them to run from his emotional pain. Going into the Navy, he continued the partying and finally received an "other than honorable" discharge. He continued all these poor choices until after a lot of drugs and sex and going from place to place he discovered he, along with his mom, also had depression, his was getting worse.

In 1994 he walked into his first Celebrate Recovery and began attending Saddleback Church, but all of this only sporadically. Finally, he was diagnosed with Hodgkin's Disease and after battling with this, he hit his bottom and was ready to get serious about dealing with the things in his life that had taken its toll on his body and mind. After realizing that Christ came to do great work in him, he began to do the hard work of letting God heal him. He has given himself to help many people through Celebrate Recovery and is presently the National Director of Celebrate Recovery Native Nations, taking the message of healing to tribes and native people throughout the United States. This is the kind of person who has helped me understand what it is to be a servant of the Lord Jesus Christ.

I was on a team that had battled many life's issues, Jana who had come from an abusive family; Linda, who had been a codependent married to an alcoholic, and me, with my own issues that were still being worked on. I began to figure out that the only ones who are useable are those who have had major struggles. I was currently struggling with one of my own that would show up in ways I didn't want to have happen. But not yet. I still had some lessons to learn that wouldn't be pleasant.

We made a game drive that evening and again the next morning. Much of the wildlife we saw did what they were designed to do: eat, mate and go about the issues of life God had given them. We saw every kind of animal in that part of Africa except rhinoceroses. The only one we saw was in Nairobi at the elephant sanctuary and it was blind and, in a cage, separated from the other animals.

What a wonderful end to a marvelous time in Kenya. I had my picture taken by Paul standing on the marker of the boundary between Kenya and Tanzania with my *Mzungu* t-shirt shirt on. The word *Mzungu* is a bantu word that has been used to describe white people, much like the word *gringo* in Spanish. It originally meant someone who traveled around a lot. I was in both countries at the same time, so I guess I fit the description—and I was white. Only a dirt road leads to the spot. A driver for some of the other groups joked that he was the customs agent for Tanzania and he would collect our visa fee. Everyone had a laugh at this, and he didn't collect any money from anyone.

Later in the afternoon we were driven with our luggage to a landing strip to wait for an airplane to take us back to Nairobi. There were several Masai-dressed people who were there, but we were told by our guides that they really weren't from the Masai Tribe, they were from some other tribe, but most of the park visitors wouldn't know the difference. At the airstrip there was a tax-free store with a few items in it, the store was mainly a tin shack hastily erected.

After a time of waiting an airplane landed, but it wasn't ours. Ours arrived a few minutes later. The airstrip was dirt and the airplanes were four-engine turbo props that could land and take off in these conditions without problem. As we were getting ready to board the plane, our guides embraced us and told us we would be missed. They had tears in their eyes as they said good-bye, so we knew they meant it. We were met in Nairobi by another driver, the one who had originally picked us up and had been our driver in the city and taken to the Guest House for one more night's sleep before we headed homeward.

The next day, we boarded the KLM Royal Dutch Airliner at Jomo Kenyatta International Airport for the trip home. Again, we had a layover in Amsterdam and I boarded another airliner that would eventually take me to El Paso. The rest of the team went on to Los Angeles.

I loved the Celebrate Recovery Summits. They were celebrations of lives changed, relationships restored and the fellowship of people from not only the United States, but all over the world. My memories of those who have served and continue to serve in this ministry sustain me and I am elated when I get to see them again. One Summit will stand out in my mind maybe a little bit more because I was asked to be on the ordaining counsel for John Baker as he was ordained following the completion of seminary studies, most of them from my alma mater. Rick Warren was one of those who prayed for my friend along with me on the Saddleback stage. I never had a picture of this group, but it is stuck in my mind.

CHAPTER 16

GETTING A HANDLE ON MYSELF

Both of our mothers had come to live with us. First my mother, who was in her late eighties and had fallen and broken a hip which was later broken again as she went into church on a Sunday morning. In Albuquerque at the Methodist church she belonged to had merged with another church which was farther from her house. She really didn't want to leave Albuquerque, the city she had lived in since 1958 continuously and had lived in before this earlier in the 50's. Dad bought a house from a friend which at that time cost seven thousand dollars. He had done some add-ons, like making the carport a dining room and adding on another room in the back for a shop area. At one time he talked me into buying a hundred chicks to raise for eggs and to eat. I agreed, and we had chickens all over the back yard. There were some eggs, but when it came time to get them ready to eat, the task was not really to my liking since we had to hang them on a clothes line, cut their throats, let the blood drain, dip them in boiling water and pluck the feathers and finally to gut them and put them in plastic bags in a freezer. I couldn't eat chicken for months, not being able to get the smell out of my mind.

Dad had other agricultural interests as well. He always grew a garden and had several crabapple trees. We all ate from the garden and at one point there were so many crabapples that he bought a juice press and made apple juice. One interest, although not agricultural, was collecting rocks. He had agates and geodes and myriad other kinds of rocks all over the back yard and in a shed, which was not attached to the house. A rock polisher and a rock saw were among his many tools that were a part of the house on 57th Street NW in that city.

There were so many memories that Mom didn't want to part with by moving from Albuquerque. My brother, Keith, asked her to live with them in Grants and her objection was it was too high in elevation and she couldn't breathe very well there. But there was another objection, the biggest of all: She didn't want to leave because she was a great fan of the University of New Mexico Lobo basketball team. She listened to every game. If it was televised, she got the picture, but turned off the sound so she could listen to the play-by-play description on KOB-AM radio, with Mike Roberts doing the play-by-play. If she moved away so far, like to Las Cruces, she wouldn't be able to get the radio station because of the distance. That wasn't exactly true, but the signal faded in and out.

I finally convinced her that I could get the games through the internet and she could listen to them in Las Cruces without interruption. She needed help because at this point she was in a walker and unable to do most of the things she needed to do to cook and clean. Finally, she agreed to move to Las Cruces with us. It was a depressing, but necessary move for her to make, but to her credit, she did it and tried to find as much positive as she could by living in the southern part of the state. It was warmer in the winter, the elevation at about 4000 feet was about 1200 feet lower than Albuquerque. She went to church with us, but never joined. She was a Methodist, and we were Baptist. The only major difference in basic beliefs was the mode of baptism, although Methodists will baptize either way.

She was accepted by those in the church and she grew to love going to church with us. At first, she came in with a walker, but finally she had to resort to a wheel chair. I pushed Mom into and out of church with a lot of satisfaction. She was my Mom and I was proud of her. She never hinted that she would change her membership, even though the church had relaxed its membership rules to allow those "not immersed" to become members, but not be given a letter to another Baptist church if requested. We were able to get her a motorized scooter and she drove it—well pretty well. We did have scars on a couple of hallway walls and the kitchen appliances, but the day she showed up driving her new, red, power scooter to church she had all eyes on her.

Fern's mother was still in Farmington and we kept getting reports that she was not doing well. Fern's sister, Jeanette, tried to take care of her, but often she would be seen out along the roadway into where she lived cutting weeds—with a butcher knife. She had back and memory problems, was bent over anyway and this was not helping. We talked her into coming to Las Cruces as well and she finally relented without conditions.

The house we bought, a double-wide modular home with 5 bedrooms, was now being used to its fullest. Each mom had her own bedroom and, when we went anywhere we went in the minivan. I had a lift for the scooter mounted in the van and I could get both the scooter and a wheelchair in, with some difficulty, but hey! We could travel now. So both mothers went to church. Fern's mom, Clodell, whom everyone called, "Granny," was a Baptist, but our Baptist church was a lot different than hers. She got used to it and enjoyed going. Our music was louder, and we didn't sing from the hymnbook.

Mom died in 2007 after I got back from Africa. She wanted her memorial service to be held in Albuquerque at the church she had been a member of there. I didn't want to go through two memorial services, so we didn't have one in Las Cruces. She was cremated in Las Cruces and I purchased an urn to place her ashes in. My brother, Keith, was given the ashes which he now has. Mom was one of a kind. She came to love Jesus deeply as she grew older. She served her church faithfully and was loved by the people in the church. She had been a Christian for most of her life but had never really blossomed until she sought out and found a congregation that taught the Word and began to live it. Many of the churches we attended when I was growing up were liberal in theology and, while they taught "morality," there was little understanding of the Holy Spirit's work in the believer. There was no personal relationship with Christ. It was through her example that Dad also became a Christian and became active in the Methodist Church.

Mom's death was at our home in Las Cruces. She had been getting weaker and weaker and Hospice had been called in to help. Fern was an angel in taking care of Mom and the two loved each other. At night

Fern would check on Mom to see that she was all right. One night she woke me up and said she thought Mom had stopped breathing. I went into Mom's bedroom with Fern and we called Hospice to put in place the taking of her body to the funeral home. We knew this moment was coming, but it was still hard. Mom was ten days away from being ninety-four. She had a relationship with Jesus and went to be with Him forever. We will see her again.

Granny's health became worse and at one point she was in the hospital in Las Cruces after dislocating a shoulder. Her dementia was now even more pronounced and her stomach problems and back were always making her feel terrible. We needed to go to California to a meeting. Since there was nothing we could do since she was in the hospital and being cared for, and Jim was there to see after her while she was in the hospital, we decided to go, but notified Jeanette. Jeanette became indignant that we would go out of state while Granny was in the hospital, so she and her daughter came and took her out of the hospital against the advice of the doctors. Since Jeanette had Power of Attorney for her mother, we had no say in the matter and Granny went to live in Kirtland, near Farmington. The trip was difficult for Fern's mom and upsetting to us.

Jeanette had become Mormon after her daughter married an LDS man. Jeanette's husband, Stanley, had divorced her after he found another woman he wanted, and Jeanette had found solace in her new faith. None of the rest of the family were very happy with any of the events, Granny notwithstanding. But with that dose of reality, we let it go. Granny lived a few months longer and after a stay in the hospital in Farmington, went to be with Christ and my mom. We went to the funeral in Farmington at La Plata Baptist Church. The Mormon Church in Kirtland had a dinner for the family after the services were over.

Mormon people are generally good people and kind. The theology, however, takes people away from a real, intimate relationship with Christ and puts them into a religion full of legalism and fantasy scripture that has no basis in history or archeology and contradicts the Bible upon which it claims to have status. Jesus is not God incarnate and there is a propensity to incorporate Masonic rites into a temple ritual that seems "holy." I was one time asked by a Mormon missionary if I had prayed to ask God if the Book of Mormon was "Scripture." I told him I had. He seemed a little surprised because I don't think he had gotten that response before.

"Well, what did God tell you?" he asked.

"God told me that the Book of Mormon came from the same place as the Koran," I replied. "Someone read the Bible and thought they had a better idea and they used their imagination to come up with something different." The reply stunned him a little and he replied, "I had never heard that before." He walked on down the street. It is not my purpose here to argue against Mormonism, but I relate this because it has affected my family. There is a very great distinction between the LDS church and biblical Christianity. In Mormonism or any other religion, sometimes even in Christian denominations—even Baptists—man tries to please God through various human efforts by following a set of rules or precepts that are believed to be sufficient to reach the Almighty or whatever the goal may be. In Buddhism a deity is not even necessary in some sects. One finds "himself or herself" through contemplation. Some religions require drastic acts such as self-mutilation or in killing those whom they deem infidels. The major distinction is that in the Bible God seeks people through the person of Jesus Christ, redeems them, and through the inner working of the Holy Spirit of God the person is to become a servant like Jesus Himself with a personal relationship with Him.

That's what happened to me. The process began when I was twelve and went to the Billy Graham Crusade in Albuquerque. It was at that point I began to know He wanted me to surrender to Him. I was stubborn, and it took the better part of my life to learn and to begin to become what He designed me for. Sometimes I am too stubborn for my own good. Most of the time I ignored the direct leading God gives me. I have had a great education, a great start in the faith, and somehow found it difficult to discover where I fit in. Pastoring seemed to me to be the only thing that was worthy of a follower of Christ, but I felt out of place as I pursued it. I had a worldly bent to my personality and wanted to find acceptance with all people, sometimes doing what I knew wasn't right to be able to fit in. I wasn't a scholar, although I loved books and wanted to learn. I had a hard time memorizing things and putting them together in a coherent thought stream. I am disorganized preferring to have a "piling system," rather than a filing system that for me works somehow better. I am able to find things I have piled up—unless someone moves them. If I try to file things, I get them out of order and often just stick pieces of paper into whatever file is readily opened at the time.

In 2009 a problem that had plagued me earlier resurfaced to the point that I was arrested for drunk driving. I had been working on my son, James' yard and had some wine to drink. Way too much wine! I remember being pulled over by a Las Cruces police officer. He told me I had gone through stop signs and was weaving all over the road. I didn't argue. He gave me a breath test, I flunked. I was cuffed and put in the police car and taken to the Doña Ana County Detention Center where I was finger printed and allowed to make a call. I called James. I was then led to a cell with several other detainees, still under the influence. One of the other inmates looked at the document I had been given with my charges and dismissed it as nothing, throwing the paper on the floor. It was time for chow and I was given a tray which I didn't eat much of. Another inmate asked me if he could have it. I gladly gave it to him.

I had fought this issue off, but with my weight-loss surgery in 2005, my propensity to drink came back with a vengeance. Somehow with the surgery a genetic predisposition toward alcoholism is triggered in some people. I was one of them. This was a serious matter and I had not wanted to tell anyone. It became a matter of pride since I was an elder in my church, a co-founder of a prison ministry, the National Director of Celebrate Recovery Inside, a movement I had helped bring into existence along with the founder of Celebrate Recovery. Who does one talk to? What would they think of me? Well, I knew I needed to get honest. I needed to stop "teaching" CR and do the program for myself. I had helped get it started at Mesilla Park, it failed, I had tried to help St. Paul's United Methodist Church resurrect theirs, it failed, and now I was failing.

I had blundered into the same problem my Uncle Gene had fought for years in his own life and that Fern's dad had struggled with. I was in denial about my alcoholic state, reasoning that if Jesus turned water into wine at the Wedding Feast of Cana, and it was "good wine," then it must be okay. I also read in Deuteronomy 14:26 that an offering was to be made, but if the distance you were to take it was too great, "*you may use the money to buy any kind of food you want—cattle, sheep, goats, wine, or other alcoholic drink. Then feast there in the presence of the Lord your God and celebrate with your household.*" I wasn't exactly following the biblical direction, but that's how in my own mind I justified what I was doing. I was conveniently forgetting what Paul said in Ephesians 5:18 Don't *be drunk with wine, because that will ruin your life. Instead, be filled with the Holy Spirit.* I had to change this way of thinking.

My guts twisted themselves into knots as I picked up the telephone to call Pastor Dennis Diaz. I asked for a time to meet with him, not telling him the reason. I remained in turmoil. My heart pounded as I reached his office at the church. After hearing me out I expected a rebuke from my pastor. What I got was a blessing. I had offered to resign as an elder, and to confess to the whole church. He assured me I had been a pastor to him. That he loved and respected me regardless of the moral failure I was confessing. He prayed for me and told me I didn't need to resign at this point, but that I would have to tell the other elders what I had told him and let any decision proceed from that meeting.

Again, my stomach churned thinking about having to lay my sin before my brothers. The evening came when I opened up to them. They listened and asked questions and to a man they said they wanted me to remain as an elder. They all laid hands on me and prayed for my recovery. I didn't know that one of my brother elders in that room was experiencing the same issue.

I told Tom one evening as we were going to the prison for Crossings, and then I had to tell the inmates I was leading in a step study what I had done. Each time I expected judgment, but I received grace. As I got honest with the inmates, they listened and when I had finished, the comment was made, "Well, now, you're one of us." I guess I was. I too had been arrested and jailed. I would be on probation for a year and I had to equip my car with an Interlock and drive with an Interlock

License. I was now an official "criminal" although it was a misdemeanor and not a felony.

At one point, the warden, Lawrence Tafoya, called me and asked me about my driver's license being suspended. He told me I couldn't come out to the prison as a volunteer. I told him what had happened and that I had the special license, and he then told me I was still welcome as a volunteer since I was legally allowed to drive.

I learned a great lesson: Get pride out of the way so God's grace can flow through my life. I'm not proud of the drinking arrest, but it has opened my eyes to the problems related to addiction. Christians, even ones who are trying to please the Lord, can succumb to weaknesses and even become addicted to drugs, alcohol, or whatever, the same as non-Christians. I was shown that I must humble myself, get real, confess my sin, be prayed for and get healed. James 5:16 says, *"Therefore confess your sins to each other and pray for each other; so that you might be healed."* I could not have been healed without sucking it up and getting real with the people who mattered to me. I could not have been healed without the inmates in the step-study of Celebrate Recovery who held me accountable and accepted me. After all, I was a member of a church that had as its motto: Real People, Growing in Real Faith in Jesus Christ, and Meeting the Real Needs of Others. Why I couldn't get real with myself? I have figured it out. I'm still fighting the battle of the flesh. Paul, in his own life put it this way: *The trouble is with me, for I am all too human, a slave to sin. 15 I don't really understand myself, for I want to do what is right, but I don't do it. Instead, I do what I hate. 16 But if I know that what I am doing is wrong, this shows that I agree that the law is good. 17 So I am not the one doing wrong; it is sin living in me that does it.* (Romans 7:14-17 NLT)

CHAPTER 17

WHY DOES IT MATTER?

Learning to be real helps others along the way. Like my son, Paul. In 2010 it was discovered that he had been embezzling money from clients of a bookkeeping agency he was working for in Aztec, New Mexico. I went to see him just before he was arrested and I confessed to him the arrest I had for driving while intoxicated. He was stunned! He had never thought that his dad, a Christian, a retired warden, a leader in his church, one who had begun a ministry in prison with Celebrate Recovery and Crossings, a basically good person, could do such a thing. Well, none of us measure up to perfection, especially the perfection we would like others to perceive us with. Jesus remarked to the rich guy who came up to him to ask him a question, "Good Teacher, what must I do to inherit eternal life?" *"Why do you call me good?" Jesus asked. "Only God is truly good."* (Mark 10:17-18 NLT) None of us humans are truly good, we all have flaws, some folks hide them like I did, and I guess in some respects still do, but I'm working on it.

He said to me, "You've been talking about Celebrate Recovery, Let's talk." So we did. I explained to him how the program helps us with our hurts, habits and hang-ups. All of us have them, everyone needs to trust Jesus Christ to be our Savior and to be able to allow the Holy Spirit of God to release us from all of those character defects that keep us bound to our old nature, when we follow Him as our Lord, our Master. One of my symptoms had recently become alcohol to excess. Another was lying to people about it, including Fern. The deeper character defect was lodged in my identity. I didn't think I was worthy of being the person I was perceived to be. Well, I wasn't. But my new nature in Jesus Christ needed to come to the front and dislodge my old inferiority complex. I struggled with this issue and usually dealt with it by trying to make myself feel good. Alcohol could do that. Having other people like me could do that. Having a good reputation could do that, but that was not living an authentic new life in Christ. When I finally got real with myself, God and those I trusted and I began to heal inwardly. I told Paul he could too.

He told me that he was as addicted to stealing money as anyone could be to drugs, alcohol or anything else; he got a "rush" from taking the money, and, having been a correctional officer and knowing what prison was like, he planned to commit suicide if he was ever caught. I was the one who was now stunned! Two people stunned in the same conversation, him and me.

Thankfully a church less than two blocks from his house was beginning a Celebrate Recovery. My grandson, Andrew, was helping to get this started, so both he and his dad began working the program. I had made a trip up to Aztec a few weeks earlier to do the training for the church. Andrew and his wife, Sondra, at the request of Lorrie my daughter-in-law went over to be with him and his plans to commit suicide were relieved by their presence. Fern and I drove up to be with them for Thanksgiving and that is when we had our talk. It was at that point he gave his life to Jesus Christ and committed himself to whatever it took to serve Him.

Paul had a three-month stint in the San Juan County Detention Center because the bail was set so high none of us could pay it and he couldn't attend the local CR, so I sent him a Celebrate Recovery Bible. When he was released as the result of being accepted in a pretrial program, he volunteered as the cook for the weekly CR meetings and became very involved in the life of the church. When he went for sentencing after pleading guilty to the charges, he was hoping for probation, but the judge looked at the previous probation he had served for forgery and gave him seven years. It was a blow, but the judge could have given him a lot more time than that since there were many charges for both embezzlement and forgery. He was led out of the courtroom in handcuffs and tears. The pastor, Kevin Parker, spoke on his behalf as did I, which may have led to the reduced sentence. Kevin has since become the editor of the Baptist New Mexican newspaper.

My other son, James, the one who bailed me out of jail, the one who followed me in a corrections career and also retired as deputy warden at the same institution I retired from was never a bad person, but he was a "wild child." During his college years he worked as a male stripper and later as a bouncer in a night club in Albuquerque. Not pleasing to his parents. One night he came home from the night club with scratch marks across his face, a torn shirt and severely scuffed snake skin western boots he had just purchased. He had gotten into a scuffle with patrons as he was telling them to leave the premises. They took exception to his position as a bouncer and the altercation became physical. I asked him how much he was being paid for his efforts. At the time it was about six dollars an hour… My question to him was, "Well is it worth it?" He couldn't answer.

This son worked his way through the Corrections Department and retired from the same position I had held. He was happy in his retirement and was on a trip to Las Vegas, Nevada with friends when he began to feel pain in his chest. They called a taxi and got him to a hospital. He was having a heart attack. They put a stint in the ailing blood vessel and he called us letting us know what had happened. After listening to him and commiserating with him about his illness I asked him a question: "Has this opened your eyes to anything God is telling you?"

His answer surprised me. "Yes, I got to thinking about my relationship with God and I have started talking to Him. I told Him I wanted to be one of His." I was elated that this had begun in him something he had been missing. As a youngster he had said he was trusting Christ as Savior and I baptized him in the river when we were serving in Ojo Caliente. He had attended church until he was in his teens and then it was a struggle to get him to go.

When he returned to Las Cruces after the heart attack he began to attend church with us at the theater church we began as we were running out of room at Mesilla Park. We had gone to 4 services at the main campus and had no place else to go so we recorded the sermon during the Saturday evening service and took it to the Cineport 10 theater in the Mesilla Valley Mall. A praise team was recruited, and we began these services not knowing how they would be received. It was a big hit with people who most likely would not go to a church building and we began to have many people trust Christ through this ministry. James plugged into this theater church and is now working the "Hub," the welcome and information center.

James was also willing to go on a Walk to Emmaus, the same weekend program that had begun to change my life. From that he agreed to work with the Kairos Prison Ministry and was a weekend leader for one of the weekends. His life changed from a narcissistic bachelorhood to one of service to others. Christ had changed another in my family. My two sons, even though the events that brought them to Jesus were tragic, could have been more tragic, but God used the prison time and the heart attack to bring life to these sons. I started Bible studies with James and when Paul was paroled, we had our studies together. Something I should have been doing when they were younger.

Throughout the years since Celebrate Recovery Inside became more and more to be accepted, I have heard stories of those who have been in prison finding a way out through Jesus Christ and by working the steps and principles of Celebrate Recovery. Numerous times I have had people come up to me during workshops at CR Summits or one-day training conferences, look me in the eye and say through tears, "Thank you for getting CR started in prison. It saved my life," or something very similar. Now it was my own sons who were being changed.

We began to be aware of more people around us who needed a real relationship with Jesus Christ. Fern and I took a box of food to a neighbor living in a trailer next to us. The original owner had died, and his niece had taken the house over. She had two boys and had just had a third child, a girl. We knocked on the door and she opened it holding and feeding the infant. She was surprised that we had a gift for her and seemed somewhat puzzled.

We got to know her and her "significant other." They had been living together for a while, but the relationship wasn't a good one. She said it was surprising that we brought the box of food to their home. They were out of food and that was something they needed. Several times I saw them in arguments that led to physical blows. One day she came over with cuts and bruises and just wanted to talk. We invited her to attend our community group sessions and she came a few times and on one occasion she prayed to receive Christ. It began to make a difference, but we found out she was addicted to methamphetamine and couldn't get off it. I found this out after I had loaned her my Ford Ranger pickup truck and she banged into someone. She was also caught on camera speeding through an intersection and was sent a citation. I stopped lending her the vehicle but offered to take her where she needed to go.

One day I got a call from her from the hospital. She had overdosed. When I visited with her the first time she was unresponsive, and I couldn't wake her up. I returned and although she was groggy she recognized me, and I asked her a simple question: "Do you want to live?" I also said that if she didn't I wouldn't help her kill herself. She said she did and I was able to get her into a transition home. I had been working with some women in a home having sessions with them using the book by John Baker, *Life's Healing Choices* as well as other studies we use in the Crossings program. When we began the Celebrate Recovery program at Mesilla Park, the women also began to come from the transition home. Sometimes I would park my car and drive the van the home owned to CR. I wish I could say the outcome for Donna was a good one, but during her transition time she was arrested for a previous charge, jailed and relapsed. I visited with her in jail a few times, but I finally lost contact with her. I still pray for her, but I suspect she has either moved from the area or is no longer living. Not all things come out the way we would want them to and I know we serve a good God. The home moved to Deming, an hour's drive away and they came for several more months but stopped after the travel expense became too great.

As I look at those who attend our Celebrate Recovery program on Monday nights at Mesilla Park Community Church, I see some who have been court-ordered to be in a recovery program, I see some I have known in prison and helped them plug in and become leaders. I see some who have been in the Large Group session at the Las Cruces Gospel Rescue Mission come and become involved in step studies and move out into the community, from homelessness to acceptance, from despair to hope. I see those in our church who are willing to take the steps of Celebrate Recovery to get through the difficult things in their lives that keep God from helping them to see the purpose He has for them and begin to take leadership in not only CR, but the life of the church as well.

One man who began to attend CR several years ago from a city about an hour away came with a challenge. "Do you think CR can help me?" he asked. "I have felt abused by women, especially my ex-wife and I am a bitter man and I don't like women." We urged him to give it a try. At first he couldn't even speak the words he wanted to say, so in open-share groups he would pass. Finally, he asked if he could read what he had written. We assured him it would be accepted. So he read, telling about the bitterness in his life and that it had caused PTSD and fear. The more he shared, the more comfortable he became with the process. He got involved with a step study, completed it, began to become involved in the audio-visual ministry of the church, also attended a CR group on Friday nights at another church in town, all while driving over an hour from his home each time. He was introduced to CR by a group in California and after he had shared his testimony at MPCC, he took a trip, first to California to share his testimony with his friends there. Then he went to the East Coast, getting to reestablish relationships along the way. He now co-leads a step study group.

A young couple with two boys in tow showed up one Sunday morning and wanted to talk to someone; that became me since I am there during the morning hours to be of help to those asking for it. They were having difficulties financially and were about to lose the home they were renting. As I got to know them better, they weren't married, had only just met, were on probation and he was headed to court. I got John Pickett involved. John had recently retired as senior pastor of University Presbyterian Church and had begun a community program with partnerships with churches and local helping agencies. We talked to them about the possibility of buying the property which was up for sale and helping them to purchase it later.

Her problem was drugs as was his. I was in court with him as he was sentenced to a rehab program. They broke up. She began coming to church, Celebrate Recovery and appeared to be doing well until she got in with a group of drug addicts and dealers. She called me one day and said she had to move to Las Vegas, New Mexico to live with her grandmother. Could I help get some men to load her truck? I could, and I did. Several of the men from Mesilla Park came and loaded her up. One of the ladies from Celebrate Recovery also began working with her and trying to help her make better decisions.

After arriving in Las Vegas, she let us know that she had begun going to church at a Calvary Chapel there. She was doing well and had been off drugs. I encouraged her to touch base with the nearest Celebrate Recovery which was in Santa Fe and she did, but the program was very small, and she didn't find the help she needed. I am continuing to work with her to get help for her boys who are being placed in a program in Albuquerque. So far, she is off drugs and I am continuing to pray that her life stays on track and that Jesus is the one she will look to continue to help her.

God has used me to be of some help to the hurting and homeless. I began working at the Las Cruces Gospel Rescue Mission. At first, they didn't have a place for me to bring my equipment to do a CR program and the attendance was sporadic. I talked it over with the administration and they decided I needed to work with the "programmers" who lived there and helped with the various tasks that needed to be done. We discovered that Friday mornings was a good time for a Large Group meeting and I began to do a version that didn't include open-share groups since I only had an hour for the presentation. I offered to get step studies going and began one for men. Mary, a CR leader said she would lead a step study for women, but this did not work either. What does work, we found out is to continue the large group with a talk-back time at the end of it. Several have begun coming to CR at the church and have joined step studies there.

One man and his sister began to attend our Community group on Tuesday nights. He was an engineer working with a fire suppression company and his sister a fifth-grade teacher. They were quiet during our discussions but began to be more involved as time went along. She moved back to Alamogordo where she had another job and was closer to her family and a boyfriend. He continues with us and approximately a year ago began to become more serious about his faith. He joined

CR and said he had always struggled with an inferiority complex and a poor relationship with his mother. He has come more and more out of his shell and recently said he feels that God is calling him into ministry, as a Christian counselor and is seeking further studies to help him to become what Christ is calling him toward. He mentioned that he began thinking about this after one of the church's men's retreats (we never call them retreats—for us they are *advances*). I had spoken on self-image and becoming great in the eyes of God by becoming a servant. It touched him.

I love the diversity of Mesilla Park. The demographics of the valley are nearly a reflection of the church composition. We called an executive pastor from California, William Dossett, an African-American man who had a diverse church in the Bay Area. He was a great addition and, while a few blacks had been a part of our church, many more found it a welcoming atmosphere. William was a great counselor and a listener who helped direct those struggling into Celebrate Recovery and to begin other ministries like Griefshare and Divorce Care. We became more of a caring church and missed William when he left to be on staff at Venture Church in Los Gatos, California, pastored by Chip Ingram.

In 2014 I got an email invitation to attend the 10th Anniversary of Celebrate Recovery in Fortaleza, Brazil. I accepted. If I could get myself down there they would give me a place to stay and they had some things they wanted me to be involved in. I accepted the invitation and began to make plans to go to Brazil. I had studied Portuguese at the University, but I had not spoken the language since. The people inviting me, Nelson Massambani and his church, Igreja Central Batista in Fortaleza, had attended a Summit at Saddleback. They wanted more information about CR in prisons and I met with them separately in a stairwell in one of the Saddleback buildings.

My getting down there was a lesson in blunder and blessing. The blunder was that I had not considered the fact that I needed to get a visa before traveling to Brazil. I discovered my error on a Sunday morning before I was to leave the following Tuesday for the conference. A thought came into my mind to check out the requirements. I did and found out that the only place I could get a visa for Brazil in that short a time was to fly overnight to New York City. I called a company that specializes in getting this accomplished and they told me I had to be in their office the next morning at seven o'clock. I quickly called and got tickets on a flight that afternoon from El Paso, taking me through Phoenix, and I landed at JFK Airport at 6 a.m. A taxi got me to the office in time to get breakfast at a Dunkin Donuts shop a couple of doors down and I was finished just as the man I was to talk to unlocked and entered the office.

I presented him with my passport and the other documents along with a photo that would be used for the visa. He told me to come back at 4:30 in the afternoon and he should have it for me. The cost was over $500 in addition to the flight from El Paso to New York. I looked at my return ticket and discovered that the plane I was to fly out on would leave JFK at 4:20 and I told him. He put his hand on his head and said, "Let me think. I think I can get it quicker, but it will cost another $75 to talk to the person at the Brazilian embassy." At that point, I was already in way over my head, so I agreed. "If I can't get it done, I will have your passport and the visa transported by FedEx and you can pick it up at the FedEx office near the airport in El Paso."

This didn't set well with me, so I silently prayed for God's favor in the matter. He then asked me why I was going to Brazil and I told him about the prison ministry I was involved with through Celebrate Recovery and how it was helping inmates to get out of prison and stay out. He told me to be back by 2:30 and hopefully the issue would be accomplished. I left and was back by 12:30. As I walked into the office a couple of the employees looked at me and smiled. "I think he will have good news for you," he said. I hoped he was right and I sat down to wait for the man's return.

As he entered the office he glanced at me, got a manila envelope and placed papers inside it. He motioned for me to come to his desk and handed the envelope to me. "We got it done," he said. "I talked to the embassy worker and he wanted to know why the hurry and I told him about your conference and that you were helping those in prison. He thought that was a good thing and hurried it up for me." Inwardly I thanked my Lord Jesus and outwardly I thanked him for his effort, even though it cost me. "By the way," he told me, "it didn't cost the full amount, only $65." I thanked him again and reached for my phone to call a taxi to take me to the airport. Mission accomplished.

The flight to Brazil was overnight. I had not slept much going to New York, the flight to El Paso arrived after midnight, I had to get back on the plane at 6:00 a.m. headed for Atlanta. The trip from Atlanta to Brasilia was interesting. I began talking to a woman next to me who, I found out, was a prosecutor in Brazil and she was interested in anything that would help inmates. We discussed CR and I gave her my testimony as to how Jesus Christ could and would help anyone, even those who were in prison.

I had to fly back to Fortaleza from Brasilia and I was met by Nelson Massambani and Armando Bispo, the pastor of the church. We deposited my luggage at Nelson's apartment and immediately went to the office of the *Secretaria de Justiça e Cidadania*, the Secretary of Corrections. The Secretary was a very pleasant looking woman, blonde, whose name was Mariana Lobo Coelho Albuquerque. She spoke English, having studied in the Dallas area and I immediately picked up on the Lobo and Albuquerque since that was the place I had lived for a number of years and the UNM Lobos are famous, at least in New Mexico.

The objective of the conversation was to officially designate Celebramos a Recuperação (Celebrate Recovery) as the official recovery program for the prisons in the State of Ceará. After some discussion she said she would do so and would sign a document during a service at the church. This was something the program had been working on for some time.

I was taken to two prisons, one in Fortaleza for women and another in Pacatuba, for men. The women's prison had been programmed with CR for several years by volunteers that had been trained at Saddleback, and I had helped train them. The men's prison was just in the beginning stages and Nelson and I did a session with the staff to help them understand the program. I was impressed with the women's prison and told a group of the women through an interpreter how CR Inside was started. The women were allowed to keep their children for a year after they were born with them in the prison and there was a separate facility for their living quarters.

I stayed at Nelson's apartment with he, his wife Roswitha and their two children and Oma, Roswitha's mother who was from Germany. The family spoke three languages, Portuguese, English and German. Often the conversations would from one language to the other in the same conversation. We ate meals that Roswitha and Oma fixed. Oma means "grandmother", but I never learned her name, since that was what everyone called her. Their dachshund dog Niki and I became fast friends quickly. Out of the window the city could be seen, tall skyscrapers that were mainly apartment buildings were readily visible.

Nelson interviewed me during the conference at the church asking questions in Portuguese and an American who had grown up as a Missionary Kid, Cameron Young, did the interpreting. The video is on YouTube. My whole time there was spent trying to overcome a huge sleep deficit starting with the New York trip and the flight to Brazil. I had forgotten medication for Restless Leg Syndrome and it took a couple of tries to find the right medication for me since the drugs are called by different names in Brazil than in the U. S. My hosts became somewhat worried about me as I was getting a little zombied out. The first couple of nights I slept on a mattress on the floor. That added to my sleeplessness, but finally the right medication was found and Rebeca, their adopted daughter, offered to switch beds with me and I finally got some rest. The Secretary came to a Sunday night church service, probably the only evangelical service she had ever been to and signed the document naming CR as the recovery program for the prisons in her state.

The night after the signing of the document at the church we went to a *tapioquera* where I experienced a different way to fix what I usually have as a pudding. Tapioca flour can be fried on a grill and filled with either meat or sweets, like a burrito. I got a meat-filled tapioca and it was delicious. We went to the waterfront and walked through the shops along the beach at night. The view of the city around the Atlantic was beautiful.

The next day we drove to a beach town, Beberibe. On the way we stopped at a sugar refining operation that sold their product. Sugar cane was harvested from the fields, squeezed of the juice and the rest of the cane used to make a fire under the cauldrons cooking the juice until it crystalized into a brown syrup. This was placed in molds to make rectangular cakes that were wrapped and sold to visitors. We went through the town and parked close to the beach, where I got wet in the Atlantic surf. We ate lunch at a restaurant and Nelson had an artist make a sand design in a glass container that showed the CR logo from Brazil. I got to experience the best of Brazilian hospitality and how the Gospel is being proclaimed there.

CHAPTER 18

I AM BLESSED

Has my life been a great one? If you consider all the blunders I have made, all the poor choices all the stupid things I have done, no. But if you look at what Jesus Christ has done in me and through me—in spite of myself—the answer is an enthusiastic *yes*! Did I set out to deliberately do the things in my life that have helped others, no. Did I blunder into things that have made a difference and was God able to use it for His glory? Absolutely.

God was able to use things in my life that brought me shame and guilt to help my own family, my church, those in prison, transition homes, the Gospel Rescue Mission and elsewhere to bless me and those I care about as well as many I have never met. When John Baker called me about putting my testimony in the Celebrate Recovery Bible, he said I reminded him of Gideon, a co-dependent who thought of himself as the least and the last. Gideon was reluctant to obey God, but God showed him that he was a "mighty warrior." (Judges 6:12) I might not have been a *mighty warrior*, but I was reluctant, like the Bible character. I didn't fit in anywhere. I really didn't know who I was or where I was going… I just went along. When things got tough spiritually, I bailed out, and then I came back.

I did other things that, when I think back on them, were quite extraordinary, like working in prison, like going on mission trips and speaking in a language which was not my most comfortable. Like standing in the middle of a prison yard in Kenya and telling the inmates there about how Celebrate Recovery can help bring them to Jesus

Christ for healing and purpose in their own lives. That's the power of God working to change lives. He changed mine; he can change yours as well.

My church, Mesilla Park Community, has sustained me and I have seen this church grow so much that it had to find a new building. The old one no longer sufficed. We had a service on Saturday evening called *"Saturday Night Life,"* other services at 8:15, 9:30 and 11:30 on Sunday morning and then we began recording the sermon on Saturday night to be used at the Cineport 10 theater at the mall on Sunday morning. We didn't have parking places for everyone. We ran out of room for the SonTown kids. Some people had to park across a main street and railroad tracks and then walk to church.

We negotiated for an abandoned K-Mart building that Dennis had been praying for over a number of years. We could pay up to three million dollars after getting qualified for a loan through the Baptist State Convention. Our negotiations narrowed down with the owner, an attorney in California who worked for the Church of Scientology, to the point we were a couple of hundred thousand dollars apart when a realtor in Phoenix bought it out from under us.

We were devastated and continued to pray. The Phoenix realtor found out we wanted the property and we began to negotiate with him. All he really wanted were two one-acre parcels along the main street, El Paseo Road. We bought the part we wanted for the price we had originally decided we could afford. A miracle from God! A couple of other hurtles were overcome, like the property being a foot or so below the flood plain. We asked for a remeasurement and it was measured at one eighth of an inch *above* the flood plain. Another miracle. There were other events that led to our praising God on many occasions as goods and services were donated just when needed.

We held the memorial service for TJ Diaz in the building even before we had the occupation permits. She had died of stage four cancer eleven years after being diagnosed with the disease and was given only two years to live at that point. She was able to see her children graduate from high school and college. Her youngest daughter was presented with her diploma by New Mexico State University Chancellor and President Garry Carrothers, the former governor who had visited our

Roswell Correctional Center years prior to this occasion. The University entourage came to the Diaz' home to do the presentation because TJ was not well enough to attend graduation. This was a miracle in and of itself. God had blessed this family and this church. We miss our TJ. She had a Christian beauty beyond her good looks. She radiated the love of Christ to everyone she encountered. Through all the cancer treatments she ministered to those who were going through it with her, never feeling sorry for herself. She left a legacy Mesilla Park will never forget. She blessed me just by knowing her and seeing her devotion to Christ and His people as well as her family.

One of the greatest honors I have received was from John Baker. He invited me to the Summits in 2016, both in Tennessee and California at CR's expense; both Fern and myself. At the Summit celebrating the twenty-fifth year of CR in Murfreesboro I was given the "Lifetime Achievement Award" for Celebrate Recovery. I took the glass award engraved with my name and the scripture from Matthew 25:23 in its box to our hotel room and on Thursday night I took it out to look at it. I discovered fingerprints, so putting it on the desk I opened a lens wipe and began to take off the smudges. It toppled over onto the desk and broke in two parts. I was devastated.

John asked me to bring the award to California for another awarding there. I had to tell him that my pride or my clumsiness—or both—had broken the glass and I was trying to find someone to repair it for me. He immediately emailed his assistant, Marnie Buhler to get another one made. That's the kind of people that built this great ministry. I think this is a symbol of my life. Even when I blunder—God through others bless me. I don't deserve it, but I love it!

The Scripture from Proverbs 3:5-6 became my life verse: *Trust in the Lord with all your heart and lean not on your own understanding' in all your ways submit to him and he will make your paths straight.* Often it wasn't my whole heart, but He took what I gave him and turned it into a blessing.

PROLOGUE

THE PSALMIST HAS SAID:

*S*ome *of you wandered for years in the desert, looking but not finding a good place to live, Half-starved and parched with thirst, staggering and stumbling, on the brink of exhaustion. Then, in your desperate condition, you called out to God. He got you out in the nick of time; He put your feet on a wonderful road that took you straight to a good place to live. So thank God for his marvelous love, for his miracle mercy to the children he loves. He poured great draughts of water down parched throats; the starved and hungry got plenty to eat.* Psalm 107:4-9 (MSG)

There are people in my life who have influenced me greatly regarding the things that have caused me to blunder. The men in my life who, not by their words, but by their actions, influenced my addiction to nicotine, and from that I learned to hide my "stuff" from others and to lie about whatever might reveal my real self to those whom I didn't want to know about the "real me" and my weaknesses. They didn't cause this in me, but I was influenced. I chose to do what I did, and I did those things willingly. My will, I have learned, must seek the will of God, not my own or the influences that come at me.

The man who brought fear into my life with a pocket knife to my throat in front of neighbors who were not so neighborly when I was a six-year-old, and my mother who would not believe me fed me lies about myself that I had little value and that my life didn't matter too much in the real world. That belief that I lived my life with, positioned me to try to be somebody, but in my own mind I always failed, because I didn't find my identity in the presence of the Creator who made me and the Christ who died for me. I tried to find it in myself, even when I knew better.

When the Celebrate Recovery Bible testimony was asked for I didn't know what to write. This was the first testimony I had done. I had not yet experienced the alcohol issue that I would later have. I didn't see myself like Gideon, but God has used me to do what I could not have done had I not been one of his "kids." What I have learned from this, though, is that I can relate to those who struggle, because I have struggled. I can understand addictions because I have felt its grip on my own life and I have found that God, in His ultimate wisdom, has created a means by which those of us who love Him and want to follow Him may do so and find support and strength along the way that we don't possess.

Celebrate Recovery is a tool to understand that process, but the process has been with us since Jesus died on the cross and rose from the grave that we might have life and have it abundantly. The Gospel and the discipleship which flows from it have been there since Jesus told his disciples: *"All authority in heaven and on earth has been given to me. Therefore go and make disciples of all nations, baptizing them in the name of the Father and of the Son and of the Holy Spirit, and teaching them to obey everything I have commanded you. And surely I am with you always, to the very end of the age."* Matthew 28:18-20 NIV

Many people have a difficult time coming out from under the lies and misinformation they have had programmed into their souls. Jesus came to seek and to save those who are lost, struggling, have little direction or no direction in their lives and to bring new life, eternal life to them. Celebrate Recovery has helped me to have a mind change about a lot of things, especially who I am.

I am also thankful for those God has put in my path at just the right time to help me, like the high school teacher who kept me after class and challenged me to do my homework so I could get my grade up in her class, and it showed me I wasn't as stupid as I had convinced myself I was and I went on to get a Master's Degree. Like Billy Hill in the Air Force who helped me find where to put my name in the "whosoever" in John 3:16. That began my life in Christ. That started me on the path to blessing. Like Dr. Richard Cunningham who taught me Bible at the

Baptist Student Union at the University of NM and then suggested I go to seminary where he went to teach. Like the Pecos Valley Baptist Association who invited me to go on four short-term mission trips to Yucatan. Like Tom Zornes who invited me to a Walk to Emmaus, and then to become involved in the Kairos Prison Ministry. Like Donna Wilpolt, Cook the Deputy Secretary of Corrections who invited me to a meeting where we discussed putting together a faith-based ministry to prisoners. Like John Baker who began Celebrate Recovery and did a workshop at a Purpose Driven Church conference my church sent me to for a totally different reason, and then became interested in what I had done with the program God had given him and invited me to help bring Celebrate Recovery to prisons and jails in the rest of the country and to the world. Like those inmates at Southern New Mexico Correctional Facility who became my accountability partners as I did the step study for myself and worked through my own issues that have plagued me throughout my life.

My pastor, Dennis Diaz, has been an inspiration and a person who has challenged me to accept grace, God's grace, and to let it flow freely through me to others. He showed me that my life could be a channel through which God could do ministry and I didn't need to be a "pastor" to let him do it. The restorative grace shown me when I had to confess my failure and the accountability with the elders which led to my helping another elder opened my eyes to a ministry within the church that is needed.

My wife, Fern, my companion for more than a half century, has been a stabling force and a very pleasant memory since we were married in 1965. We have had few disagreements, no fights, and she has stood by my side no matter what. She was always willing to move when my assignments changed, to go to seminary and help by working to keep the family in the black. I prayed for God to lead me to the woman who would be my help mate and there has never been a doubt that my prayer was unanswered. She has a pleasant disposition that always showed that she loved me and has been a great mother and grandmother. This is a treasure I will take to heaven when I go. She has been my therapy when I needed it. As her memory follows the path her mother's dementia took and she is unable to do things that require thinking through a process, even to the point she gets confused about things, I find it is my turn to serve her and to love her through the hard times. It is my joy to do so. I love her and I always have.

I also learned that we don't need any self-help books or special philosophy to travel the road of life, we need Jesus; but also, we need those who have traveled the road before us and with us to show us the pitfalls and the crevasses that can derail our progress. Perfection? It's not possible this side of heaven, but progress definitely is. Thanks to God, I'm not who I was, blundering and staggering, but I'm not who I really want to be yet. I need God's chisel to keep chipping away at my character defects. I will continue to find help and support and people who keep pointing to my Lord Jesus in Celebrate Recovery and in my church. May you, who have read this find the Holy Spirit ready and willing to do in you what you can't do for yourself as you open yourself to God's will daily. He will take you from blunder to blessing like He did for me.

---

1.   The 1980 New Mexico Prison Riot. University of Colorado, Boulder. Colvin, Mark.

www.ingramcontent.com/pod-product-compliance
Lightning Source LLC
Chambersburg PA
CBHW060909120626
46553CB00001B/260